WHO'S IN THE MONEY?

www.edinburghuniversitypress.com/series/tiac

WHO'S IN THE MONEY?
The Great Depression Musicals and Hollywood's New Deal

Harvey G. Cohen

EDINBURGH
University Press

For J.C.S. . . .

a true partner in the struggle
for nearly a quarter-century

Edinburgh University Press is one of the leading university presses in the UK. We publish academic books and journals in our selected subject areas across the humanities and social sciences, combining cutting-edge scholarship with high editorial and production values to produce academic works of lasting importance. For more information visit our website: www.edinburghuniversitypress.com

Edinburgh University Press Ltd
The Tun – Holyrood Road
12 (2f) Jackson's Entry
Edinburgh EH8 8PJ

Typeset in 10/12.5pt Sabon by
Servis Filmsetting Ltd, Stockport, Cheshire,
and printed and bound in Great Britain by
CPI Group (UK) Ltd, Croydon CR0 4YY

A CIP record for this book is available from the British Library

ISBN 978 1 4744 2940 5 (hardback)
ISBN 978 1 4744 2941 2 (paperback)
ISBN 978 1 4744 2942 9 (webready PDF)
ISBN 978 1 4744 2943 6 (epub)

CONTENTS

FIGURES

ABBREVIATIONS

AMPAS Academy of Motion Pictures Arts and Sciences
FTC   Federal Trade Commission
IATSE International Alliance of Theatrical Stage Employees
IBEW   International Brotherhood of Electrical Workers
MPDDA Motion Picture Producers and Distributors of America
NIRA   National Industrial Recovery Act
NRA   National Recovery Administration
SAG   Screen Actors Guild
SBA   Small Business Administration
SDG   Screen Directors Guild
SWG   Screen Writers Guild

ACKNOWLEDGEMENTS

This has been a multi-decade, mostly joyful journey of love. It started for me as a teenager in the Film Studies department at UC Santa Barbara, when Professor Charles Wolfe screened the key film considered in this book, *Footlight Parade* (1933), and discussed some of the history behind it. Watching it that day, and over the ensuing decades, I sensed that more lay hidden beneath the story, that it held a wider significance and subtext that would reward investigation. This was not the average Hollywood film, artistically or politically. It embodied the combination of struggle, pain, cathartic achievement and subsequent rapture that most of my favourite artists traffic in: Pedro Almodóvar, Frank Capra, Charles Chaplin, Ray Davies, Duke Ellington, Antonio Carlos Jobim, Joni Mitchell, Mavis Staples, Rufus Wainwright, and many more. Hopefully, this book and its research shed new light on some films and a period in American history that I've been chasing since the twentieth century.

In researching this book, I am indebted to the expertise and generosity of archivists and librarians. Thanks to all of them, especially at:

- The Warner Bros. Archive at the University of Southern California, where Sandra Garcia-Myers proved an experienced guide, and strongly but respectfully disagreed with my interpretations concerning Jack L. Warner.
- The British Library's now-defunct Colindale branch, with its endless supplies of newspapers and magazines. The new British Library newspaper reading room (where I also spent time) in central London

is very nice, but doesn't have the musty old-fashioned atmosphere of Colindale. When you walked in, you already felt you were entering another world. Which is cool if you're a nerd historian.

- The British Film Institute's Reuben Library (and its older research library); there was no film-related US or UK resource they did not possess. And such a nice place to work. Thanks especially to Ian O'Sullivan, who explained some new technology to me that saved a ton of time.
- The Margaret Herrick Library at the Academy of Motion Picture Artists in Beverly Hills, which supplied a number of the local Hollywood-related documents, such as the final NRA motion picture code.

Thanks to the insightful readers of my book: Dennis F. Mulqueeney (who heroically read the manuscript twice and, especially, helped with financial nomenclature); Marvin Schulman; and Edmund F. Wehrle (Eastern Illinois University). As usual, of course, the mistakes are mine. Gratitude to various anonymous readers of this book who pointed the way towards further revelations; I think I know who they are, but I shall name no names here.

Appreciation to Philip John Davies (De Montfort University), Iwan Morgan (University College London) and David Somerset (British Film Institute), for allowing me a test run of the ideas from this book during events at the British Library and BFI Southbank. Professor Morgan's comments and efforts on behalf of this book were especially helpful. Special thanks to my dad, Jay L. Cohen, and his wife Gale, for housing me during the weeks of Los Angeles research, lending me a (very necessary) car, and enduring hearing probably more than they expected about 1930s films and politics.

A spiritual shout goes out to my grandmother Pearl Lentz Horowitz Guest, aka 'Grandma G', who had many conversations with me about the history of Hollywood films and studios, and fondly recalled seeing movie stars like Clara Bow when she worked in downtown LA during the 1920s, as well as her conversations with W. C. Fields in the mid-1940s. Also, more unrepayable thanks to her daughter, my mother Joyce Lynn Cohen, who watched and discussed dozens of old movies with me over the decades, and recommended many. Mom, you put the bug in me.

INTRODUCTION

Over eight decades later, it is still not as appreciated as it deserves, perhaps because it contrasts so starkly with the usual vision of the great American movie musical. But that distinction forms a significant part of what makes the film so unique. There are no legendarily talented dancers or singers out front, no Judy Garland or Gene Kelly, though there is spirited hoofing and vocalising figure throughout. The grim economic upheaval of the Great Depression is omnipresent, instead of the idealised fantasy world favoured by, for example, the Astaire and Rogers musicals.

But *Footlight Parade* belongs on any list of all-time great musicals, both for what is achieved on-screen and how it reflected the historical reality of the period, as well as for what transpired behind the scenes politically and financially in Hollywood during the momentous year of 1933. By the end of that year, the way the Hollywood studios went about their business, and the way their workers saw their roles within that tightly held system, would never be the same. This book covers these developments in a roughly chronological fashion, as well as the stories and significance behind the other two Great Depression Musicals (as they are now called) that preceded *Footlight* that year (*42nd Street* and *Gold Diggers of 1933*), and more.

Footlight Parade, written, produced and released in 1933 by Warner Brothers Pictures, Inc., is one of the most curious combinations of politics and entertainment ever issued by a major American studio. It marked the third, and best, of the Warner Brothers Great Depression musicals – a series of mostly successful films released during the 1930s that helped the studio stave off the bankruptcy and receivership other studios faced during that decade. The fast-moving and witty script provided a view of theatre life on every social level during America's worst economic crisis, from rich (and larcenous) investors to struggling 'chorus girls'. James Cagney made his singing and dancing debut in the film after more than a dozen tough guy starring roles for Warner Bros., and the studio and the public were not sure if he had the talent to branch out into this different genre. Nevertheless, he acquitted himself brilliantly. The film's technically magnificent, absurdly ambitious musical numbers may represent choreographer Busby Berkeley's best work ever, and almost seem as if they were concocted with current-day computer graphics though they were, of course, painstakingly created on the Warner soundstages in Burbank, California, by crews and cast working fourteen-hour days. *Footlight*, released just months before a mandated stricter adherence to the Production Code circumscribed the adult content allowed in major studio films, also featured a surprisingly salty script, with more sexual innuendo and invidious corruption included than today's audiences usually expect from films made during Hollywood's classic era.

The details briefly described above are unique enough, but part of what set *Footlight* apart from other films of the time and even those of today was

Figure I.1　President Franklin Delano Roosevelt is saluted on-screen near the rousing conclusion of the third of the Warner Bros. Great Depression Musicals, *Footlight Parade*. (Warner Bros., 1933)

its blatant political messaging, especially in the climactic number 'Shanghai Lil'. The sequence, set in a bar near the port of Shanghai, features a surprisingly rowdy, risqué and internationally diverse cast of participants, as well as opium, alcohol, prostitutes and the US Navy. Near the end, filmed from directly above, dozens of American troops hold up flash cards to the camera that, when joined together, complete a graphic of the American flag. The soldiers in the middle of the flag then turn their cards over to reveal a large portrait of the new US president, Franklin Delano Roosevelt, superimposed upon the flag. The sailors then quickly rearrange themselves into the Blue Eagle, the central symbol of Roosevelt's New Deal programme, firing their rifles in salute. Companies, stores and movie theatres nationwide were being encouraged at the time to place Blue Eagle signs on their front windows to demonstrate their participation in Roosevelt's approach to combating the Great Depression. The Blue Eagle symbol showed that the bearer agreed with the ethos of Roosevelt's National Recovery Administration (NRA), a programme which reorganised most of the American economy, compelling both workers and bosses to sacrifice in the short term for the greater long-term economic good of the country and their fellow citizens. This organisation and approach, like all of Roosevelt's New Deal programmes, encountered fierce resistance from millions of Americans even after it was passed into law in June 1933, yet here it was, being celebrated in patriotic fashion within a mainstream, heavily promoted Hollywood studio film.

For 1933 audiences, the Blue Eagle's appearance in *Footlight Parade* would be instantly familiar, making it plain that the film and the Warner Bros. studio supported Roosevelt's policies. And indeed, at the time, they did. The two main brothers who ran the studio, Harry and Jack, were among Roosevelt's most important advocates and fundraisers during the 1932 presidential campaign. Warner Bros. advertisements throughout 1933 featured New Deal imagery and slogans. The overt political symbolism featuring Roosevelt and the Blue Eagle was singular – such straight-up propaganda and fervent support for a current President and his political agenda in a feature film had rarely if ever been seen in major studio American cinema before or since (except for perhaps the depiction of President John F. Kennedy's bravery during World War II service in *PT 109* [1963]). One could not imagine such a heroic image of a sitting president emanating from today's major studios, all of them owned by multinational corporations, eager not to offend either the public or stockholders by affiliating their films with any political party.

But the movie existed in one milieu, and Hollywood's soundstages and corporate offices represented quite another. While *Footlight Parade* was in production and Roosevelt's policies were being enacted, the Warner brothers especially, along with the heads of production of all the major Hollywood studios, did all they could during 1933 and afterwards to undermine New Deal legislation. They subtly worked to curtail workers' rights and salaries instead of bolstering both sides of the labour/management divide, as they publicly claimed they were doing, and were supposed to do under NRA regulations.

As part of an exploration of the connections between the Warner Bros. Great Depression Musicals and Roosevelt's New Deal, this book features a detailed examination of the months-long struggle in Hollywood during 1933 to create an NRA code of practice for the notoriously bitter and divided motion picture industry. This months-long battle impacted every level of film industry workers from executives to extras, as well as distributors and exhibitors nationwide. The proposed code of practice pitted independent studios and theatres against the major studios' powerful vertically integrated economic system, as well as newly organised movie stars and writers against studio management. Through their manipulation of this New Deal legislation, the Warners (even more than other studio moguls) attempted to ensure that the economic pain of the Depression was served as much as possible upon artists and craftsmen, not owners or management. While the Warners, as personal friends of Roosevelt, posed as exemplars of the New Deal in real life, in their marketing and in their released movies, they were attempting to reverse his policies within their studio and their industry just as the cameras were rolling on *Footlight Parade*, the movie most epitomising their supposed dedication to Roosevelt.

This book uncovers how such compelling entertainment came to be created and filmed despite the resentful conflicts raging in Hollywood, with plenty of newly uncovered production and political stories. It also demonstrates how the 1933 Warner Bros. Great Depression Musicals reflected this crucial period in American history with humorous yet cutting dramatised situations, as well as heroic and inspiring portrayals. Audiences reacted positively to these characterisations; net profits for *Footlight Parade* in America equalled roughly 150 per cent of the original budget, and *42nd Street* and *Gold Diggers of 1933* ended up being two of the three top-grossing films of the year. Behind the scenes at Warners, the creation of *Footlight Parade* (as well as the film itself) embodies a story of financial survival, political intrigue and backstabbing amid a volatile labour and political atmosphere between the Hollywood studios, their workers, independent film businesses and the federal government in the midst of the worst of the Great Depression. This book provides a history of the American film industry, focusing particularly on the succession of controversial and influential events that roiled the studio system during 1933, which set the stage for the system's fall from dominance in the years following World War II. It surveys the labour environment for stars, craftsmen, writers, producers and 'chorus girls'. It also briefly examines the Great Depression musicals Warner Bros. produced after 1933, and the ultimate fate of the NRA nationally, particularly in Hollywood.

While several scholars have touched upon some of the subjects covered here, this book combines these topics in new ways with new research from the perspective of US cultural and political history. Rather than the usual escapism employed by movie musicals, the Great Depression Musicals of 1933 reflected and invented new ways of viewing the unprecedented political order embodied in Roosevelt's New Deal. They represent important historical documents, revealing as much about the period as traditional primary sources such as government documents and newspapers. To a degree, these films reflected the reality of the period or at least a political standpoint that proved phenomenally popular – this represents one reason they remain resonant and fresh to audiences today, including those who have viewed the films in my history classes over the past few years. They serve as a useful lens for examining the effects of and resistance to Roosevelt's landmark attempts to significantly alter the political and economic direction of the United States. The visions of work, art, freedom and responsibility portrayed in the Great Depression Musicals, and how those same attributes were acted out in the Hollywood studios and labour market, were markedly different. This book exposes and addresses the balance between these make-believe and real-life worlds.

1. THE WARNERS AND FRANKLIN ROOSEVELT

To [the older and more established] Hollywood [studios], Warner's primacy is an odd and faintly distasteful fact. People in show business, by and large, are inclined to resent the Warners ... [Goldman Sachs banker and film financier Waddill] Catchings describes the movies as a rat-in-the-corner industry. Developed late, its laws are rat eat rat. Under these laws the Warners have fought their way to the top against the opposition of the whole amusement world ... The fight has left its mark on the brothers. They have not yet lowered their guard. They are neither in Hollywood nor of it ... Their production methods, in many respects unique, are mostly self-developed. Their personnel turnover is small, their interior discipline almost grim. The Warner brothers trust few people outside their own camp, but in each other they have the most implicit confidence. 'Warner brothers personally', as Harry [Warner] once put it, 'have always construed themselves as one'.

– *Fortune* magazine, December 1937[1]

Like all major American movie studios in Hollywood during the 1930s, Warner Bros., Inc. possessed its own personality.[2] Even if you were held up buying popcorn in the lobby and walked into the theatre a few seconds late, missing the film's initial seconds when the Warners' corporate logo flashed on-screen, audiences then and scholars now could easily recognise a Warners picture. They were usually darker, photographically and thematically; less glamorous than the products of other studios; the characters more likely working-class, urban, striving underdogs. Happy endings were not a given, escapism not guaranteed. The films often shared a low budget, yet a carefully considered and crafted aesthetic. The foundation for these artistic and commercial motifs lay in the personalities of the Warner brothers themselves. They boasted a biography different from their fellow studio moguls'. To a large extent, the Warner studio's themes and values, including those featured in the Great Depression Musicals, are foreshadowed by the history of its founding brothers, and their unique way of doing business, starting from the beginning of their career, far from Hollywood.

The Warners endured a hardscrabble history in their early years, living the familiar tale of struggling immigrants in the turn-of-the-century United States.[3] The family patriarch Benjamin emigrated from Poland in 1883, initially leaving his family behind for the vaunted promise of better economic times in America. Whatever the future held, it had to represent an improvement over the pervasive anti-semitism and pogroms Jews like Benjamin Warner (and most other Jewish families that produced the eventual first generation of Hollywood studio moguls) faced in eastern Europe, drastically limiting their financial opportunities. Benjamin bounced around the eastern end of North America for years, starting in Baltimore, heading off to Canada for a short spate in fur-trading, then back to Baltimore. Finally, aided by the labour of most of his nine children, the family found limited stability operating a grocery store in Youngstown, Ohio, located in the then-booming industrial belt in America. The Warners' struggle to gain a foothold in America, according to biographer Michael Freedland, taught the siblings 'that the day was meant for working, and that you didn't waste God's given time doing anything else'.

Youngstown proved significant in the story of the Warners' rise. Most of the other Jews who ended up running the nascent Hollywood film industry learned their entrepreneurial skills in major metropolitan areas like New York City, Boston or Chicago. As author Neal Gabler put it, 'culture and class distinctions were less readily apparent' in Youngstown. The Warners were underdogs, operating in somewhat of a cultural backwater far from established entertainment centres. They needed to prove themselves and exhibit moxie to move into the big leagues of entertainment in urban cities. Such qualities were not learned in school, and none of the Warner siblings finished his studies; ambition and family survival loomed too large. But another quality the brothers and their father possessed that their fellow future moguls also shared was varied retail experience. Through hard experience, they learned, often after disastrous failures, how to move product, developing a sense of what worked in the market-place and what did not. By the time they entered the exhibition side of the film business, showing the hit short *The Great Train Robbery* (1903) in their yard, the Warner brothers and their father had worked in shoe and bicycle repair, perishable and general goods, butchery, soap and ice cream sales, carnival barking, snake charming, and more. In his attempts to start a career as a child singing star, future production chief Jack L. Warner became the earliest Warner to develop a taste for show business. As a young man, he briefly pursued such ambitions, going on the road for a season billed as Leon Zuardo and doing a blackface act as the mass commercial appeal of minstrelsy was winding down in the United States. Jack and his eldest brother Harry would eventually become the two main brothers who ran the Warner Bros. studio.

The Warner reputation for scrappiness and drive emerged at these first movie screenings. Sister Rose played accompanying piano, brother Jack performed illustrated songs, and the older brothers ran the projector and took tickets. According to Clive Hirschhorn, the brothers' new enterprise, funded by their father's selling of an old watch chain and horse, made 'more money than Benjamin Warner made in a month selling meat'. There existed little doubt where their future lay; soon thereafter, the brothers started taking their projector on the road to other film-starved communities in Ohio and Pennsylvania, eventually settling down and opening a movie house in New Castle, Pennsylvania. By 1907, they had started a film distribution company, making it easier to get new films to underserved communities, and eventually sending their burgeoning library of film titles as far afield as Norfolk, Virginia and Portland, Oregon.

Entrepreneurs like the Warners, and their future studio brethren like Adolph Zukor and Louis B. Mayer (and others), could see before most that movies were not being developed to anywhere near their true business potential. Most investors steered clear of this art form, which many at the turn of the century thought of as a smarmy fly-by-night operation catering to immigrants and uneducated blue collar workers, figures frequently exploited and demeaned in America. But these budding movie executives collectively realised that the appeal of this fledgling art form would spread and multiply exponentially, providing power and riches to those who could streamline the business and create product that would expand its audience. Though the Warners were slower to achieve such heights than other Hollywood studios (perhaps because of their relatively slow start in Ohio), they eventually wielded a huge influence in this process.

But first, the Warners, and other independent film companies, needed to displace a large obstacle.[4] The [Thomas] Edison Manufacturing Company and other companies which held the patents that made motion picture production, distribution and exhibition possible were frustrated that independent concerns like the Warners' film exchange were making significant money, using their inventions without paying for the privilege. The nine companies, including Edison's, established the Motion Picture Patents Company (MPPC) in 1910, a trust levying high licence fees upon anyone buying film stock, opening a theatre venue, or using a film projector or camera. The MPPC monopoly briefly put the Warners out of business, although the brothers re-established themselves by 1916.

Edison was highly skilled at creating (or at least enabling his employees to create) much of the key technology of film production and viewing, but he had no clue how to attract a paying audience. He possessed the same talents and blindness in the recorded music industry as well. The MPPC's aggressive actions inspired the new indie film companies to fight against the fees in court and pack up their equipment and move thousands of miles away to Hollywood, where Trust employees in the days before easy cross-country travel found it difficult to prosecute and physically assault offenders, as they commonly did on the East Coast. By the time the US Supreme Court declared the MPPC's monopoly behaviour unconstitutional in 1915, the independent film companies had established a profitable beachhead on the West Coast. To the Trust's chagrin, their business strategy, relying on legal restraints of others, unwittingly had the effect of bringing forth the birth of the modern American film industry with Trust partners frozen out of it, the names of their film companies consigned to the past by the end of the 1910s. While the Trust emphasised collecting fees, other companies and executives (such as Carl Laemmle, who would later go on to found Universal Pictures) found ways to innovate and reach mass multi-class audiences, construct superior distribution frameworks, and capture long-term economic success and influence.

Another essential division existed: the Trust partners were almost exclusively white Anglo-Saxon Protestants, while the independent producers who fled to Los Angeles and built the eventually highly profitable world-conquering Hollywood studio system (including the Warners) were almost exclusively Jews, a group still facing discrimination in business, education, social clubs and more during this period. Yet, the movie business the Jewish studio heads created (and the early moguls were all Jewish, except for Walt Disney and Darryl Zanuck) became a respectable cornerstone of American life, business and culture as the twentieth century unfolded. And those Jewish outcasts, first- and second-generation immigrants to a man, got in on the ground floor by creating their own opportunities, as successful immigrants usually do.

The Warners began producing their own low budget films by 1910, but found limited success until 1917. In 1918, two patriotic anti-German World War I films initiated their first attempts at major features. One of these, *My Four Years in Germany*, grossed $1.5 million with a net profit of $130,000, the first step in the making of Warner Bros. as a major studio. A slow climb followed: they built their own studio facility in Hollywood in 1919, and in the 1921–2 period managed to release only six feature films. By 1923, the studio had introduced its first major star, the expressive well-trained dog

Figure 1.1   The Warner brothers, with Harry Rapf, a successful producer for decades
at MGM, in 1918: (L to R): Rapf, Sam Warner, Harry Warner, Jack
Warner, Abraham (usually known as Albert) Warner. (Warner Bros./The
Kobal Collection)

Rin-Tin-Tin. 'Rinty', as fans called him, starred in nineteen lucrative films,
'keeping the studio buoyant throughout the silent era and [saving] many theatres from closure', according to Clive Hirschhorn. Thousands of pieces of fan
mail arrived for the dog every week at the Warner lot, where he was reportedly
known as 'the mortgage lifter'. Not only that, but the studio's legendary head
of production from 1929 to 1933, Darryl F. Zanuck, the man who greenlighted
the Great Depression Musicals, initially came to the studio's attention because
of his authorship of over a dozen Rin-Tin-Tin scripts, though he admitted
later that 'he disliked the dog and hated writing for him'. In appreciation for
enabling Warners to vastly increase profits and production, the dog received
movie star perks: a small orchestra on-set to maintain actorly inspiration, a
diamond-studded collar, steak at mealtimes, and a $2,000 weekly salary (over
$28,000 in today's money).[5]

The embrace of new technology catapulted the fledgling Warner studio into
the big leagues in 1927 when they became the first to capitalise on the commercial potential of 'talking pictures'.[6] One could easily argue that the brothers'
struggling second-rate industry status compelled them towards an innovation
that revamped and rejuvenated the film world. The established Paramount

Figure 1.2   The first major movie star at Warner Bros., Rin-Tin-Tin, who ensured the economic survival of the company in its early years, with his trainer Lee Duncan *c.* the mid-1920s. (The Kobal Collection)

and MGM studios, with their more spacious lots, higher budgets, more tightly packed release schedules, exclusive theatre chains and superior profits had already constructed a successful business model and were loath to take chances on an unproven innovation that risked upsetting their financial projections. Many at the time viewed talking pictures as an evanescent gimmick that would demean the art of filmmaking. Besides, introducing sound into motion pictures would represent an expensive proposition for a product doing just fine without it.

But the Warners were underdogs, searching for a way to climb into the top tier of their profession. As part of their striving towards this goal, they cemented an alliance with Goldman Sachs financier Waddell Catchings in 1925. Catchings and most other Wall Street executives had previously avoided investing in Hollywood, judging the industry unstable or not organised well enough to merit serious investment. But, according to scholar Douglas Gomery, Catchings felt impressed by Warner Bros' 'strict control of production budgets', and 'extremely economical methods in building their studio lot'. For the first time, he saw an efficient motion picture operation worth a major risk, as long as they allowed him 'to dictate a master plan for long-term growth'. The Warners quickly acceded to his plans; their former ways of funding their business usually cost them more than 100 per cent interest; Wall

Street offered much better terms – the initial deal brought a $3,000,000 credit line at just 5 per cent interest, and initiated an alliance between Wall Street and Hollywood financial interests that continues to this day. Developing sound films put Warners ahead of competitors, but they never could have funded that development, and the retrofitting of theatres nationwide with sound equipment, if not for Catchings' far-sighted observations and investment.

Warner Bros. initially moved to secure their advantage in 'talkies' by signing a deal with Western Electric in 1925, a subsidiary of the nation's largest company, American Telephone and Telegraph. Western Electric, which brought out the first electronic public address system in the early 1920s, had been experimenting with sound recording and film for years. This transaction allowed Warners access to the engineers and experience to help them develop motion pictures with sound.

Western Electric and the Warners dubbed their system 'Vitaphone'. Sam Warner, the third son in the family line, drove these efforts over the initial objections of his brothers. He viewed the new technology primarily in terms of providing orchestral accompaniment for films, particularly musical shorts screened before Warner features. He was not initially thinking about recording actors' dialogue, which represented a more difficult technical feat than presenting performing musicians. This explains why producers originally planned on *The Jazz Singer* featuring sound only during its musical segments, as had been the case with 1926's moderately successful first Vitaphone feature *Don Juan*.

By the time *The Jazz Singer* premiered in the fall of 1927, the investments needed to jump-start Warners' experiment with sound totalled $5 million (about $68 million in today's dollars). The future of the studio rode on this bet. During the preceding year, Warners had produced over a hundred short musical films with sound for the 200 theatres equipped with the expensive and somewhat clunky Vitaphone sound system, with the film's sound emanating from recorded discs instead of a magnetic strip on the celluloid. The bravery of Warners' insistence on pursuing sound was also demonstrated when Western Electric forcefully renegotiated their original deal with Warners, stipulating that all of the movie studios, not just Warner Bros. could access, for a price, Vitaphone technology. Luckily for Warners, the other studios, save for half-hearted efforts by Fox, declined that opportunity, deigning to wait until an industry standard became established. This meant Warners had the lead in developing 'talkies'. Harry Warner felt that the other studios purposely let his studio develop sound on their own because 'they wanted him to go broke'. There is no proof concerning this supposition, but it does illustrate Harry's (and his other brothers') highly competitive and slightly paranoid state of mind.

The gamble paid off more spectacularly than anyone could have imagined. *The Jazz Singer* included the first words spoken on-screen in a major studio film, unleashing an explosive commercial impact, selling millions of tickets, and forcing rival studios to adopt sound so they could compete with the huge lead Warners established. Though corny, stilted and still silent at times, *The Jazz Singer* represents one of the few movies in history that decisively changed the industry, along with *The Birth of a Nation* (1915), which proved the viability of feature films, and *Bonnie and Clyde* (1967), whose success alerted the major studios that they needed to change the content and marketing of their films to attract a younger baby boom audience.

The effect of *The Jazz Singer* on Warners itself was perhaps even more explosive: the introduction of sound dramatically increased the company's stock price, from $9 to $132. They also made a royalty on every motion picture sound system sold to theatres by Western Electric. It paid to be the pioneers: while the top three film studios saw profits rise from 3 to 7 million dollars between 1928 and 1929 as they began releasing sound pictures, Warners' profits were up $14 million over the same period. Moreover, Warner produced 86 films in 1929, more than doubling their output in just two years, another windfall emanating in large part from Catchings' financial restructuring.[7]

The brothers, all major stockholders, could have become incredibly rich quickly. Yet, under the leadership and discipline instituted by Harry, they smartly used their new cash resources to consolidate gains and transform their studio into one of the industry leaders, instead of lining their personal bank accounts. They upgraded their studio sound facilities, and more importantly, used the bulk of their recently arrived millions to purchase over 500 movie theatres. The studio also bought First National, a film production and distribution company whose fortunes were declining, but which owned a huge film studio in Burbank, a few miles north of Hollywood, which would serve as the foundation for the Warner studios. Renovated and enlarged numerous times over the decades, this location is still the centre of Warner Bros. production today. By 1930, the brothers had marshalled a national distribution system showing exclusively Warner pictures ably competing against the similarly massive theatre chains owned by other large movie studios. Warners was now a player in Hollywood.

They made further moves that went beyond the business vision of the time. Realising that the advent of sound films created new financial opportunities, Warners invested some of their new capital into record companies, radio stations and music publishing companies, creating corporate synergy. Most 1930s hit songs emerged from films – 'soundies' represented an excellent promotional device for music. The song that alerted Warner executives to this potential was 'Sonny Boy', a DeSylva–Brown–Henderson composition sung by Al Jolson in *The Singing Fool* (1929). According to film historian John Kobal, the song 'became one of the biggest selling hits in the history of popular music, it was sung repeatedly in the film, and sold over two million copies'.[8] Warners ensured maximum revenue from music featured in their sound movies; when audiences heard a song in one of their films and wanted to buy a record of it or the sheet music, Warners earned additional profit on the music as a result of their investment in these ancillary firms. Music from Warner films airing on Warner radio stations helped sell movie tickets for Warner features and sheet music, all of which aided the company's balance sheet. As *Motion Picture Herald* reported in 1933, a couple of months after the premiere of the first Warner Bros. Great Depression Musical, music publishers

> learned quickly that the exploitation [of songs in movie musicals] sky-rocketed their earnings. Warner sold 500,000 sheets of '42nd Street' music, at 40 cents per copy, grossing $200,000. Sales of records, too, improved considerably. '42nd Street' record sales have totalled 100,000 to date at 75 cents each, representing a gross of $75,000. The average high mark for sheet music sales is said to approximate 150,000 copies. Obviously, the Warner activities more than tripled this total, with still more sales in the offing.[9]

The studio's embrace of radio was particularly telling. Other major studios viewed the medium, which aired comedy and drama material not far removed from offerings in local movie theatres, as a threat to their business, and 'tried to do everything they could to discourage the listening habit' in audiences, according to Freedland. By the end of 1930, Warners owned 51 subsidiary companies, their stock was valued at $200 million, and they had $230 million in gross assets (up from $16 million in 1928), employing 18,500 people. Warner Bros., and eventually all the major studios, moved beyond the film world during this period, diversifying into various strands of the mass media. Markets were expanding, and Warners, once the struggling underdog, was now out in front.

However, not all the changes ushered in by the coming of sound were viewed as advantageous by Warners and other companies. Sound made film production several times more expensive and required more extensive financing. As author Scott Eyman has argued, it also 'made unions inevitable', since so many of the elite new personnel hired for work in sound films (particularly 'journalists, sound engineers and Broadway actors' and writers) had enjoyed a long history of union membership and protection and saw no reason why they could not enjoy such privileges in the notoriously anti-union environment of Los Angeles. As will be discussed in a later chapter, the leaders of the Hollywood unions that coalesced during 1933, the Screen Writers Guild and the Screen Actors Guild, were often drawn from those demographics, and the studio moguls, particularly the Warner brothers, were dead set against new union recognition for film employees.

Sam Warner, the force behind 'talkies' at Warner, never saw how his efforts transformed his brothers' lives and the industry. The day before *Jazz Singer* premiered in New York, he died of a cerebral haemorrhage in Los Angeles. This served as a tragic parallel to the film itself, in which the rabbi who resisted his son's career in pop music dies before he sees his son's breakthrough success. 'When Sam died, and there is no doubt that *The Jazz Singer* killed him, something went out of our lives', wrote Jack L. Warner in his autobiography. Besides losing a brother and a visionary executive, a bridge was lost between the two most volatile Warner brothers and the two most central to their business: the usually calm, pious-minded Harry, who strove after respectability, and the 'crude, vulgar' Jack. 'There was a time when they did not see each other', recalled Darryl Zanuck. 'Harry hated Jack.' Their physically and verbally violent fights and arguments were legendary, and became worse after Sam's passing. He seemed the only one who could bring them together at tough times for the sake of the studio and the family. As Neal Gabler wrote in his history of the Jewish Hollywood moguls, after the massive success of *The Jazz Singer* established Warner Bros. as a major studio, 'the Warners would never be a family again',[10] a sad and frustrating situation for the only family-owned and -operated major Hollywood film studio.

Even before they amalgamated into a studio, the Warner brothers showed an interest in making what later scholars would term films of 'social relevance'. This decision was grounded not just in the brothers' nature and history, but in the philosophies of Harry Warner, who viewed the studio's film presentations as a responsibility, as well as a route to profit. 'The motion picture presents right and wrong, as the Bible does', he once said. 'By showing right and wrong, we teach the right.' *Fortune* magazine, in a lengthy 1937 profile of the studio, wrote that Harry 'has two major interests: business and morals . . . [he] has a violent hatred of human prejudice and persecution.' The move towards socially relevant films may have also served as an attempt to counter and reverse the anti-semitism that plagued American Jews, especially directed at those who headed the Hollywood studios. 'Both before and after Pearl Harbor, books were published that cast suspicion upon the motives of Jewish producers and studio owners like [Harry] Warner', reported Nancy Snow. 'With titles like *Hell Over Hollywood: The Truth about the Movies*, *What Is Wrong with the Movies* and *An American's History of Hollywood – The Tower of Babel*, American readers were exposed to ugly stereotypes of greed and immorality surrounding Jews.'[11]

The Warner Bros. films of 'social relevance' were usually concerned with justice broadly defined, standing against hypocrisy and exploitation, and identifying with the hard-working little guy who, in the American tradition, pulls himself up by his own bootstraps. This trend largely started with the studio's

World War I-era films, which took strong stands against what were viewed as German perpetrators of unnecessary conflict. As scholar John Davis points out, the trend of anti-war films (particularly concerning World War I) released by Warner Bros. continued well into the late 1920s and 1930s, even before Universal Studios' Oscar-winning pacifist hit *All Quiet on the Western Front* (1930).[12]

With the coming of the 1930s, Warner Bros. came into its own, crafting a house style that characterised the studio for decades.[13] In 1930, Zanuck was made head of production, and he, Harry and Jack Warner made the decision to specialise in low-budget production, partly because of the studio's hardscrabble early years and the Great Depression, partly due to the unavoidable large cash outlays for sound film technology and studio construction, but also owing to the scrappy nature and history of the brothers, their studio, and the way in which they viewed the world. The studio continued its tradition of paring film budgets to the bone. 'Listen, a picture, all it is is an expensive dream', Harry maintained. 'Well, it's just as easy to dream for $700,000 as for $1,500,000.'

Zanuck spearheaded the drive towards realism, veering away from the typical Hollywood happy ending whenever possible. According to biographer Leonard Mosley, Zanuck ordered director William Wellman to excise all sentimentality from *The Public Enemy* (1931), the film that introduced James Cagney to film audiences and began the profitable and influential trend of Warner gangster films. 'People are going to say the characters are immoral, but they're not because they don't have any morals', Zanuck said he told Wellman. 'They steal, they kill, they lie, they hump each other because that's the way they're made, and if you allow a decent human feeling or a pang of conscience to come into their make-up, you've lost 'em and changed the kind of movie we're making.'

Throughout the 1930s, expensive prestige pictures were limited in numbers at Warners and budgets slashed. Between 1931 and 1932, for the most part, Harry and Jack forbade musicals, because of their expense, and because the industry released a spate of them (mostly unsuccessful) in the late 1920s and in 1930 after the coming of sound. In 1933, with the advent of the Great Depression Musicals, Warner Bros. would revive the genre in spectacular and profitable fashion, but these musicals also acquiesced to the low-budget and social relevance aesthetic, particularly in their non-musical sequences.

Film scholars agree that the Warner studio was a tightly run ship, implemented by firm executive control. Thomas Schatz's research into the company files revealed a 'factory-based assembly-line production system' with no room for 'excess', 'a model of narrative and technical economy'. As the main music composer for the Warner Bros. Great Depression Musicals put it, 'the Warner execs were obsessed with economy'. He recalled endless pre-production meetings when production costs formed the only item on the agenda. 'Anyone who got over $2000 a week [Harry] hated instantly even if he never met him', recalled Zanuck. 'In Harry's mind everybody was a thief, including Jack for condoning extravagances.'

As was often the case at the Hollywood studios during this period, directors were usually hired only to supervise the shooting of a film, sometimes with every shot carefully proscribed in the script and no creative latitude. They were often given little input into pre- or post-production, which is why Warners' most active directors during the period, such as Lloyd Bacon, who helmed *Footlight Parade*, had the time to direct as many as four or five films per year, a schedule inconceivable in today's industry.[14] Retakes of scenes done after principal production, common at most other studios and usually expensive, were rare at Warners, only allowed if 'the preview [screening was] extraordinarily sour'. Producers went uncredited on-screen for most of the 1930s, and after Zanuck exited in 1933 no 'producing genius' like Irving Thalberg at MGM was hired to take his place. Instead, Warners' production slate was constructed and maintained by 'jocular penny-pincher' head of production Jack, plus 'methodical assistant Hal Wallis, and half a dozen almost anonymous supervisors'. The strategy kept salaries low, ensuring that focus centred on the studio, its product, and maintaining profit, not artistic egos. 'Many of Hollywood's first citizens, especially over at the Metro-Goldwyn-Mayer studio [where generous film budgets were common, even during the Depression] think that Harry's cut-rate dreaming is the worst possible formula for making pictures', reported *Fortune*. 'And yet by all movie standards – Hollywood's, the box office's, and the critics' – Warner Bros. is conceded to make very good pictures indeed.'

These business conditions, as well as the Warner tendency towards films of social relevance, marked the Warner house style. Their films tended to be darker, with more shadows displayed within the cinematography, and in the background, as well as on actors' faces. When the *mise-en-scène* was lashed in chiaroscuro or when close-ups were used extensively, sets could be cheaper and less detailed, sometimes even non-existent. An exhibitor in Harrisburg, IL, writing in *Motion Picture Herald*, appreciated the difference, noting that Warner Bros. 'are making good box office pictures without spending a million doing it'. This house style also made the films seem more dramatic, personal, more like real life captured on celluloid, stripped of the usual fancy Hollywood key-lit and back-lit photography tricks. In a 1932 article, Zanuck championed Warners' successful embrace of 'headline films', drawn from current events and everyday reality, a theme he introduced during his short reign as head of production. 'You can't go on telling the same story forever. The triangle is rusty', he wrote. 'That is why we originally adopted the headline type of story, and that is why we intend to continue with it.' With the coming of sound, as Nick Roddick points out in his study of 1930s Warner films, the Hollywood studios 'were making a very different kind of movie [than previously] ... in a word, more realistic ... no studio made this shift more decisively than Warner Bros.' But Roddick's book concentrated on gangster, prison, historical films and other dramas produced by the studio during the 1930s – the Great Depression Musicals also strongly reflected this sensibility of 'social relevance', and have often been ignored by authors attempting to tease out the character and history of Warner Bros. during this era.

The Warner films of the 1930s usually offered a unique combination of bleak realism, fast pacing and quick snappy dialogue. They were a world away from 'glamorous and glossy' high-budget star-studded films such as *Grand Hotel* (1932) released by MGM, Hollywood's top-grossing studio of the period. As Leo Rosten wrote in his 1941 anthropological examination of Hollywood, 'Warners specializes in emotions, not manners'. While other studios fashioned fantasy worlds on-screen that were meant to transport audiences far from the misery of the Depression, one of Warner's biggest hits of the early 1930s was *I Am a Fugitive from a Chain Gang* (1932), based on a true story steeped in dirt, injustice and frustration. It was directed by Mervyn LeRoy, one of the most prolific and successful Warner directors, a man seemingly tailor-made for the aesthetic Zanuck established. He grew up amid 'life in the raw' in turn-of-the-century San Francisco. 'I met the cops and the whores and the reporters and the bartenders and the Chinese and the fishermen and the shopkeepers', LeRoy recounted. 'I knew them all, knew how they thought and how they loved and how they hated. When it came time for me to make motion pictures, I made movies that were real, because I knew at first hand how people behaved.'[15] LeRoy earned the reputation of a quick director, filming twice the amount of usable footage per day as other directors, a skill deeply appreciated by a studio management team that needed to economise wherever possible during the Great Depression. Fewer production days equalled lower production costs, more opportunity for profit. LeRoy helmed roughly half a dozen films per year between 1930 and 1933, and was a studio loyalist – he married Harry Warner's daughter Doris in 1934 (an occasion recorded by Vitaphone cameras) and their first son was named Warner. These connections and his early box-office successes earned him control over his budgets, the rare ability to have some 'players under personal contract', and profit-sharing on his films.[16] The Warner Bros. production style in some ways made it easier for staff directors to crank out movies quickly – most Warner footage did not need the sheen and glitzy design of MGM spectaculars; in Burbank, anonymous office sets and plain dingy rehearsal spaces were the norm with little set-up time required.

Chain Gang focuses on James Allen (played by Paul Muni, Oscar-nominated for the role), a talented, hard-working World War I veteran who upon returning home wishes to elevate his status by becoming a civil engineer. Through a series of unlucky breaks, he is wrongly accused of robbery while on the road looking for work and sent to a notorious Georgia chain gang. While Allen is on the road, we see him riding the rails like a hobo in scenes resonant of the Depression, interacting with others in the same plight. The chain gang scenes are even more wrenching, their reality underscored by the technical advice of the true life James Allen (the man's actual name was Robert Burns), who endured the ordeal portrayed on-screen: we see the men perpetually in chains, even while asleep; how they face beatings if they do not ask for permission before wiping their brows as they break rocks in the hot sun; how the State of Georgia continually refuses to release Allen even after promises of clemency for good behaviour.

This film presents an unrelenting nightmare of struggle that does not end happily. On the run after escaping the chain gang for a second time, James has a brief reunion in a dark Chicago parking lot with his true love. He tells her he has 'no friends, no rest, no peace' and is always wary of authorities wishing to apprehend him. 'How do you live?', she tearfully asks. 'I steal', he replies with a mad look on his face, and then disappears back into the night, as the film suddenly ends. Several theatre owners quoted in *Motion Picture Herald*'s 'What the Picture Did for Me' column felt this ending 'spoil[ed]' the film. 'My personal opinion is that [the film] would do 25 per cent more business if it had a happy ending', complained an exhibitor in Montpelier, Idaho, adding that fifty of his patrons agreed with this sentiment. 'Too depressing', noted another exhibitor in Piedmont, Missouri. 'Several women walked out.'[17]

Yet, this film enjoyed the rare distinction of playing across America for more than a year, according to the *Herald*. People went to see it in much greater numbers than other prison films that ended happily or with justice meted out; perhaps it better suited the tenor of the time. As the Missouri theatre owner further stated, the film 'drew fairly well, considering [it was] Lent and rain'. Depression audiences probably needed catharsis and realism as much as escapism. The Warner brothers, as well as LeRoy and Zanuck (both of whom claimed they wrote *Chain Gang*'s final scene), understood that better than their competitors, although, as Schatz's research demonstrates, the legal and sales departments, a story editor and the first director assigned to the project felt it too 'morbid' and 'violent' for the public to embrace.

Another way in which *Chain Gang* reflected reality was in its pre-Production Code frankness concerning adult lives: when he returns from the Army, Allen says he's 'S.O.L.' (short for 'shit out of luck'); the film portrays blacks and whites suffering together, acting as friends and equals in the chain gang even if the bosses segregate the men at night; during his first escape from the chain gang, Allen accepts the free services of a prostitute; later on, his landlady openly bites her fingers in lust looking at him and they live together without being married, a situation that depicts love as an immoral game; the Georgia state law authorities dissemble and repeatedly go back on their word, denying Allen justice and a chance at the career as a civil engineer that he has earned. Such situations of depravity, racial equality, abuse of authority and non-married sexual behaviour would not be permissible on-screen two years later in 1934, when the Production Code Administration mandated that all major studio films present a conservative morality on-screen. But *Chain Gang*, one of the hallmark Warner films, went out of its way to present an adult reality. Many films of the pre-Code period raised the quantity of sex and violence in their movies (including *Footlight Parade*) to lure in poverty-stricken Depression audiences, but *Chain Gang* and *Footlight* purposely added such details to increase their verisimilitude, not just raise their titillation quotient. Warners' efforts at verisimilitude certainly convinced the state of Georgia, which brought a libel suit (ultimately dismissed) against Warner Bros. because it objected to *Chain Gang*'s portrayal of its penal system. According to film historian William Meyer, the Warner brothers and director LeRoy were warned not to enter the state of Georgia in the months after the film was released. LeRoy maintained in later decades that he had had no intention of preaching any particular message about the Depression or prison reform in *Chain Gang*; he had just wished to present a great story, and, he maintained, this intention animated all of his work as a director,[18] including the Warner Bros. Great Depression musical *Gold Diggers of 1933*, which he would helm the next year.

Wild Boys of the Road (1933), released the same month as *Footlight Parade*, mined similar disturbing territory as *Chain Gang*. With their childhood homes about to be foreclosed upon and their parents out of work, two teenage boys decide to cease being an economic burden on their strapped parents. They leave their comfortable high school world in order to ride the rails in search of work, hoping to send money home. Numerous shots display a multi-racial group of hobos riding the rails, desperate for employment. In a particularly beautiful and tragic scene, the boys leap off moving trains as they get close to a station, breaking into a run to avoid the railroad police; one boy accidentally hits his head on a pole as he leaps off, and lies half-conscious on the railroad tracks as his leg is run over by a train. In another scene, the boys realise they hold a numerical advantage over the railroad 'dicks' and fight back and win against them (unfortunately, as most boys hurl rocks and eggs against the cops, the black kids use minstrel-stereotyped watermelons). It's a spontaneous joyful rebellion, but one careful not to display hints of communist revolution or social blame during a period when the Communist Party was gaining a small number of adherents in the United States. As screenwriter Andrew Bergman argued in his book describing films of the Great Depression, Warners' 'social consciousness films . . . [demonstrated] both a gritty feel for social realism and a total inability to give any coherent reasons for social difficulties'.[19] Certainly, stockbrokers, for example, were not indicted in these films for their encouragement of buying on margin, which allowed their clients to purchase stocks while putting down only 10 per cent of the cost, creating a huge bubble in the market which led to the 1929 market crash that initiated the Depression's economic dislocation. There existed no room in the plot for such detail in this or probably any other Hollywood film.

But as *Wild Boys* closes, it is obvious that something is wrong in the United States, that justice and opportunity is not being made available to all Americans, even the most vulnerable citizens. In a crowning speech at the close of the film, the main character, Eddie, tells a judge:

> I'll tell you why we can't go home, because our folks are poor, they can't get jobs, and there isn't enough to eat. What good will it do you to send us home to starve? You say you gotta send us to jail to keep us off the streets. Well, that's a lie. You're sending us to jail because you don't want to see us, you wanna forget us, well you can't do it 'cause I'm not the only one, there's thousands just like me and there's more hitting the road every day . . . I'm sick of being hungry and cold, sick of freight trains, jail can't be any worse than the street, so give it to me!

Eddie's friend Tommy, the one who lost his leg in the rail yard, chimes in as well, arguing that if the banks, soldiers and breweries get 'help' from government, then they should too: 'What about us?', he asks. 'We're kids.' At the last second, upon hearing their story, the judge, who slightly resembles President Roosevelt and has an NRA Blue Eagle insignia hanging above his chair, relents and releases Eddie from a sentence for a crime he did not commit. Eddie then starts a job as an elevator boy, but the two friends he has journeyed with throughout the film and most of the hobos they encountered along the way are clearly nowhere near as lucky and will still need to struggle.

The World Changes (1933) represents another example of Warner's 'social relevance' films. It traces decades of American history, from hard-working pioneers heading west in the 1870s to the Wall Street greed and deteriorating morals supposedly characterising the 1920s. In *Five Star Final* (1931), Edward G. Robinson portrays a New York newspaper editor pressured by the paper's owner to include more lurid and gossipy pieces to increase circulation and profits. When his reporters unearth and write about a woman who killed a man in self-defence decades before, even though she has been a non-newsworthy mother and wife ever since, the editor fails to kill the story, even though he knows the ensuing publicity threatens the woman's daughter's wedding. When the mother commits suicide over the shame she feels and the groom's family wants him to back out of the wedding, the daughter and her fiancée excoriate the editor, owner and reporter, attacking the morality of their profession: 'It won't do any good to tell you what you've done. You'll go on hunting little unimportant people who can't fight back . . . You've grown rich on filth and no one's ever dared rise up and crush you.'

Not everyone admired the hard-hitting approach of many Warner films, as a perusal of *Motion Picture Herald*, the national magazine representing the interests of exhibitors, indicates was the case during 1933.[20] Similar in plot and spirit to *Chain Gang*, *Heroes for Sale* (1933) left its honourable, talented and innocent protagonist wandering homeless through America at the close of the film. It drew criticism from theatre owners: 'too gruesome . . . a cheerful ending would have played better' (Selma, LA); 'could be a wow [if it had a] a happy ending' (Lebanon, KS); and 'people do not seem to care for this type of story' (New York City). Dr L. D. Whitaker, a Farmville, VA theatre owner, pleaded with Hollywood to issue more 'happy films':

> God knows there is enough tragedy in the everyday life of people . . . For the life of me I cannot see why the producers fail to realize that they are seriously hurting the entire industry by the types of pictures they are now presenting to the public . . . Within the past few months I have seen picture after picture that contained tragedy and unhappiness, and left the audiences leaving the theatre with long faces that gave them the appearance that they were returning from a funeral instead of from what was supposed to be a house of entertainment.

Many other Warner titles of the period continued the 'social relevance' theme as the main basis throughout a film, and even more films featured the motif in certain individual scenes.[21] A slogan that the studio used throughout the 1930s highlighted these tendencies: 'Combining good picture-making with good citizenship.' But an in-depth profile of the company published in *Fortune* in 1937 made clear that such concerns were not of the bleeding heart variety, and that in the end the bottom line drove the 'social relevance' films: 'Most Warner executives are quick to disown the role of crusader for social justice; they protest that their only purpose in treating these "controversial" themes is a harmless passion for gold.' The article also hinted that for Harry Warner and his moralistic sensibility this might have been somewhat less the case. The magazine noted that 'Warner is the only major studio that seems to know or care what is going on in America [today]'. Harry downplayed this theme in interviews since a priority of social crusading would have alienated the Republican-leaning Wall Street crowd the studio relied on for financing, but films quickly produced based on current events evinced an immediacy that attracted audiences, and could be filmed for less money than films featuring lavish sets. The drive for profit was paramount, and, as will be seen in future chapters, employees were at times not treated with the kind of justice often championed in many Warner films of the decade. The 'rat eat rat' ethos applied not just to the competitors of the Warner Bros. studio, but also, seemingly, to their own employees.

The brothers were ruthless in running their business efficiently. Jack Warner's job was 'not to make artistic triumphs', according to *Fortune*, 'but to make sixty pictures a year on a budget of $25 million in a carefully organized and controlled system of "factory production"'. And Jack was quite skilled at this: 85 per cent of the 214 Warner releases between 1933 and 1937 more than made back the cost of production and distribution, a figure several times greater than Hollywood's batting average in the present day. 'This does not mean that they were very good pictures', lauded *Fortune*. 'It means that they didn't cost very much to begin with and that every one of them hit the budget on the nose . . . a famous Jack Warner specialty.'[22]

As the Warners made their way to the top echelon of their field, Franklin Delano Roosevelt also reached the top of his, developing a reputation for scrappiness, character and innovation. Roosevelt, born in 1882, grew up on his family's Hyde Park estate along the Hudson River about ninety miles north of New York City.[23] He possessed an aristocratic background. His family's neighbours were people like the Vanderbilts and Astors – though the Roosevelts, who traced their American ancestry to before the American Revolution, did not occupy the highest realm of wealth. They were more than comfortable, however, with Roosevelt's father leaving an estate of $300,000 (over $9 million in today's money) while Cornelius Vanderbilt left more than $72 million. Franklin's mother Sara wished for him to live in patrician comfort on the family estate, but this lack of activity did not interest her son. Young Franklin travelled to Europe several times, and attended upper-class schools Groton and Harvard. Biographer Frank Friedel noted that Rector Endicott Peabody at Groton served as a key early influence in Roosevelt's life, 'leading him toward Christian service to the nation and those less fortunate than himself', in the style of the Social Gospel movement which reached its zenith during the 1890s. Like his fifth cousin President Theodore Roosevelt, Franklin believed in *noblesse oblige*, the notion that the well-off had a duty to give back to society in recognition of the advantages and riches they enjoyed. Historian David Kennedy noted how another experience at school may have influenced Roosevelt's ability to see beyond his upper-class background: 'The one disappointment of his undergraduate years was his failure to be elected to membership in Porcellian, an upper crust [Harvard] club whose rejection stung him deeply and may have contributed something to his later animus against the American upper crust, an animus that would in time earn him a reputation in the wood-panelled clubrooms of America's self-styled aristocracy as a "traitor to his class".'

After a year at Columbia University Law School, Roosevelt passed the bar and served as a lawyer in a Wall Street firm, concentrating less on corporate and banking law and focusing more on cases where, in the words of Friedel, 'he learned first hand about the problem of poverty'. Most observers, however, noted that his ambitions lay in the political realm, tracing the path of his cousin Theodore – supposedly Franklin confided to his fellow law clerks his desire to emulate Theodore's career. After three uneventful years in law, he did: becoming Assistant Secretary of the US Navy, involved in the New York legislature (as a State Senator), running for Vice President of the United States (and losing, unlike Theodore), and in 1928, becoming governor of New York, his eventual springboard to the presidency.

Franklin's contracting of polio at the age of 39 also heightened his empathy for those who struggled. The disease left him incapacitated, mostly residing in a wheelchair, able to walk just a few halting steps at a time, and those steps accomplished only with uncomfortable metal braces lashed to his withered legs. Roosevelt spent much of the 1920s rebuilding his body, learning how to live and thrive with his disability, and building ties with both the north and south wings of the Democratic party from his rehabilitation centre in Warm Springs, GA, in the middle of the Old South. Before Roosevelt's election to the presidency in 1932, his party, the Democrats, had lost three presidential elections in a row, mostly because of their inability to resolve the differences between its northern urban and southern rural factions. But Roosevelt was a master at bringing previously irreconcilable groups together, as seen in his ability to unite Tammany New York City voters with more conservative rural upstate New Yorkers to win the governorship in 1928, or in his eventual ability to win an unprecedented four presidential elections in a row.

Roosevelt successfully campaigned for the presidency during the Great Depression. It is difficult to overstate the extreme economic calamity of the period – no conditions near as dire were experienced in the United States before or since.[24] When Roosevelt assumed the presidency in 1933, income was down 50 per cent from four years previously. Unemployment reached 25 per cent across the country and almost twice that in urban centres like Cleveland and Detroit. Among minorities and immigrants, the numbers were worse. And about a third of those lucky enough to have employment could only secure part-time work as the economy severely contracted. US Steel, for example, had no full-time workers on its payroll as Roosevelt began his presidency, down from 225,000 in 1929. Over 5,000 banks had closed and millions of personal bank accounts were lost, wiping out at least $7 billion (over $125 billion in today's dollars) between the crash and Roosevelt coming to power. Many more banks temporarily closed just before Roosevelt's inauguration, waiting for action from the new president to shore up the banking system. As is often the case in American history, farmers took it on the chin: farm income dropped from $6 billion in 1929 to just $2 billion in 1932. And there were virtually no government benefits to help those who sorely needed it. Local, state and national governments lacked the infrastructure to deal with the unprecedented poverty and deficiency of opportunity racking the country, especially since their tax revenues plunged along with the consequent drop in employment and consumer activity. The city of Chicago, for example, could not pay its schoolteachers during the winter before Roosevelt assumed the presidency. The anomie unleashed by the vastly reduced circumstances reached into Americans' personal lives: marriage fell 22 per cent between 1929 and 1933, and 15 per cent fewer children were born. In historian Arthur Schlesinger's telling, the burden resting on FDR's shoulders represented no less than 'a matter of staving off violence, even (at least some so thought) revolution. Whether revolution was a real possibility or not, faith in a free system was plainly waning.'

Roosevelt faced a daunting job after swearing his oath of office on 4 March 1933, a job that not everyone in the country felt could be accomplished. The effects of the Depression made many Americans wonder if such failure signalled that capitalism was untenable.[25] Interest in communism and socialism spiked during this period, especially since positive Soviet propaganda spread through the press provided a rosier picture of life in the Soviet Union than was later found to be the case. The Communist Party gathered 102,000 votes in the 1932 election, its best showing in American history, yet statistically insignificant compared to Roosevelt's 22 million votes, and the 15 million amassed by the Republican Party. While no efforts were ever uncovered of American communists actually planning to bring down the government (although some argued it needed to be done), there existed areas of the country where beliefs in communism and socialism were paid attention to more seriously. Rural farm communities represented one of those areas, as communists helped organise actions in several states, and another was the Hollywood film colony. In Hollywood, the numbers of those interested in communism enough to join the party were only a few hundred (out of tens of thousands in the industry), but represented a particularly threatening prospect since the town dominated the most powerful form of mass media. This circumstance inspired two decades of harsh vitriol, a 'red scare', in the Hollywood labour community beginning in 1933, just as President Roosevelt's New Deal programme unfolded, and the Great Depression Musicals were being produced and released.

During 1932, the interests of Democratic Party presidential candidate Franklin Roosevelt and Harry and Jack Warner converged, as the brothers became among the most high-profile contributors and advocates in the Roosevelt campaign.[26] The support from the Warners was surprising; the Jewish movie moguls, including Harry and Jack, were usually reliable Republicans, the party viewed, then and now, as more friendly towards business. As journalist

Ronald Brownstein reported in his history of the links between moviedom and Washington, DC politicians, as regards the Hollywood studio heads, 'as entrepreneurs who had scrambled up the hard way, their vague political views were anchored in an apostolic belief in hard work, bootstraps and the American dream; practically, that translated into the right of those who had scrambled so fiercely to keep what they earned without much government intrusion'. Judging from the many Warner films that reflected the suffering of the Great Depression, this general situation, and President Herbert Hoover's inability to offer solutions for it, may have played a role in the Warners' political switch. Jack Warner seemed to confirm this interpretation, recalling Harry telling him in 1932 that 'the country is in chaos. There is revolution in the air, and we need a change.' *Fortune* magazine reported that Jim Farley, chairman of the Democratic National Committee and a key force in the ascension of Franklin Roosevelt to the presidency, convinced Harry to back his man.

Another important reason for the Warners' ticket jumping probably emanated from Harry's unhappiness concerning 'a Senate investigation of a stock sale of his during the Hoover administration'. Though not yet an illegal offence, Harry and the other main three brothers in the business appear to have been engaging in what would today be termed insider trading, using private company knowledge to make a profit in the stock market. Harry sold shares at $54 per share, probably knowing that they were headed for a fall, then bought them back again at less than half the price. He claimed that he and his brothers sold the shares because the company needed the capital as the failing economy kept sliding, but, as Freedland reported, 'the brothers admitted making a profit of $7 million in their own share deals during 1930 – not a popular thing to do while the Depression wrapped itself around America like a racoon coat'.

The brothers were asked to help Roosevelt become better known on the West Coast and drum up support among their media mogul peers, especially William Randolph Hearst, whose nationwide network of newspapers included 20 per cent of Sunday circulation, and almost half of California circulation. Jack embraced his new role for the Democrats wholeheartedly, becoming the party's Hollywood figurehead during the election much as Louis B. Mayer had done for the Republican Party in the 1920s. During the 1932 campaign, Mayer served as the vice-chairman of the California GOP and as chairman of the Republican State Central Committee. Mayer was a good friend of Hoover as well as Hearst, with Mayer providing a home at his MGM lot for Hearst's independent Cosmopolitan Pictures company. Hearst and his papers supported Republican presidential candidates in 1924 and 1928, and the Roosevelt campaign wished to see his political affiliation change in 1932. 'Jack Warner has gone in for politics on all four[s]', reported *Variety* six weeks before the election. 'There is no train that comes in with a visiting Democrat

Figure 1.3   Former Republican president Calvin Coolidge with Hollywood's premier
Republican and MGM studio head Louis B. Mayer on the MGM lot, 19
February 1930. Behind them and to the right are (L to R) the legendary
actress/producer/writer Mary Pickford, probably the most famous
woman in the world during the silent film era, and Coolidge's wife
Grace. (Getty Photos)

not met by Warner and his staff.' Jack L. Warner's reputation within the industry for not tolerating any lack of work initiative among his staff was surprisingly put on hold for two hours when he brought Boston's fiercely Democratic
mayor to Warners to let him 'lace it to Hoover' before an audience of all the
studio's 'stars, directors, writers and executives'. *Variety* reported that Jack
had assumed the chairmanship of the 'local motion picture division of the
Democratic campaign' and had donated $50,000 to Roosevelt's campaign in
the early going.

The 'Motion Picture Electrical Parade and Sports Pageant' formed the highlight of the Warners' efforts on Roosevelt's behalf, held at Los Angeles' new
Olympic coliseum (the city hosted the Olympics that summer) on 24 September
1932.[27] While not a formal campaign or fundraising event, it generated enormous publicity for Roosevelt's campaign, and marshalled the resources of
Hollywood, its stars and media power behind a presidential candidate in an
unprecedented manner. The event featured, according to the *Los Angeles
Times*, 'twenty massed bands' and 'a glittering procession of beautiful floats'
sponsored by most of the major studios, festooned with movie stars. The

Figure 1.4   Franklin Delano Roosevelt, the New York governor, on the stump during his successful 1932 presidential campaign. (The Art Archive/Culver Pictures)

Republican-leaning *Times* gave the event prominent coverage the day before and after the event, and estimated 60,000 people in attendance, though a picture of the event included in the coverage makes it seem as if that number were actually much higher, since the 100,000-seat coliseum looked packed to the rafters as Roosevelt addressed the crowd. The proceedings proved as absurd and surreal as any celebrity event of the present day: a trained horse named Redhead jumped through fire, Hollywood notables played polo on the field, and the studios' floats paid tribute to, among others, George Washington (Fox), Cleopatra (RKO), 'old Spain' (Goldwyn), the Rock of Gibraltar (Columbia) and, in Warner Bros/First National's case, the 'Goddess of Beauty', who, aided by 'a moving elevator ... played in a silver fountain' at the top of a 'silver tower lighted with colored globes'. MGM, the studio headed by Mayer, the most famous Republican in Hollywood, did not contribute a float to the proceedings and barred his stars from attending. Cars featuring luminaries such as Charles Chaplin, Claudette Colbert, Clark Gable, Stan Laurel and Oliver Hardy and many others circled around the Olympic track, waving at the crowd (strangely, no Warner stars were reported present). Besides candidate Roosevelt's brief bow and speech to the crowd, the highlight appeared to be remarks by humourist and movie star Will Rogers, whose semi-political gibes delivered with an 'aw, shucks' attitude appeared on the front page of the *Times* in a regular column. Los Angeles radio stations KHJ and KFWB (the latter owned by Warner Bros.) covered the event live.

Jack Warner claimed in his autobiography that his offering of a share of the proceeds from the pageant to Hearst paramour and movie star Marion Davies' favourite anti-vivisection charity 'guaranteed the backing of the Hearst newspapers'. The rest of the funds raised went to the Motion Picture Relief Fund, which supports retired and poverty-stricken film workers. But it should be noted that Jack was a notorious tale-spinner; whether or not the event inspired Hearst's support is not known; it is a boast that should be viewed with caution. But, in the days preceding the pageant, the *Times* featured stories about the growing links between Roosevelt and Hearst, and the two men met privately for 25 minutes during Roosevelt's brief and event-packed day in Southern California. On the day Roosevelt arrived, a *Los Angeles Times* front-page editorial acidly noted that Hearst and his news-papers were vociferous opponents of Roosevelt's bid for the Democratic presidential nomination just three months before, but now Roosevelt was appearing in Los Angeles 'under the aegis of the Hearst newspapers'. No source from the period mentioned Jack Warner's supposedly high-profile role in the Roosevelt/Hearst rapprochement. Hearst's behaviour was not unusual in this or any other election. Foes of candidates during the presiden-tial primary season often coalesce around their party's eventual nomination for the office. But the *Times* was probably trying to spotlight dissension and possible hypocrisy within Democratic ranks.

In any case, six weeks later, Roosevelt took California (Hoover's home state and usually a Republican stalwart), and the entire country, by a landslide in the general election. For the first time in sixteen years, a Democratic presiden-tial candidate took Republican-leaning Los Angeles County, a feat probably relished by Jack Warner. *Variety*, the most influential show business industry periodical now and then, proclaimed in a front page banner headline that the election comprised 'America's Greatest Show', noting that it 'sway[ed the] entire populace', amid some grumbles that the 'ballyhooed' occasion sent entertainment grosses downward nationwide for weeks, including an esti-mated $50 million loss at film box offices alone.[28] Rumours swirled that Jack might become Roosevelt's official government liaison to the film industry. That did not occur, but Roosevelt later invited Jack to the White House, where he stayed overnight in the famous Lincoln bedroom. Jack also maintained for many years, including in his autobiography, that the president had offered him an ambassadorship in thanks for his service during the campaign, but he claimed that he refused it, telling Roosevelt that 'I think I can do better for your foreign relations with a good picture about America every now and then'. Such boasts were apparently hyperbole. Jack Warner, Jr (as well as others) stated that no diplomatic post was broached: 'I heard [Jack Sr.] say he wished it was true, but his old presidential pal never came across.'

The brothers also arranged for a 'special gold-leafed Pullman' train of Warner stars, including James Cagney (the future star of *Footlight Parade*), Bette Davis and Ginger Rogers (the future star of *Gold Diggers of 1933*), to barnstorm across the country on the way to attending the presidential inauguration in Washington in March 1933.[29] Jack Warner told the press that 'the contingent ... includes all Warner stars except those actually engaged in productions at the time of the departure'. This public relations stunt provided positive publicity opportunities for the studio as well as the new administration, one of the first of many future political and economic links between Hollywood and the White House. Press reports indicated two names for the train: 'the 42nd Street Special', named after the film that premiered four days after the inauguration, the first of what would later be known as the Warner Bros. Great Depression Musicals, and 'the Warner–GE Better Times Special', which registered the fact that General Electric co-sponsored the train, paying most of the $60,000 expense for the trip, and providing lighting on the outside of the cars so fans along the way could see the stars even during night appearances. The corporation, the parent organisation of the NBC radio network, ensured that live radio hook-ups were available across the United States, airing publicity about Warner Bros. and GE in numerous local communities. Zanuck and Jack Warner made speeches sending off the train in Los Angeles. At seventeen stops across the country, elected officials or their representatives praised Roosevelt, and twelve 'chorus girls' from the *42nd Street* cast performed dance routines from the film.[30]

In her autobiography, Davis claimed that the actors aboard worried about parading such luxury across an economically devastated country, and said she felt they should have been promoting a hypothetical musical called *Let 'Em Eat Cake* instead of *42nd Street*. 'Not only did we blind the poor with our glitter, we even had one whole car fitted with sand, water and suntan lamps that transformed the Pullman into a mobile Malibu beach', she recalled. 'The whole affair was fabulous – traveling in such luxury during a depression. We were afraid we might incite a revolution; but unlike the eighteenth-century Frenchmen, Americans love their royalty and we were welcomed everywhere with open arms, although a few did stick their tongues out at us.' According to scholar Charles Eckert, luxuries on the train also included a fully equipped kitchen of new GE appliances, and an entire car for a horse named King, ridden by western stars Leo Carrillo and Tom Mix at events staged along the route. In larger cities, these events were usually held in GE showrooms.

The Warner/GE train promoted other movies and stars, as seen in an 18 March ad in the *Motion Picture Herald* picturing a beaming Bette Davis sitting amid a pile of inauguration clippings: 'The "42nd Street Special" Made Her Famous – [her new film] Will Make Her A Sensation!' Warner Bros. made a short film documenting and promoting the train's exploits, which was shown before features during 1933. As an announcer bellowed during the film, 'Hollywood is on its way to Washington!'

MGM also commissioned a train for the inaugural. Their Traveling Studio car made the Roosevelt inaugural the first stop in what purported to be a four-year tour, screen-testing potential local movie stars and promoting MGM films at whistle stops nationwide. The publicity surrounding MGM's train seemed less connected to the Roosevelt administration than that conceived for the Warner train, although an MGM ad in *Motion Picture Herald* on inaugura-tion day featured a painting of the new president alongside a short note to him about how 'proud' they were to have a 'place in the Inaugural Parade', adding that their train 'will carry from Washington the good-will message of the screen to the nation', a much more vague statement than seen in the Warner ads concerning the import of the day. Contemporary MGM train publicity did not name 'stars' that rode on their train for the inauguration or afterwards; it seems their biggest names were absent, perhaps not a surprising circumstance for the studio headed by Hollywood's most famous Republican. In the same issue of the *Herald*, Warner Bros. reminded the film community of their par-ticipation in the day's events. One ad proclaimed 'Saturday[,] America gets that New Deal!', but most of the ad was devoted to promoting *42nd Street* and the inaugural train that bore its name. Another ad in the same issue, spanning two pages, bragged in huge letters about 'the inaugural parade of hits' Warner would supply to theatres during 1933.

Warner Bros. also sponsored a float in the inaugural parade called 'Better Times', and made sure it carried no company designation because, as Harry Warner maintained, 'commercializing the inauguration would not be digni-fied'. This seemed at least in part a dig at rival MGM's train in the parade, which apparently featured a visible MGM logo. Harry and Albert Warner, along with several Warner executives, attended various inaugural balls that evening. Never before had the motion picture industry been so intimately and prominently involved with a presidential inauguration.

Warner Bros. led the way in associating itself and its products with Roosevelt and the New Deal, his legislative programme that sought to solve the crisis of the Great Depression. A week prior to the inauguration and the premiere of *42nd Street*, a two-page ad in *Motion Picture Herald* explicitly linked the two events in bold all-caps lettering: 'The inauguration of our new president, the inauguration of a new deal in entertainment', the ad proclaimed, adorned with pictures of the US Capitol and lounging chorus girls. In the month after the inauguration, various Warner full-page or two-page ads adopted govern-ment and/or Rooseveltian imagery. In two different ads they boasted of their

'10-week reconstruction program' featuring their 'inaugural parade of hits' that they predicted would lift box-office figures, while another ad extolling 'the Warner spirit' included a row of white stars resembling those on the American flag. Besides the many references to Roosevelt and the New Deal in the 1933 Great Depression Musicals, *Heroes for Sale* featured a scene among struggling hobos where one fears 'the end of America' because of the widespread misery, while the other reassures him by confiding: 'Maybe [it's] the end of us, but it's not the end of America . . . you read President Roosevelt's inaugural address? He's right, you know it takes more than one sock on the jaw to lick 120 million people.' Other studios also partook of the optimism surrounding the first weeks of Roosevelt's presidency, with Columbia Pictures in one ad proclaiming 'Happy Days Are Here Again!' (Roosevelt's campaign song), and predicting that the administration's opening of banks, legalisation of alcohol and providing of unemployment relief would help drive up theatre receipts. However, throughout the first ten months of 1933, more than any other studio, Warner Bros. identified publicly, repeatedly and loudly in their films and in motion picture industry periodicals with the incoming administration.

But the Warner/Roosevelt train was not destined to run smoothly for long.

NOTES

1. [Uncited author], 'Warner Bros.', *Fortune* (December 1937): 110–11.
2. The concept of the personality of Hollywood film studios in this period is also discussed in Neal Gabler, *An Empire of Their Own: How the Jews Invented Hollywood* (New York: Anchor, 1988), Chapter 6; Leo Rosten, *Hollywood: The Movie Colony, The Movie Makers* (New York: Harcourt, Brace & Co., 1941): 242–5. Chapter 4 of the Gabler book deals with the history and personality of the Warner Bros. studio.
3. This history of the pre-film industry Warners is based on the following sources: Michael Freedland, *The Warner Brothers* (London: Harrap, 1983), Chapters 2 and 3; Gabler, 120–36; David Thomson, *The New Biographical Dictionary of Film* (London: Little, Brown, 2003): 919–20; Clive Hirschhorn, *The Warner Bros. Story* (London: Octopus, 1979): 8–23; Jack Warner with Dean Jennings, *My First Hundred Years in Hollywood* (New York: Random House, 1965), Chapters 1–8. Sources differ on whether the Warners showed *The Great Train Robbery* in their yard at first or in an Ohio store. I've used Gabler's information since his research is more documented than the other authors' cited here.
4. Sources for this section on the MPPC: Jeanne Thomas Allen, 'The Decay of the Motion Picture Patents Company', in Tino Balio, ed., *The American Film Industry* (Madison, WI: University of Wisconsin Press, 1976); Robert Sklar, *Movie-Made America: A Cultural History of American Movies* (New York: Vintage, 1994), Chapter 3; David Thomson, *The Whole Equation: A History of Hollywood* (New York: Vintage, 2004), Chapters 2 and 4.
5. Freedland, 20; Hirschhorn, 14–22; Leonard Mosley, *Zanuck: The Rise and Fall of Hollywood's Last Tycoon* (London: McGraw-Hill, 1984): 98–102; Susan Orlean, 'The Dog Star: Rin-Tin-Tin and the Making of Warner Bros.', *The New Yorker* (29 August 2011): 34–9; Thomas Schatz, *The Genius of the System: Hollywood*

Filmmaking in the Studio Era (New York: Henry Holt, 1988): 61–2; [uncited author], 'Warner', *Fortune*, 111.

All financial estimates of dollar value inflation over time in this book are from: https://www.measuringworth.com/uscompare/ (last accessed 23 February 2017).

6. This section on the adoption of sound in motion pictures by Warner Bros. is from the following sources: Scott Eyman, *Empire of Dreams: The Epic Life of Cecil B. DeMille* (New York: Simon & Schuster, 2010): 258–9; 269–71; Freedland, Chapters 4–6; Gabler, 136–46; J. Douglas Gomery, 'The Coming of the Talkies: Invention, Innovation and Diffusion', in Balio, ed., *American Film Industry*; Douglas Gomery, 'Tri-Ergon, Tobis-Klangfilm, and the Coming of Sound', *Cinema Journal* 16:1 (1976); Douglas Gomery, 'Writing the History of the American Film Industry: Warner Brothers and Sound', in Bill Nichols, ed., *Movies and Methods, Vol. 2* (Berkeley: University of California Press, 1985); Donald Grafton, *The Talkies: America's Transition to Sound, 1926–1931* (New York: Charles Scribner's Sons, 1997): 72–113; Hirschhorn, 30–4; Mosley, 124–46; Schatz, 62–6, [uncited author], 'Warner', *Fortune*: 112, 206–10; [uncited author], 'History, Warner Bros. Studio Facilities', from http://www2.warnerbros.com/wbsf/#/geninfo/history/ (last accessed 8 November 2011; [uncited author], 'Western Electric: A Brief History', available at http://www.porticus.org/bell/westernelectric_history. html#Western%20Electric%20-%20A%20Brief%20History (last accessed 7 November 2011).

As Gomery explains in detail, there were several antecedents for talking pictures going back at least fifteen years before the release of *The Jazz Singer*, including some pioneered by Thomas Edison and various German scientists and companies, but none of them worked as well technologically and commercially as the Vitaphone system used by *Jazz Singer*. The Fox studio also contributed to the eventual success of 'talkies'. If the German economy had not been experiencing such profound problems during the mid-1920s, scientists and companies from that country might well have beaten Warner Bros. and Western Electric to the international motion picture market-place.

7. About half of those 86 films were produced by or made under the banner of First National, of which Warner Bros. took full control in 1929: Hirschhorn, 66.

8. John Kobal, *Gotta Dance Gotta Sing: A Pictorial History of Film Musicals* (London: Hamlyn, 1971) 24–5; Thomson, *Equation*: 122; Russell Sanjek, *American Popular Music and Its Business, Volume 3, 1890–1984* (New York, Oxford University Press, 1988): 54–5, 72–5.

A Nashville, IL theatre owner mentioned the plugging of songs from *42nd Street* on the radio as an important factor in making the film a hit at his theatre: H. R. Hisey, in 'What the Picture Did for Me' [column], *Motion Picture Herald* (22 April 1933).

9. [Uncited author], '84 Features with Music Available for Booking in the Next Few Months', *Motion Picture Herald* (20 May 1933).

10. Freedland, 58–9, 62, 74, 97–8; Gabler, 120–2, 145–6; Mel Gussow, *Zanuck: Don't Say Yes Until I Finish Talking* (London: W. H. Allen, 1971) 40; Jack Warner, *My First*, 181; [uncited authors], 'Radio Sponsors' 'Stay Home' Plea Widens Breach with Exhibitors', *Motion Picture Herald* (3 June 1933); 'Radio Competition', *Motion Picture Herald* (30 December 1933).

11. Gabler, 196; Nancy Snow, '"Confessions" of a Hollywood Propagandist: Harry Warner, FDR, and Celluloid Persuasion', in Martin Kaplan and Johanna Blakley, eds, *Warners' War: Propaganda, Politics and Pop Culture in Wartime Hollywood* (Los Angeles: Norman Lear Center Press, 2004): 61–71; [uncited author], 'Warner', *Fortune*, 208, 220.

12. John Davis, 'Notes on Warner Brothers Foreign Policy, 1918–1948', *Velvet Light Trap* (Winter 1977): 19–22. Andrew Bergman analysed Warners' tendency towards films of 'social consciousness', but his arguments are much the same as Davis's for 'social relevance': Andrew Bergman, *We're in the Money: Depression America and Its Films* (New York: Harper & Row, 1971).

13. This section on the Warner Bros. house style is based on: Gussow, 50; Mosley, 157–63; Nick Roddick, *A New Deal in Entertainment: Warner Bros. in the 1930s* (London: British Film Institute, 1983): 20–8; Rosten, 243, 282–3; Schatz, Ch. 9; Thomson, *Equation*, Ch. 12; Darryl F. Zanuck, untitled column, *Hollywood Reporter* (24 December 1932); [uncited author], 'What the Picture Did for Me [column]', *Motion Picture Herald* (11 March 1933); [uncited author], 'If You Can Make 'Em Sit Forward You've Got a Picture, Says LeRoy', *Variety* (26 December 1933); [uncited author], 'Warner', *Fortune*, 110, 215–18. The Warren quotation is from: Tony Thomas, *Harry Warren and the Hollywood Musical* (Secaucus, NJ: The Citadel Press, 1975): 39.

    Various authors have cited various dates concerning the year Darryl F. Zanuck became head of production at Warners. Schatz says it is 1929 on p. 66 and 1930 on p. 136 of *Genius*, David Thomson (in his encyclopedia) claims 1931, and Mosley claims 1925. I think that, over the years, there has been confusion about job titles. Trying to piece this together, it seems Zanuck became the senior producer at Warner in 1929, and head of production the year after. I'm basing this on David Thomson's nomenclature, but on dates provided by Schatz, since he has made a broad investigation into studio files. Hirschhorn also lists the 1930 date.

14. One source contends that at Warner Bros., 'Directors participated in cutting unless shooting took them away' and cites several pictures from the second half of the 1930s. During the period covered by this book, especially with directors like Bacon and LeRoy who were helming four to five movies yearly, they probably did not have much time to contribute to editing: David Bordwell, Janet Staiger and Kristin Thompson, *The Classical Hollywood Cinema: Film Style & Mode of Production* (Oxon: Routledge, 2002): 326.

15. William Meyer, *Warner Brothers Directors: The Hard-Boiled, the Comic and the Weepers* (New Rochelle, NY: Arlington House, 1978): 223.

16. Bordwell, Staiger and Thompson, *Classical*: 326.

17. For exhibitor reaction to *Chain Gang*, including the columns referenced in the text, consult: [uncited authors/various exhibitors], 'What the Picture Did for Me [column]', *Motion Picture Herald* (11 March 1933, 23 April 1933, 27 May 1933, 10 June 1933, 24 June 1933, 16 September 1933, 30 September 1933).

18. Meyer, 227–31.

19. Bergman, 92–102. The quotation is from p. 92.

20. Sources for this paragraph, all from the *Motion Picture Herald*: Dr L. D. Whitaker, 'Wants Happier Films: Exhibitor Finds Explanation of Losses in Multitude of Depressing Pictures in These Times' (4 March 1933); 'What the Picture Did for Me' [column] (28 October 1933, 4 November 1933).

21. Some further examples of Warner Bros. social relevance films in the 1929–33 period, taken from the aforementioned Bergman, Hirschhorn and Roddick books, the Zanuck and *Fortune* articles, as well as my own viewing: *The Gamblers, The Time, the Place and the Girl, Madonna of Avenue A, Fast Life* (all from 1929); *Dawn Patrol, Son of the Gods, Doorway to Hell* (all from 1930); *Little Caesar, The Public Enemy, Smart Money, The Finger Points* (all from 1931); *Silver Dollar, The Famous Ferguson Case, Two Seconds, Life Begins, Cabin in the Cotton, The Mouthpiece, Taxi!* (all from 1932); *20,000 Years in Sing-Sing, The Mayor of Hell,*

Heroes for Sale, and of course the initial three Great Depression Musicals *42nd Street*, *Gold Diggers of 1933* and *Footlight Parade* (all from 1933).

22. Freedland, 2, 60; [uncited author], 'Warner', *Fortune*, 214–15.

23. This pre-1932 biography of Franklin Delano Roosevelt is based on the following sources: David Kennedy, *Freedom From Fear: The American People in Depression and War, 1929–1945* (Oxford: Oxford University Press, 1999): 94–115, Frank Freidel, *Franklin D. Roosevelt: A Rendezvous with Destiny* (Boston: Little, Brown, 1990): Ch. 1, Michael Simpson, *Franklin D. Roosevelt* (Oxford: B. Blackwell, 1989): Ch. 1.

24. Sources for the information cited concerning the depth of the misery during the Great Depression: Kennedy, 85–91, 160–6; William E. Leuchtenburg, *Franklin Roosevelt and the New Deal, 1932–1940* (New York: Harper & Row, 1963): Ch. 2; Sylvia Nasar, 'Keynes: The Sunny Economist', *New York Times* (18 September 2011); Arthur M. Schlesinger, Jr, *The Age of Roosevelt: The Coming of the New Deal* (Boston: Houghton-Mifflin, 1960): 3.

25. Sources for this brief discussion on communist interest in the United States during the Depression: Friedel, 206–7; Kennedy, 221–4; Leuchtenburg, 25–7, 111–14, 281–3, Schlesinger, Jr, 49–51, 54, 263–4.

26. Except where noted, this section on the Warners and Roosevelt during the 1932 election is based on: [uncited author], 'Inside Stuff – Pictures [column]', *Variety* (20 September 1932); [uncited author], 'Will It Be Sheehan of Warner? Coast Specs on Roosevelt Aide', *Variety* (15 November 1932); Richard Barrios, speaking in the *42nd Street: From Book to Screen to Stage* short documentary, on the *Gold Diggers of 1933* DVD (Warner Bros., 2008); Ronald Brownstein, *The Power and the Glitter: The Hollywood–Washington Connection* (New York: Pantheon, 1990), Chapters 1 and 3; Davis, 22; Freedland, 63–5; Steven J. Ross, *Hollywood Left and Right: How Movie Stars Shaped American Politics* (New York: Oxford University Press, 2011), Chapter 2; Snow, ibid.; Cass Warner Sperling and Cork Millner with Jack Warner Jr, *Hollywood Be Thy Name: The Warner Bros. Story* (Rocklin, CA: Prima, 1994): 161; Bor, *Clown Prince of Hollywood: The Antic Life and Times of Jack L. Warner* (New York: McGraw-Hill Ryerson, 1990): 93–4; J. Warner, 207–24; [uncited author], 'Warner', *Fortune*, 212. The *42nd Street Special* promotional Warner Bros. short film is available on the *Gold Diggers of 1933* DVD.

27. Sources for the section on the 24 September 1932 pageant: Sperling, ibid.; [uncited author], 'McAdoo to Join Roosevelt; Senatorial Aspirant to Fly North on Speech Tour Today and Bring Candidate Here Later', *Los Angeles Times* (20 September 1932); [uncited front-page editorial], 'Hearst and Roosevelt', *Los Angeles Times* (24 September 1932); [uncited author], 'Roosevelt's Day Here Will Keep Him On Jump', *Los Angeles Times* (24 September 1932); [uncited author], 'Film Pageant On Tonight; Electrical Floats and Twenty Bands Ready for Studios' Charity Fete at Coliseum', *Los Angeles Times* (24 September 1932); [uncited author], 'Brilliant Screen Floats Parade and Sports Pageant Thrill Thousands at Stadium; Notables and Charity Fete', *Los Angeles Times* (25 September 1932); Doug Douglas, 'Film World Pageant Goes on Air; Radio to Bring Word Pictures', *Los Angeles Times* (24 September 1932); Kyle D. Palmer, 'Campaign Issues Are Ignored by Roosevelt; Large Crowds Hear Candidate's Appeal but Learn Little of Where He Stands', *Los Angeles Times* (25 September 1932); Mark Wheeler, 'The Political History of Classical Hollywood: Moguls, Liberals and Radicals in the 1930s', from Iwan Morgan and Philip John Davies, eds, *Hollywood and the Great Depression: American Film, Politics and Society in the 1930s* (Edinburgh: Edinburgh University Press, 2016): 32.

Steven Ross (p. 71) claims that Louis B. Mayer was the 'modern pioneer' of 'celebrity-studded' publicity events for presidential candidates because of a MGM star-saturated evening at the Shrine Auditorium in Los Angeles six days before the 1932 election, but the 'Motion Picture Electrical Parade and Sports Pageant' was held more than a month before.

28. [Uncited author], 'America's Greatest Show: Elections Sway Entire Populace', *Variety* (1 November 1932 [top front page article]); [uncited author], 'Presidential Air Ballyhoos Kept $50,000,000 Worth of Customers Home', *Variety* (15 November 1932).

29. Sources for the material on the Warner and MGM trains attending the 1933 Roosevelt inauguration: Barrios, ibid.; Danae Clark, 'Acting in Hollywood's Best Interest: Representations of Actors' Labor During the National Recovery Administration', *Journal of Film and Video* 17:4 (Winter 1990): 8–12; James Cunningham, 'Asides & Interludes [column]: From Capitol Hill When the Industry Attended the Inaugural', *Motion Picture Herald* (11 March 1933); Bette Davis, *The Lonely Life* (New York: Putnam, 1962): 124–6; Charles Eckert, 'The Carole Lombard in Macy's Window', in Christine Gledhill, ed., *Stardom: Industry of Desire* (London: Psychology Press, 1991); Sperling, 161; [uncited author], 'WB's $60,000 Special Train Tour as Bally for "42nd St." Premiere', *Variety* (20 January 1933); [uncited authors], 'MGM's Traveling Studio to Head Inaugural Party Contingent', and 'Warner Train Speeds Up Records at Stops Tied to Film Openings', *Motion Picture Herald* (4 March 1933); [uncited author], 'Warner 42nd Street Train in New York for Premiere', *Motion Picture Herald* (4 March 1933); [uncited author], 'Warner Special Train Arrives in Town Today', *Los Angeles Times* (17 March 1933).

30. Contracts for the 'chorus girls' riding on the '42nd Street Special' indicate the Warner brass's concern about the behaviour of the women on the train, perhaps worried that any potential trouble could reflect badly upon the Roosevelt administration during the inauguration, so they installed a strict morals clause into their contracts, insisting the chorus girls could not do anything that will cause 'public hatred, contempt, scorn or ridicule … insult or offend public decency'. They faced immediate termination for 'any infringement thereof'. Also, perhaps because lodging and food were paid for by the studio, the chorus girls were paid only $25 per week on the train, whereas their wage during filming was $66: 'Dancers 42nd Street Contracts for Chorus', and 'From 42nd Street Contracts for Chorus', (both 2803 special), *42nd Street* file, Warner Bros. Archives, University of Southern California, Los Angeles.

2. THE GREAT DEPRESSION MUSICALS

It took a couple of years, but the Great Depression finally caught up with Hollywood in 1931.[1] As the studios consolidated and sound films emerged, the industry grew exponentially during the 1920s. By the end of the decade, according to *Film Daily Year Book*, the American film industry boasted more employees than Ford and General Motors. The novelty surrounding 'talkies' held audiences in theatres for a surprisingly long time after the 1929 stock market crash, with 45 million admissions per week in 1931 in a nation of roughly 120 million.[2] As the Hollywood studio system entered what many historians term its Golden Age during the 1930s and 1940s, one reason behind its success was this kind of guaranteed audience and market saturation, which rose overall over the 1930s and for most of the 1940s. For comparison, in 2011, movie admissions dwindled to just 1.3 billion per year in a nation of about 300 million, very close to a historic low[3] – each American went to the cinema on average only four times per year.

After the dramatic growth of the 1920s, attendance and profits finally fell dramatically during 1931. A financially desperate period in Hollywood began, which didn't start to reverse until 1934. Part of the problem stemmed from the fact that production costs had doubled and exhibition costs soared because of the introduction of sound. But the economic dislocation of the period remained the main reason. The studios' customer base shrank significantly. 'Draconian' budget cuts slashed Hollywood's annual payroll from $156 million in 1930 to $50 million in 1933. During 1931 and 1932, 6,500 American movie theatres were shuttered, about a third of them. To attract audiences, tickets were discounted. Product giveaways and bingo games were staged to entice customers. Foreign revenue dived. The studios took a battering. The film historian Tino Balio reported:

> Fox suffered a loss of $3 million [in 1931] after a $9 million profit the year before; and RKO's $3 million surplus from 1930 turned into a $5.6 million deficit. Paramount remained in the black that year, but [studio head Adolph] Zukor saw his company's profits fall from $18 million to $6 million and by 1932 he had a deficit of $21 million.

By 1933, Paramount, RKO and Universal were in receivership, one step away from bankruptcy, and Fox underwent reorganisation. Of the eight biggest Hollywood studios, only MGM stayed in the black throughout the Depression, and even increased its corporate assets during the mid-1930s, though it veered close to red territory in 1933. The stock value of these major studios dropped from $960 million in 1930 (over $13 billion in today's dollars) to $140 million four years later. Paramount's stock had gone from a 1930 high of 77¼ to a 1934 low of just 1½. No one knew whether Hollywood would ever recover from this devastating tailspin.

The economic boom Warner Bros. experienced in the wake of introducing sound films, and the brothers' multiple investments in ancillary businesses and movie theatres, helped them survive the period without entering receivership, but they endured years of losses. The studio's annual financial report announced a $7 million profit for 1930, followed by nearly $31 million in reported losses over the next four fiscal years. The low-budget aesthetic described in the previous chapter doubtless helped them survive, but they also produced fewer movies, going from a high of 88 releases in 1929 to about 55 films per year between 1931 and 1936. Tension was palpable during those years. Harry Warren, the Oscar-winning composer for most of the Warner Bros. Great Depression Musicals, recalled arriving at the studio for the first time in summer 1932 to write the songs for *42nd Street*. The parking lot was 'almost empty – they had laid off most of their people', he said decades later. The studio was 'in real trouble, and there was quite a bit of [initial] opposition in the company to making [an expensive musical like] *42nd Street*'. In 1937, *Fortune* magazine reported that 'litigious stockholders' unsuccessfully tried to toss the Warner brothers out of their own company for allegedly poor management and failing to pay dividends between 1930 and 1937. 'And yet Warner Bros. has been the only big theatre-owning company . . . excepting MGM's parent, Loew's Inc. – to have ridden the depression without resorting to bankruptcy, receivership, or reorganization of any kind', concluded the magazine. '[But] the tide has left Harry [Warner] with a nervous stomach, which keeps him at times on a light diet of steak and potatoes.'

This economic situation guided studio decisions in this period, including the decision to buck current industry thinking which viewed musicals as a moribund genre fallen out of favour with the public, and launch the series of Great Depression Musicals. In reviving and transforming the movie musical, the studio produced three musicals in 1933 that still hold up today. These films took audiences on flights of fancy, while also registering the tough and dire situation inhabiting the national and international landscape. Part of the reason these films have proved powerful and enduring, then and now, is their unique melding of struggle (during their dialogue sections) and release (during their fanciful and romantic musical numbers). Americans needed an escape from misery and Warner Bros. provided it in a style unprecedented in Hollywood history. Even more importantly from the perspective of the bottom line, the 1933 Great Depression Musicals were significant in keeping the studio afloat during the worst times of the Depression in Hollywood.

The edict against musicals by head of production Darryl F. Zanuck and Harry and Jack Warner probably went into effect in 1930, a year in which Warner Bros. issued ten musicals, most of which evinced little box-office effect, despite featuring songs by such luminaries as Jerome Kern, Richard Rodgers and Lorenz Hart. Over the next two years the studio released only seven musicals, with low budgets and little executive support behind them.[4]

The novelty of musicals in the wake of the birth of talking pictures had worn off by the early 1930s.[5] According to writer Tony Thomas, Hollywood released 50 musicals in 1929, almost one per week, while another 100 releases 'dragged in a song or two' to get in on the fad. No wonder a glut ensued. As Zanuck indelicately remarked, 'there were so many musicals you wanted to vomit'. The expense also proved a factor in the studios staying away from them after 1930. Costs were exacerbated during this period by studios bringing in top Broadway stars and songwriters to adorn their early musicals. For example, John McCormack, the famous Irish tenor, received $50,000 per week (over $700,000 in today's money) for ten weeks' work, and Marilyn Miller made $1,000 an hour for 100 hours of work on *Sally*, a Warner Bros. film.

While artistic and commercial successes such as Rouben Mamoulian's *Applause* (1929) and King Vidor's *Hallelujah* (the first African American musical – racially progressive for the period, though less so today) were produced, most musicals from this period did not get anywhere near the standard set by those two films. Two hit MGM films from 1929 demonstrate the primitive state of film sound and the low standards audiences had for the novelty of musicals at this time. *Hollywood Revue of 1929* featured an all-star cast in a variety show format surrounded by under-rehearsed chorus girls filmed mostly in proscenium style, with the camera almost always planted in the position of an audience member, with little editing or camera movement. Such static film construction doubtless had to do with the limited technology available during the early days of 'soundies', when the camera's whirring noises were contained within an awkward booth that proved difficult to move. Uncomfortable silences are legion, corny vaudeville humour reigns, and comedy legends Buster Keaton and Laurel and Hardy are not used to their best effect. *Broadway Melody* somehow won the Oscar for best picture, and shares with *Revue* proscenium framing and a lack of camera movement, along with some unbelievable plot twists and a sparkling cinematic presence in actress Bessie Love.

Later observers have argued that audiences were also alienated by the large number of operettas (such as *Bride of the Regiment, Dixiana* and *The Rogue Song*, all from 1930) released, which were behind the times, to say the least. 'Instead of exploiting [the musical] to convey the zesty, energetic *modernity* of America, [the industry] seemed to waste [the form] – and our time – on wallowings in outmoded, old-fashioned Europeania of our parents' generation', according to scholar Anthony W. Hodgkinson. Similarly, Lary May and Stephen Lassonde marshalled convincing evidence showing that while 1920s film audiences flocked to theatres (the Egyptian, the Chinese, etc.) and

Figure 2.1   A sequence from the 1929 MGM musical *Broadway Melody*, which won the Best Picture Oscar. It's an example of the stage-bound non-cinematic proscenium style of framing that the great majority of movie musicals featured during the first glut of them from 1929 to 1930. Out front (L to R): Anita Page, Charles King and Bessie Love, nominated for the Best Actress Oscar for the role. (MGM/The Kobal Collection)

movie stars (Gloria Swanson, Rudolph Valentino) that flaunted exotic, foreign upper-class sensibilities, 1930s Great Depression audiences tended to avoid those tropes, supporting instead films with American themes and characters, and more simply designed, less ornate movie theatres.[6] For this reason as well as others, European-style operetta productions tended to do poorly. In 1930, Warner released two such films. *Golden Dawn* took African colonialism's worst racialist clichés, adorned them with minstrel slang, blackfaced whites posing as Africans, and operetta-styled songs like 'My Bwana' and 'Get a Jungle Bungalow'. The magnetic Marilyn Miller starred in *Sunny* as a cruise ship stowaway. The film sported an unbelievable plot, stilted dialogue and unrealistic romantic situations set to operetta music, not the modern and snappy pop music featured in the Great Depression Musicals. Sometimes in both these Warner releases, the music seems added mostly to indulge in the current fad. Neither film features more than three short songs (and in the latter's case, three short dance sequences) and each could have easily done its job without the musical accompaniment.

By 1931, the fad faded, Hollywood released fewer than twenty musicals, and those imported Broadway musical stars and songwriters had long since boarded the four-day train back to Manhattan. Film audiences no longer purchased tickets just to view dancing and singing on the screen; that was old hat. They needed more: a dramatic plot, well-written dialogue, star appeal, spectacle that could not be duplicated on a live stage. As legendary film producer Sam Goldwyn wrote to Florenz Ziegfeld, Broadway's greatest musical impresario, when they worked together briefly on a film in 1930, musicals had to give 'regard to screen requirements'. One film that pointed the way in stretching the musical's boundaries was Rouben Mamoulian's *Love Me Tonight* (1932), which featured an innovative approach to sound (especially in the bravura opening sequence that unfolds in the streets of Paris) as well as placing music in unexpected cinematic settings, but it still featured a plot that could have been lifted from the nineteenth century, with unlikely mistaken identities and a romance between a princess and a tailor. The songs by Rodgers and Hart are memorable, yet rendered with operetta pretensions. Hollywood slowly learned that the old rules of Broadway did not apply to film musicals. Basically, the musical film genre had not yet been properly developed: its potential lay largely unexplored during this initial period. And it seems likely that American audiences needed a more uniquely American reinterpretation of the musical reflecting the spirit of the times.

Starting in the summer of 1932, against prevailing business wisdom and trends, two men at Warners, Zanuck and choreographer/director Busby Berkeley, mapped a new approach to musicals. For Zanuck, Warners had relied too much on the gangster genre in recent years and it was played out – he viewed musicals as a potentially profitable venue for the studio to explore if produced correctly and with verve. Together, Zanuck and Berkeley created the blueprint for the successful modern film musical, before Astaire and Rogers, Bing Crosby, McDonald and Eddy and other successful practitioners of the form later in the decade.

Zanuck boasted an impressive Hollywood résumé even before joining Warners as a screenwriter in 1924, at the age of 22.[7] His determination surfaced early in life, when he left school to join the US armed forces during World War I, lying about his age to serve his country. His career as a writer began in the field of pulp fiction, and a collection of his short stories, all concerned with 'liquor, hop and women' according to biographer Mel Gussow, received a positive *New York Times* review, and served as 'progenitors of the movies that Zanuck was to make in the 20s and 30s'.

In the film colony of Hollywood, Zanuck first earned notoriety for his mastery at cranking out complete if corny film scripts quickly, sometimes in a weekend. In 1925, for example, he authored nineteen scripts for Warners under three pseudonyms, twelve of which made the studio money. At one point, MGM sought to hire Melville Crossman, one of his three pseudonyms. When Zanuck started in the business during the early 1920s, he got his first major break working for Universal Pictures, not yet a major studio. Under the leadership of founder Carl Laemmle, Universal had a reputation as a place where enterprising young people could get their first experience writing, producing and directing, provided they didn't mind being paid next to nothing while working on films with minimal budgets. Some of the best filmmakers of Hollywood's Golden Age learned their craft there before moving on to greener vistas, somewhat like the function played by Roger Corman's American International Pictures in the 1960s for the film makers of the so-called 'Hollywood Renaissance' of the 1970s. At Universal, budding executive Irving Thalberg, who would become head of production at MGM and one of Zanuck's fiercest competitors as an executive, gave Zanuck his first assignment as a screenwriter. Soon Zanuck moved on, writing gags for a year, almost always uncredited, for Mack Sennett's Keystone Films, the company known worldwide for slapstick comedy. He followed this gig by working separately with the legendary silent screen comedy triumvirate of Charles Chaplin, Buster Keaton and Harold Lloyd, eventually becoming alienated by their refusal to apportion on-screen credit for his contributions. Zanuck subsequently arrived at Warners, where his numerous scripts for Rin-Tin-Tin established his worth. The Warner brothers praised Zanuck as 'the savior of our operation', making him their senior producer in 1929, and head of production the next year at $5,000 per week.

Busby Berkeley proved nearly as instrumental in establishing the 1930s Warner Bros. house style as Zanuck himself.[8] He became the leading force transforming musicals into a dynamic cinematic medium as a creator and director of dance sequences. His work in the Great Depression Musicals made his reputation. He came from a theatrical family and as a young man performed in musical revues, gaining a reputation for staging musical numbers. Berkeley's first choreography experience was arranging military parades and marches, hence his emphasis on regimentation in his routines, though this was far from his only cinematic signature. By the late 1920s, he was a well-known Broadway choreographer, working on Rodgers and Hart's *A Connecticut Yankee* (1928), among at least twenty other shows. As is often the case in this period, Broadway approbation led to Hollywood offers, but Berkeley initially had no interest when the William Morris Agency pressured him to accept one of the proposals: 'I had seen a few film musicals and I was not impressed; they looked terribly static and restricted.' When the Morris agents kept pestering him to accept Hollywood's lucrative deals, 'I finally said "All right, you get me a great star, a great producer, and a great property, and I might consider it".' The agency assembled *Whoopee* (1930), which included Ziegfeld (one of the few times he worked on a film), Goldwyn and hot comedian/vocalist Eddie Cantor. 'With a barrage like that there wasn't much I could do but agree', Berkeley recalled. After the film's completion, with work on musicals drying up, Berkeley returned to Manhattan to work with Broadway producer Billy Rose. When *Whoopee*, adorned by new Berkeley routines specially designed to work with cameras, proved a hit, Goldwyn rehired Berkeley and he came to Hollywood full-time, eventually landing at Warners in 1932.

Berkeley's tableaux were lavish and beautifully organised, with a seemingly 'non-Warners' high budget aesthetic. When his sequences arrive in the Great Depression Musicals, the sudden shifts in mood and image transport the viewer into a nearly impossible romanticised fantasy world, intoxicating and jarringly different from the quotidian trappings that characterised the rest of the screen time. While Berkeley imparted a new and uniquely cinematic zeal to his musical routines, film historian Martin Rubin documented how his approach represented 'something of a retrogression in terms of the history of the musical theatre'. Berkeley's style strongly echoed nineteenth-century entertainment traditions such as P. T. Barnum's wildly eclectic American Museum, minstrel and medicine shows, British panto, Parisian 'large scale' revues, and of course Ziegfeld Follies' showgirl-ogling tendencies. He was bringing audiences 'back to the future' in many respects, using film ingeniously to make old forms new, just before those stage traditions became extinct on Broadway after a long life. Perhaps this historical familiarity helped make his creations so popular with film audiences in the first half of the 1930s. Also, Berkeley's use of treadmills, revolving sets, regimented dancing and 'human platforms' of barely clad showgirls had their antecedents in his Broadway shows of the late 1920s.

In Berkeley's best work, reality is gloriously thrown out the window. Such fantasy, however, cost a good deal of money. Great Depression Musicals composer Harry Warren recalled the resistance Berkeley received from Warner's tight-fisted top brass and how Berkeley fended them off:

> About the only thing [songwriting partner Al] Dubin and I enjoyed at the preproduction meetings was watching Berkeley con the executives. He seldom had any idea what he was going to do until he got on a set, and mostly you would see him sitting there with his eyes half-closed, as if in a trance. But at the meetings he would be required to explain what he wanted and how he was going to do it. He would give them long-winded explanations in double-talk that would confuse all of them. Their final question was always the same: 'How much is it going to cost?' He was the bane of the production chiefs. They would come onto his sets and see a hundred girls sitting around doing their knitting while he thought up his ideas. They just couldn't figure him out. Neither could we much of the time. We used to call Buzz 'the Madman'.

Zanuck believed musicals would reap big profits for Warners – if the form were skilfully renovated and brought up to date.[9] Jack and Harry Warner initially fervently opposed the idea; musicals were expensive and the public was tired of them: 'Oh Christ no, we can't give them away', they protested. Zanuck quietly put a new Warner musical into production anyway, aided by Berkeley and Mervyn LeRoy, the studio's premiere film director. Cameras were no longer relegated to static composition as they were during the earliest days of sound; LeRoy and Berkeley were kindred souls, anxious to push the genre to new limits. In a 1933 interview, LeRoy recommended that film directors 'make 'em [films] hot, with realistic hard-punching folk of a crisp, fast-moving modern world . . . stories with action, with typical American movement and swing'. No wonder he and Zanuck got along so well. LeRoy ended up not directing *42nd Street* because of illness, but did helm the next Great Depression musical, *Gold Diggers of 1933*.

Zanuck saw the vehicle for a musical that could combine the 'headline' style of films he had brought to Warners, while unleashing the talents of Berkeley to full effect. In August 1932, Zanuck bought an unpublished novel by Bradford Ropes entitled *42nd Street*, which shared a gritty aesthetic with many of the recent films Zanuck had commissioned. The cut-throat reality of the Broadway theatre world is presented, with more slang, drug abuse, violence and sexual activity (gay and straight, as well as adulterous) than would be allowed even in pre-Production Code Hollywood. The Broadway star's secret lover is more obviously a gigolo in Ropes' book, and Peggy, the somewhat corny and one-dimensional ingénue eventually played by Ruby Keeler, has much more depth than in the film as she learns first-hand how cruel and decadent 42nd Street can be. But still, much of the honesty and immediacy of the book transferred to the film, giving it a more convincing sense of verisimilitude than previous movie musicals. The film's first shot is a hand-held slightly shaky pan of New York City from a skyscraper perspective; soon after, our first view of the rehearsal stage is another shaky hand-held shot from an audience perspective that moves down towards the stage – an exciting cinéma vérité feel one rarely sees in major studio films of the period. The same technique is used as the penultimate shot of the last Berkeley musical sequence near the end of the film, as the camera pans up a prop Manhattan skyscraper where Keeler and fellow star Dick Powell are perched at the top as lovers. What Zanuck provided to the first three Great Depression musicals was what he had added to earlier Warner successes: a dose of realism. Where most films of the period ignored the economic situation, the Great Depression Musicals acknowledged its presence front and centre, at least some of the time, especially in the three Warner musicals released during 1933.

42nd Street's budget totalled $400,000, large for the time, especially for the parsimonious Warner studio. To avoid resistance from Jack and Harry, Zanuck 'worked on' two different scripts for 42nd Street, one with musical numbers and one without. 'I decided to shoot the musical numbers without Jack knowing it at the Vitagraph studio [in Hollywood] at night', with the dialogue scenes shot at the Warner studio in Burbank, part of the reason why the musical and dialogue sequences of the film are so differentiated. 'He never knew until it was screened that it was a musical', bragged Zanuck decades later. Such effrontery could have landed Zanuck in hot water with the brothers, but luckily, Jack and Harry 'loved' the picture, as did the public.

The realism featured in 42nd Street separated it from previous musicals, but also fitted well within the Hollywood studios' efforts to use increased sex and violence in films to draw more patrons to the Depression-era box office. When a chorus girl sitting on a man's lap is asked 'Where are you sittin', dearie?', she replies, 'On a flagpole'. The audience is told that a 'good girl' in the chorus line 'makes $45 a week and sends her mother $100 of it'. Dorothy, the established Broadway star, is perilously two-timing her show's principal investor. In a sequence set to the song 'You're Getting to Be a Habit with Me', she happily swaps affection with four different men. Peggy, the ingénue who becomes a star at the end of the movie, first sees her true love in his dressing room in his 'BVDs'. Throughout the film, the Broadway world is viewed as an ultra-competitive, sensual, even promiscuous area – 'naughty, bawdy, gaudy', as the lyrics claim. Film historian John Kobal observed that much of the film's appeal

> lay in the reincarnation of the chorus girl: once a demure non-participant [in previous films] she now became a predatory calculator, deceptively

soft in garters and silk. Her crude, gutsy and very funny line of repartee made her eminently capable of coping with the wolves and sugar-daddies, swapping fast lines, outsmarting the Babbitts and generally casting a caustic look at the world around her.

This spotlight on chorus girls may have had its roots in Berkeley's approach. He claimed that he directed the first close-ups of chorus girls in movie musicals in his sequences for *Whoopee*, and the trend continued throughout his career. It represented another way in which he could delineate the movie musical from the stage musical. Backstage musicals existed before *42nd*, but the Warner Great Depression Musicals presented a more unvarnished and close-up glimpse at this world.

The backstage environment of *42nd* was also characterised by hard work and long hours. Warner Baxter, loaned from the Fox studio, plays Julian Marsh, the embattled director of the show. His doctor has advised him to quit directing, but the show needs to go on for him; his back is against the wall after his savings disappeared in the stock market crash. 'Did you ever hear of Wall Street?', he asks his doctor. Though in poor financial and physical health, Marsh gives his all: 'it's gonna be the toughest five weeks you ever lived through', he tells his players, warning that they'll be working day and night, but assuring them that a successful show will make their marathon efforts worthwhile for their careers. The Depression haunts the characters, just as the Depression haunted the Hollywood community in real life. It's part of why the actors and dancers work so hard – so they won't be relegated to the street. Dorothy's secret beau puts his boutinnière in the refrigerator at night so he can keep it fresh and use it to look classy the next day with less expense. When the main backer of the show threatens to pull the plug after he hears of Dorothy's indiscretions, Marsh, the director, in yet another impassioned speech, gets him to change his mind by reminding him of the 200 electricians, chorus girls and staff that will be thrown out of work if he follows through with his whim.

The film's approach to sensuality was reflected in Berkeley's first dance sequences for the Warner studio. As was often the case, Berkeley's elaborate productions are piled at the end of the film, with each succeeding tableau more elaborate. This sets up a template for the Great Depression Musicals: for the first hour, a struggle behind the scenes ensues; the 'sweat and blood and tears' it takes to put on a show are depicted, followed by a dramatic shift in tone as Berkeley goes into action. Within his sequences, the theatre has been abandoned and the audience is transported to an environment where anything can happen, a performance space that could only exist in the movies. Berkeley gave credit to Zanuck for allowing him the 'necessary freedom to revolutionise Hollywood's concept of the movie musical', adding that achieving this goal engendered a lot of trust between them: 'I explained to Zanuck that I couldn't show him exactly what he would see on the screen' before he shot it. Zanuck felt so excited by the early stages of what Berkeley devised for *42nd* that, even before the released film became a hit, he signed Berkeley to a seven-year contract with Warners.[10] As usual, Zanuck proved a shrewd judge of talent.

Berkeley enjoyed an unusual amount of creative freedom for any director, but especially a director at Warners. While most researched accounts of the Golden Age of Hollywood stress the collaborative nature of film production, Berkeley flew solo to a surprising degree. 'There was no collaboration; I did everything myself', he asserted in later decades. 'From the conception to the execution, every step of the way, no matter who the director of the film, the musical numbers were entirely my own. I was alone on the stage, with my own collaborators.' Berkeley explained that he brought 'sheets of paper covered with notes' to his soundstages, but 'it's what's in my head that counts, what I see, what I imagine'. The usual studio procedure entailed using four cameras to ensure that coverage existed for the film editor to have several options for editing any scene. Berkeley did away with all cameras on his sets but one. He knew what he wanted from each shot, and filmed one shot at a time, allowing no flexibility for an editor, and not allowing the cameraman to choose the framing for a scene – this singular system ensured that the on-screen vision represented pure Berkeley. The dance sequences in his films never existed as whole numbers; they were painstakingly perfected one shot at a time, then pieced together exactly as Berkeley designed. It was in its way as megalomaniacal a style as the way he usually restricted his dancers to stiff and limited (yet cinematically effective) poses and moves. Before he arrived in Hollywood, Berkeley claimed that he was 'as ignorant of the ways of filmmaking as he had been in the techniques of dancing', but his inexperience and imagination worked well, enabling him to abandon common practice, and craft his own inimitable and recognisable style.[11]

Three Berkeley-designed sequences close *42nd Street*. 'Shuffle Off to Buffalo' follows a honeymoon couple (Keeler and an unidentified groom) boarding a train for their trip. It's a set that could just about be constructed on a theatre stage, but stage audiences would never be able to aggressively zoom into the sleeper cars with a camera, as Berkeley does, to produce the feeling that audiences are eavesdropping on passengers behind the curtains at bedtime. Chorines played by Ginger Rogers and Una Merkel perch on one of the sleeper bunks, eating fruit (including a banana) and casting aspersions: 'Matrimony is baloney', 'She'll be wanting alimony', they sing. At the end of the number, in a Berkeleyesque combination of innocence and knowing sexuality, the camera pans in on gorgeous women in pairs in their sleeper bunks wearing silky lingerie as they play peek-a-boo with the curtains that allow them privacy. Ultimately, black curtains close each of the couples into a private space, including the newly-weds. At the end of the scene, Keeler opens the curtains a little, leans out of the sleeper bunk, utters a tired but sprightly 'Ooh!', looking weary and satisfied, and drops her bridal shoes on the floor for the porter to clean.

The next sequence, 'Young and Healthy', boasts a more elegant setting and costuming choices, introducing a Berkeley set-piece that recurred over the course of his career: dancers, particularly attractive women, filmed from above, forming geometric kaleidoscopic patterns – something a theatre audience could never see from their seats, made possible by use of the camera. The *Hollywood Revue of 1929* briefly featured a similar fleeting shot, but here Berkeley exploits the device more fully, artistically. Cast members – men in tuxedos and women in clinging see-through stockings and as little clothing as could be allowed – are arrayed on enormous revolving black Lazy Susans. Since the floor is usually moving underneath the dancers, they don't always have to move; sometimes all they do is run arm in arm to keep up with the speed of the wheel, hardly a complicated dancing manoeuvre, and this quality forms another Berkeley motif. Often, in his sequences, dancers don't dance. Instead they establish a formation and the camera dances around them, or mechanical devices move them. It's a uniquely filmic and visually exciting device that separated the 1933 Warner musicals from their preceding competition. The chorus girls are often still or close to it, carried on the shiny black circular wheel as if arrayed upon an assembly line, or on high-fashion display. At such points, and in such fanciful sequences throughout his career, Berkeley is the star, not the on-screen talent.

The 'Young and Healthy' sequence finishes with the famous, some might argue infamous, tracking shot where the camera hugs the ground and follows a circular path through a tunnel of dozens of spread female legs clad in the shortest skirts possible. At the end of the shapely tunnel, Dick Powell and his date (who during this sequence only smiles, never speaks or sings and is led by men most of the time) lie close together on their stomachs, his arm wrapped tight around her supine body, grinning at the intimate scene they find themselves in. This sequence particularly illustrates how, in the words of director John Landis, Berkeley 'used the frame in a three-dimensional way – in, out, around, behind'. With its sleek yet simple set design and surprising geometric patterns, it also demonstrated how, as director John Waters has observed, Berkeley routinely 'made a black and white movie look better than a color movie'.[12] Other period musicals featured similar magnificent sets, fanciful costuming and barely clad women like Berkeley's films, but these earlier films viewed the proceedings mainly from a stage audience's perspective, with proscenium-style camerawork, and static editing composition – an atmosphere that owed too much to the theatre. Berkeley broke the camera free and allowed it to travel anywhere, and that spirit of freedom contributed to the sentimental and romantic aura of dreams that the Great Depression Musicals often trafficked in. 'I work, I create, solely for the camera', Berkeley proclaimed in the mid-1960s.[13]

For the concluding *42nd Street* number, Berkeley constructed an idealised cleaned-up New York City set far from reality. The elaborate tableau went on for blocks, featured cruising taxi cabs and police on horses, numerous store-fronts and buildings, as well as a gigantic elevated Manhattan subway track impossible to render on the live stage. It is made obvious, as so often happens in the Berkeley oeuvre, that the theatre where this scene began has now been abandoned. The audience is transported to a dimension where anything is pos-sible. Part of what makes this scene work so effectively is Berkeley's decision to start the sequence with Ruby Keeler singing and dancing in front of an ordi-nary painted background of a Manhattan scene, as one would typically see at a theatre show, before the sequence mushrooms into almost absurd proportions. Yet, in the midst of the fantasy on display, reality intrudes, and the mix of the incongruous themes and visions is what makes this production number work even 85 years later. Keeler's character praises 42nd Street as a place 'where the underworld can meet the elite', where one can find 'sexy ladies from the 80s who are indiscreet'. In one scene, a woman escapes from a man abusing her by leaping off a first floor window into another man's arms. After they dance for a few seconds, her tormentor returns to stab her in the back. Dick Powell, dressed like a dandy, watches this scene from the first floor of the same build-ing with a drink in his hand, nonplussed, as if this kind of drama happened every day.

Berkeley's signature style, while thrilling to cinema audiences, usually didn't attract the best vocal and dance talents like an Astaire or a Garland. Why should such gifted specialists appear in a Berkeley film, and get paid superstar rates when the staging represented the paramount concern and attraction? James Cagney starred in *Footlight Parade* a few months after the release of *42nd Street*, but no one knew what a dynamic musical performer he turned out to be after previously being known only for tough guy roles; he never appeared in a Berkeley film again. Berkeley's style evinced an easy appeal to a studio administration wanting to economise on talent costs (with the costs incurred by Berkeley's extravagant sets, they probably needed to economise elsewhere). Even in *42nd Street*, top-billed stars like Warner Baxter and Bebe Daniels exist, but it is probably no accident that the actors who received the most attention and gained the most lift in their careers from the film were Ruby Keeler (playing her first film role) and her romantic interest Dick Powell (who had only begun his Warner Bros. career the previous year). They went on to star in many other 1930s Warner musicals, often paired together; Baxter and Daniels never did a Warner musical again. Keeler appears ungainly at times in her tap solo during the concluding *42nd Street* number, and another dancer seems to be standing in for her during the close-up shot. She also tends to do the same steps repeatedly in the Great Depression Musicals. Her singing voice, like Powell's, is not especially memorable. Both of their voices grate at times.[14] Actors with less talent could flourish in Berkeley musicals since the imaginative choreography functioned as the star of the show. But this Berkeley aesthetic also served the premise of the film: Keeler's character Ruby is not burned out or cynical like most of the Broadway guys and dolls we meet in the film. She's fresh and enthusiastic; her eyes sparkle, even in monochrome black and white. *42nd Street* is a film in which the veterans make way for the young, where anyone with the right spirit and attitude can become a star, aided by a little luck. As the character Dorothy in *42nd Street* observes, 'most anyone can have success with the proper breaks'. That theme, combined with a Zanuckian dose of realism and Berkeley's lavish appointments, established the fantasy that, to this day, in all its revivals over the decades, makes *42nd Street* such an enduring and influential American musical.

The songwriting of Al Dubin and Harry Warren also helps to explain the success of the Warner Bros. Great Depression Musicals.[15] The duo were brought together by Zanuck to fashion songs for *42nd Street*, and ended up

Figure 2.2   The songwriters for most of the Warner Bros. Great Depression Musicals, three-time Oscar winners Harry Warren (music) and Al Dubin (lyrics). Many of their hits (such as '42nd Street' and 'We're in the Money', both from 1933) are still well-known today. (The Kobal Collection)

composing 43 musicals for Warner Bros. in five years. Despite winning three Oscars for songwriting, enjoying more songs (42) on the *Your Hit Parade* radio programme than Irving Berlin (33) between 1935 and 1950, being consistently employed by the major Hollywood studios for more than a quarter-century (a claim no other songwriter can make) and having 50 million pieces of his sheet music issued, composer Warren is rarely known or discussed other than by aficionados. Lyricist Dubin shares a similar undeserved anonymity. This might be because, unlike composers such as the Gershwins and Berlin, Dubin and Warren never enjoyed large success on Broadway, and writing songs for film was viewed by many at the time as a lesser skill (although both did work on Broadway and wrote hit songs separately before uniting in Hollywood). They also eschewed publicity about themselves, while Berlin and the Gershwins served as regular gossip column fodder. Hit lyricist Mack Gordon recalled that Warren once hired a public relations person, but fired him when stories about him began appearing: 'He said it was embarrassing to see stories about himself. And he let the guy go.' But Dubin and Warren didn't mind briefly appearing in *42nd Street*, Warren had a Warners film short dedicated to his music that he appeared in, and one of the funniest moments in *Gold Diggers of 1933*, for those in the know, occurs when a Broadway producer, impressed with the songs written by the character played by Dick Powell, announces 'I'll cancel my contract with Warren and Dubin, they're out'. Of course, the songs in question were actually Warren and Dubin compositions.

Dubin and Warren were unconcerned with personal publicity. They earned four-figure pay cheques in addition to publishing royalties at Warners during a period of general economic calamity, and more importantly, their songs spoke for them. Their best compositions were not only extremely catchy, but featured the same kind of witty dialogue and crackling urban slang that accounted for the most effective non-musical moments in the Great Depression Musicals. They complemented the flavour of the productions, with a similar melding of optimism and grit. Biographer Tony Thomas argued that although Berkeley deserved and received a lot of the credit and accolades for the sequences he designed and directed in the Warner musicals, 'it must be remembered that the songs came first and that in almost every instance the idea for the production began with Al Dubin'.

And a large number of the Dubin and Warren songs have remained ever-green. In the initial rush to make musicals in 1929–30, Hollywood brought west some of the most famous Broadway songwriters. But after the bottom fell out of the initial market for musicals, most of those easterners returned to New York. When Warners revived the musical genre in 1933, the songs mostly came from writers the studios cultivated, like Dubin and Warren, who had not previously had massive success on Broadway. Film composing connoted a different kind of task from scoring a Broadway musical. A full score was rarely needed, and only half a dozen songs or fewer were required, but such songs not only had to forward the plot and theme of the film, but also had to work in a uniquely cinematic fashion. Warren and Dubin's output during the mid-1930s frequently lit up Berkeley's imagination, and that lit up the box office and eventually the top 40 radio airwaves, sheet music and record sales, in all of which Warners held a stake. Jack Burton, in his work on Hollywood musical songwriters, argues 'this renaissance [in film composing] marked the opening of a prolonged battle royal between four new teams of songwriters who punched their way to the top of the 1933 Hit Parade': Sam Coslow/ Arthur Johnston, Leo Robin/Ralph Rainger, Mack Gordon/Harry Revel, and Dubin/Warren. But the songs of the first three teams mentioned, although frequently well-crafted, have not survived and thrived during ensuing decades as much as the songs Dubin and Warren wrote for Warner Bros.: '42nd Street', 'I Only Have Eyes for You', 'You're Getting to Be a Habit with Me', 'We're in the Money', 'Lullaby of Broadway', 'Boulevard of Broken Dreams' and more. Another reason for the lasting popularity of their songs was Dubin's disciplining of himself early in his career to aim his lyrics towards the market of young girls aged 15–25, who he believed bought the majority of sheet music, the dominant money maker in the music industry until at least the mid-1930s.

Low respect for songwriters among the public and film executives also contributed to Warren and Dubin's lack of fame. Jack Warner, infamous for his mania to cut studio costs, once asked Warren how long it took him to write a song. 'Three weeks', replied Warren. Jack expressed scepticism. 'Three weeks to write a *good* song', Warren clarified. The craft of songwriting, especially in popular music, went mostly unrecognised at this time. As Warren recounted to Tony Thomas in the 1970s:

> It's a mystery to me that almost all the movie producers with whom I've worked have been musically ignorant people, even those who were making musicals, and they never seemed willing to give us the respect they would give to actors or technicians. I remember playing a waltz for one of the top producers at Warners. It was short and took only about a minute and a half to play. All he could say was, 'It couldn't have taken you very long to write that.'

Warren makes a valid point here, but it should also be pointed out that Warren's greatest visual interpreter, Busby Berkeley, who helped sear Warren's compositions into the public's consciousness, freely admitted that he didn't know 'one note of music from another'.[16] Warren, however, made an exception for Zanuck, who contrary to other producers he worked with over his career 'was interested in every phase of production, which is what made him a first-class producer . . . Perhaps it was because he had been a writer, but he was interested in what [Dubin and I] were doing.'

The new multi-format marketing Warner Bros. devised to promote the Great Depression Musicals also contributed to their success. The PR campaign for *42nd* dwarfed campaigns for their previous musicals, according to the Warner Bros. files. The *Motion Picture Herald* maintained that Warners also took the marketing of *42nd* to new heights within the industry. 'All too rarely do we find the opportunity of waxing enthusiastic over a press sheet, but here is one that leaves little or nothing to the imagination', enthused the regular columnist Chick: 'Page after page is crammed full of carefully thought-out ideas to bring business to the box office.' The team at Warners realised their new approach to musicals needed a similarly new marketing approach, and delivered. One full-page ad for the film, which opened four days after Roosevelt's inauguration, proclaims it is 'inaugurating a NEW DEAL in ENTERTAINMENT!'. A section of the ad not seen in magazines, but presumably seen by exhibitors and journalists, lists the national publications the ad will appear in, bragging it will reach nearly 12 million Americans. 'Get your share of business from this advertising', the copy advises.[17] With each of the next two Great Depression Musicals premiering in 1933, ever more involved and detailed publicity campaigns and pressbooks would be mounted. Because *42nd* finished filming in 1932, and did not premiere until March 1933 (a longer post-production period than usual), it's possible that Warner Bros. purposely delayed its release to take advantage of the massive publicity generated by the cross-country train filled with movie stars commissioned by the studio to arrive in Washington, DC for Roosevelt's inauguration. Or perhaps, realising they had a potential smash hit on their hands that renovated the musical genre, they took their time fashioning a more detailed and sizeable public relations package than usual. Or both.

With the marketing of *42nd Street*, strategies for promoting musicals at Warners changed in ways that broadened and strengthened their box-office appeal.[18] Previous musicals such as *Crooner* (1932) featured a harder-edged 'scorching' appeal in ads, especially in matters of sex, promising to reveal 'the naked truth' about 'radio crooners' and let viewers meet 'the bimbo who put sex appeal in a microphone'. 'They met at nine, they danced at ten, they kissed at eleven and were married at twelve', bragged the marketing copy for *Dancing Sweeties* (1930), which also promised 'a comedy drama of young sinners and their gay goings-on'. The materials promoting *42nd Street* still featured chorus girls in skimpy costumes, but the sexuality of the characters on-screen and in the ads is more implied than explicitly spelled out. A more wholesome family appeal applied to *42nd* with its focus on the young and somewhat naïve couple portrayed by Keeler and Powell. Additionally, the chorus girls are viewed more as hard-working than as sex bombs. Perhaps this drive towards enhanced propriety was also reflected in the higher-quality look of the publicity materials produced for *42nd*, printed on more high-quality glossy paper while previous musicals' publicity materials appeared on newsprint. Combined with the expensive celebrity-adorned cross-country train ride, the campaign gave *42nd* the aura of a classy show business event rather than a controversial and prurient expose.

The racier elements from *42nd Street* attracted attention from the censors of the time, but they had not yet acquired the power to mandate wholesale cuts or changes.[19] The drive towards installing some kind of national moral control over the film industry had been building for over a decade. Inspired by scandals involving stars and directors during the early 1920s (as well as competition from the nascent radio industry), the major studios initiated a trade organisation called the Motion Picture Producers and Distributors of America (MPPDA) to collectively deal with these potentially damaging issues, and deliver a unified and respectful image of their industry. The moguls now were represented by one voice promoting, lobbying for and defending the film industry, and that voice belonged to former US Postmaster General Will Hays. Over the next quarter-century as president of the MPPDA, Hays unleashed numerous articles and speeches aggressively vouchsafing the artistic and moral integrity of Hollywood product. His imprimatur and stern presence so shaped the image of his bosses and their companies that the MPPDA was commonly known in the movie colony as the Hays Office.

But the centre only held for a few years. By the end of the decade, religious groups, particularly the Catholic Church, inveighed against how Hollywood's films promulgated what the Church viewed as the immorality of the 1920s. Sociologists provided (now mostly discredited) data demonstrating how American youth were being corrupted by cinematic exposure. Talk of boycotts by millions of religious Americans simmered in the media, an unsettling thought for the studios at the dawn of the Depression. To placate concerns, Hays and the MPPDA commissioned a Production Code, written in 1930 by two prominent Catholics, Father Daniel Lord and Martin Quigley, editor of the conservative *Motion Picture Herald*. The eventual document produced, 'deeply Catholic in tone and outlook', hoped to serve an honourable purpose, according to film historian Thomas Doherty:

> The Code was a sophisticated piece of work. Contrary to popular belief, the document was not a grunted jeremiad from bluenose fussbudgets, but a polished treatise reflecting long and deep thoughts in aesthetics, education, communications theory, and moral philosophy. In the context of its day, the Code expressed a progressive and reformist impulse . . . It evinced concern for the proper nurturing of the young and the protec-

tion of women, demanded due respect for indigenous ethnics and foreign peoples, and sought to uplift the lower orders and convert the criminal mentality. If the intention was social control, the allegiance was on the side of the angels.

They produced twenty pages of guidelines. The Code's authors mandated, among other things, that in Hollywood films all crimes should be punished by prison or death, that evil could not be 'presented alluringly', that 'vulgarity' and 'obscenity' be banished as well as 'Kooch' and 'Can-Can' dances, that religion be respected, and that romantic relationships should only exist between two people of the opposite sex and needed to stress the institutions of marriage and home, avoiding depictions of 'arousal'. This litany satisfied Hollywood's critics, but not for long since the Code arrived with no enforcement mechanism. The studios claimed they would honour the Code, and thanked the authors and the pressure groups publicly for their guidance, but no penalties were established for violating the code, which was supervised by a mostly powerless organisation called the Studio Relations Committee (SRC). Officials from the SRC read movie scripts ahead of time, and made suggestions for cuts, but studios were under no pressure to make the cuts and often ignored the advice or reversed committee decisions. In 1934, a renewal of moral disgust by many of the same religious groups led to a stricter Production Code regime led by a strengthened Production Code Administration (replacing the SRC), which not only imposed severe financial penalties for studios that flaunted Code violations, but could actually stop the release of a film if it did not measure up to Code standards. For most of the period covered by this book, however, this innovation lay in the future. The 1930–4 period is now known among film scholars and the general public as the pre-Code era, a time when Hollywood studios generally ignored the 1930 Code, increasing portions of sex and violence in their films to attract dwindling audiences. The Warner Bros. Great Depression Musicals, like many films of this period, would be able to feature amounts of sex, violence and salty language that post-1934 Hollywood product would not be able to duplicate for a quarter-century or more.

In letters to Darryl Zanuck during the last months of 1932, SRC officials suggested cuts to *42nd Street*, including a scene where a character claimed that a character known as 'Anytime Annie' 'only said no once and then she didn't hear the question'.[20] Most of the suggested cuts were ignored, illustrating Zanuck's determination to strike a realistic tone in Warner films. Since the early 1920s, dozens of individual American states had maintained censor boards that ruled on every exhibited Hollywood film; each state could mandate different cuts, a time-consuming and costly process that was one of the reasons studios accepted the more powerful Production Code Administration (PCA) in 1934 – they only wanted to have to cut their films once for family consumption.

When it came to *42nd Street*, for example, the state of Pennsylvania insisted on the most cuts, including the flagpole line and Keeler's 'ooh!' when she drops her bridal shoes. Massachusetts wanted Warner to 'eliminate scenes showing girls in extreme décolleté', which would have been a difficult if not impossible job necessitating the elimination of many minutes from the finished product. They also objected to 'the bridge of legs' in the 'Young and Healthy' number. As the studios well knew, not all audiences wanted their films shorn of spicy content. In the *Motion Picture Herald*, a theatre owner in Columbia City, IN noted the audience reaction to 'Shuffle Off to Buffalo', a 'ribald song' from *42nd Street*: 'It went over [with my patrons] and regardless of the demand for no more spice in pictures, they [the censors] had better consult the average audience and see if they don't want some of it.'

But censors of the period were probably less worried about the Great Depression Musicals than other films resorting to more realistic and tarted-up visions of romance to garner larger audiences.[21] The same week in June 1933 that *Gold Diggers of 1933* premiered in Los Angeles, a large-font ad for MGM's *Today We Live* asked:

> CAN *ANY* WOMAN BE FAITHFUL – in the heart of one man and in the arms of another? . . . her conscience in combat with her yearnings . . . she dare not stop to think! A flaming symbol of rebellious womanhood . . . grasping at ecstasy of the moment.

Paramount's main feature that week, *The Story of Temple Drake*, based on a 'flaming novel' by William Faulkner, attracted paying customers by warning them to 'please do not bring your children to see this picture'. 'As long as there are girls like Temple Drake you ought to know about them!', the copy leered. 'S-h-h-h! They have whispered about girls like this for generations . . . now for the first time somebody has the courage to frankly tell you about them!' Both women in these ads, Joan Crawford and Miriam Hopkins respectively, boast come-hither looks. Compared to such advertisements that flaunted prurient alternatives to Production Code morality, the images of Berkeley's fantasy-laden sets adorned with smiling showgirls for the Warner Bros. musicals, even if they sported little clothing, seem almost innocent. They certainly do not depict tableaux that could be duplicated in real life, and a celebration of traditional romance and marriage was guaranteed at the end of a 1930s movie musical. The line stressed the most in the *Gold Diggers* ad is: 'The screen awakens to a new conception of spectacle and beauty!' Such different emphasis probably marked another reason why Warner Bros. tended to ignore SRC comments about their musicals – they knew they weren't the main or worst offenders. When the public started clamouring for more censorship, they rarely if ever cited the Great Depression Musicals.

In a letter from 1936, when the Production Code was in full force, three years after *42nd Street*'s original release, PCA chief Joseph Breen informed Jack Warner that the film required numerous cuts for a legal rerelease. It would not pass muster in the new, more restrictive climate. The studio had no choice but to comply if they wanted to reissue the film. Luckily, in this period when the major studios were usually unconcerned about film preservation, Warner Bros. kept the original print from 1933 as well as the re-edited 1936 release, so the prints and DVDs in circulation today are the uncensored versions. Similar situations, in 1933 and 1936, occurred for the films *Gold Diggers of 1933* and *Footlight Parade*.

Initial reactions to *42nd Street* showed that Zanuck's goal of renovating the movie musical struck a chord with critics and audiences.[22] Edwin Schallert, the *Los Angeles Times* reporter who covered the financial end of the motion picture business as well as reviewing its products, noted that the film was 'different from some of those that came and went – and whose passing was distinctly not regretted a few years ago – it has more of real material and purpose than its predecessors'. He praised its emphasis on 'the business of show-making' and rated it overall 'the best musical film since the early days of the talkies', words close to those used by Mordaunt Hall at the *New York Times*: 'the liveliest and one of the most tuneful musical comedies that has come out of Hollywood'.

Financially, *42nd Street* exceeded Warner Bros.' expectations, despite the national bank holiday that occurred during its premiere week.[23] Aided by the promotion of the '42nd Street Special' Warner/GE train, it did 50 per cent more business in its first week than *I Am a Fugitive from a Chain Gang*, the studio's biggest hit of 1932, in Philadelphia and Memphis, and doubled *Fugitive*'s opening week grosses in Denver, St Louis and San Antonio. Special 9:00 a.m. and midnight shows were scheduled at Warner's flagship Strand theatre in New York City to handle the overflow. Nationwide, it was held over for a second week in 95 per cent of its initial first-run engagements, a rare feat, particularly during the Depression, and it ran for nine weeks in New York City (with 450,000 paid admissions) and five weeks in Los Angeles when the great majority of films from the period ran for a week or less. According to the *Motion Picture Herald*'s 'Asides' column, no other film possessed the box-office longevity of *42nd Street*. It ended up being the top-grossing film in America during March 1933, and the third-highest grossing film in April. Theatre owners throughout the country praised the film over the next few months in the *Motion Picture Herald*'s 'What the Picture Did for Me' column: 'If we could only have a few more like this we would have no worry about banks' (Nashville, IL); 'Did the best third night's business my house has ever done, so I can give it no higher praise' (Pierre, SD); 'Business beyond compare!

Thanks a thousand times, Warner Bros.' (Morris, IL); 'the greatest box office attraction I have had in two years' (Montpelier, ID). The latter theatre owner spotted many of his patrons coming to the show two nights in a row.

The next Warner Bros. Great Depression Musical had been on the boards since at least the previous autumn, when it was known as *High Life*. Sometime around the turn of the year its title changed to *Gold Diggers of 1933*. [24] Much of the material concerning showgirls and their encounters with high-class men emanated from a 1919 play entitled *The Gold Diggers*. According to film writer Martin Rubin, Warners originally bought the material intending to develop it as a drama, but the success of *42nd Street* inspired them to change its emphasis. This production history could explain why there appears to be such a noticeable difference of quality between the musical and dialogue portions of the film. Variety called it 'the first of the "second editions" of film musicals', what we would today call a sequel, since Warners had previously released a much less successful film entitled *Gold Diggers* in 1929. It also served as a sequel, with its similar aesthetic and stars, to *42nd Street*.

As the *Gold Diggers* script underwent development, and Roosevelt won and assumed office, more Great Depression themes were incorporated. The opening and closing numbers, which openly reference the Great Depression in lyrics and images more explicitly than in *42nd*, were the last sequences to be created and filmed. As late as February 1933, two months before filming ceased on *Gold Diggers*, the 'We're in the Money' and 'Forgotten Man' sequences were not in the script, although the former number is hinted at in Zanuck's copy of the revised temporary script from January with stage directions that do not exactly coalesce with the scene as eventually filmed: 'Dancing madly ... no depression – forget the blues – throw your money away – as they throw handfuls of gold coins wildly into air.' The 'We're in the Money' number would be optimistic, but not wildly optimistic. How could it be? As the two Depression-themed musical bookends of the film were being mapped out and brought before the cameras, the nation and the new Roosevelt administration were facing some of the darkest days in American economic history.

According to a Warner press release as well as the film's work schedule, *Gold Diggers* had to be rush-produced and rush-released because 'fifteen musical films went in production on the West Coast as a direct result of the fact that "42nd Street" has broken box office records wherever it has been shown'. Actually, that figure represented a severe under-estimate; *Motion Picture Herald* reported in May 1933 that 68 musicals from American studios were due in the next year, all hoping for a piece of the boffo *42nd* business, as well as a 1933 Goldwyn musical starring Eddie Cantor and featuring dance routines designed by Berkeley. In the same press release, Albert Warner, the company's treasurer and head of distribution, complained that 'it is a most unfortunate state of affairs when a company which anticipates the trend of public taste accurately, as we have done in the present case of musical motion pictures, is immediately penalized by the production of a flood of imitations'. Then as well as now, copycat productions of established hit films were no novelty in Hollywood, as he must have known. Among the 1933 offenders Albert probably had in mind were Walter Winchell's *Broadway Through a Keyhole* (released by Twentieth Century), featuring chorus girls dressed remarkably like Berkeley's, and Universal's *Moonlight and Pretzels*, which included 'Dusty Shoes', a Great Depression-themed closing sequence with a remarkable resemblance to the first and last scenes in *Gold Diggers*, but adorned with less budget, less imagination, and an annoying operetta-like melody a decade or two out of pop music fashion. As is often the case with quickly produced copies of successful culture formulas, there wasn't much in such films for geniuses like Berkeley to worry about. Albert Warner went further and claimed that the studio would produce 'no more musical feature-length pictures, at least during the present season and until the imitative season dies down'. Perhaps he was just trying to lead other studios off the scent with this last statement, as he must have known that, more than a month before *Gold Diggers* premiered in early June, his brother Jack had already bought the rights to the next Great Depression Musical, *Footlight Parade*, and a script was well under way.[25]

In a departure from the others in the initial trio of Great Depression Musicals, *Gold Diggers of 1933* starts with a bang, an elaborate Berkeley sequence with no plot explanation beforehand. It proved much more fitting to the theme of the film than the original 'dancing madly, singing happy' directions in the earlier version of the script. After a credits sequence that features the cast superimposed on coins, Ginger Rogers in a close-up, adorned in shiny coins and not much else, proclaims in song: 'I've got good news to shout in your ears, the long lost dollar has come back to the fold . . . Old Man Depression you are through, you done us wrong!' While portrayed in close-up, she's allowed for a few seconds to tell the story without the elaborate sets of the usual Berkeley musical enterprise. She announces at the outset and makes it obvious that this will be a movie about the Great Depression. As the camera eventually pulls back, we see the usual bevy of Berkeley beauties dressed similarly, holding huge coins in each hand with another huge coin not adequately covering their hips. They're prancing (as usual for Berkeley's charges, not dancing) on a cavernous set adorned by coins close to forty feet high. Out of a huge onstage building with a twenty-foot-high dollar sign on it, more chorus girls wearing even less emerge with their change-jingling outfits closely examined by a medium shot.

The spell of flashy and fleshy reverie is broken when about a dozen men from the Sheriff's office rudely interrupt the number and insist on repossessing the costumes, sets, even the sheet music. 'We got a great show, it opens tomorrow night', protests the show's producer Barney Hopkins, played by Warner regular Ned Sparks. 'You can't do this to me just because I don't pay a few bills – when the show opens, I will pay them.' The cop in charge replies: 'Tell it to the sheriff.' The showgirls are inured to this situation: 'this is the fourth show in two months that I've been in and out of'; 'they close before they open'; and Ginger Rogers, who began the sequence, finishes the scene with a note of disgust: 'the Depression, dearie'. Film historian Richard Dyer has observed that this scene with its 'piles of women' particularly demonstrates the Berkeleyian view of 'women as sexual coinage, women – and men – as expressions of the male producer'.[26] And when the show closes before it opens because of the producer's financial troubles, the pay cheques of those women, as well as those of the dozens of staff, vanish.

The film then concentrates on the personal lives of the chorus girls during the Great Depression. They sleep late because they have no food and no work. As one of them steals a bottle of milk from a nearby apartment ledge, they reminisce about the days when they lived in luxury, enjoyed spending money and nice things, and had gentlemen taking care of them. Hopkins comes to visit them, and shares an idea for a 'new, different' show that he thinks is sure-fire. 'What's the show about?' asks one of the girls. 'It's all about the Depression', he replies. Joan Blondell, the feisty star of both *Gold Diggers* and *Footlight Parade* as well as many other 1930s Warner films, replies with a serious tone in her voice: 'We won't have to rehearse that.' When the girls' neighbour, an unproven songwriter played by Dick Powell, auditions one of his numbers for Hopkins, the song continues the Depression motif. 'I couldn't sing a gay song, it wouldn't be sincere', goes the Al Dubin lyric. 'I could never croon a happy tune without a tear.' After hearing Powell's idea for a song about the 'forgotten man' in the Great Depression, Hopkins reveals his vision:

> That's it! That's what this show's about. The Depression, men marching, marching in the rain. Doughnuts and cruellers, men marching, jobs, jobs . . . A blue song. Not, not a blue song, but a wailing . . . . the big parade of tears. That's it . . .

> 'Isn't there going to be any comedy in this show?' [asks one of the chorus girls]

> Plenty. The gay side, the hard-boiled side, the cynical and funny side of the Depression. I'll make them laugh at you starving to death, honey. Be the funniest thing you ever did.

But from this scene on, except for a scene where Powell is convinced to take the place of an ailing singer on-stage because otherwise the show will close and the 'kids' in the show will 'have to do things [you] wouldn't want on your conscience', the film and music lose much of their poignancy and connection to the Great Depression theme. Until the end of the film, it is hardly mentioned, perhaps because the film makers felt that relentless identification with it could be off-putting to audiences, but more likely because they grafted the Depression themes at the last minute onto a musical they had been developing for months. It's almost as if the musical splits into two irreconcilable parts, always a danger when the Berkeley sequences in the Warner Bros. musicals were already markedly different from the dialogue sections.

Figure 2.3   The 'Pettin' in the Park' sequence from *Gold Diggers of 1933* remains a primary example of choreographer Busby Berkeley's boundary-pushing approach to sexuality and reality. To close the sequence, the character Brad uses a can opener to cut Polly out of an iron maiden metal bustier. The characters were portrayed by Warner Bros. Great Depression musical stalwarts Dick Powell and Ruby Keeler. Warner Bros.' consistent promotion of Keeler during this period as a wholesome, even innocent young woman may have made the imagery of this shot seem even more incongruous. (Warner Bros./The Kobal Collection)

The first number in Hopkins' musical, as shown on-screen, is 'Pettin' in the Park'. It's a wide-ranging Berkeley sequence full of both lyrical and filmed double entendres of various couples engaging in the practice, including Keeler and Powell, a couple of chimpanzees, and couples of various ages and races, including non-stereotyped African American and Asian couples, and children. It's another tableau that could only occur on-screen, never in a live theatre of the period. Somehow, dozens of roller-skating women become involved, as does the young dwarf Billy Barty playing a slightly overgrown baby, who ends up curled underneath the legs of dozens of policemen who roller-skate around his prone body, spreading their legs apart so they won't hit him, a strange counterpoint to the end of the 'Young and Healthy' segment in *42nd Street*. A bit later, Barty frolics in a snowstorm with dozens of women, and then suddenly is transported to a park in the spring where he is playing on the grass with a ball that rolls near a woman lying on the grass in a long white dress with her thighs almost fully exposed next to a man in a suit and straw hat. Around them are many couples dressed exactly the same. A downpour ensues, and the women change behind a back-lighted scrim; their back-lit silhouettes as they undress leave little to the imagination. Barty wants to raise the scrim while the women are naked, poised between their wet clothes and their dry clothes. At the end of the sequence the rain continues pouring upon the assembled couples, and Powell begins cutting Keeler out of an iron maiden bustier with a can opener as the audience bursts into applause.

Frank boundary-bending sexuality frequently existed in Berkeley's work, but 'Pettin' in the Park' goes particularly far in this area; everyone is getting wet, so to speak. It would not have passed muster under the stricter 1934 PCA rules. Roy Hemming, in his history of movie musical songwriters, noted that the composition was 'risqué and daring in its day, when public "petting" was landing people in jail in some cities as part of the morals crusade sweeping the country'.[27] The whole sequence has little to do with the usual musical dance number – this is cheesecake titillation fantasy transformed onto celluloid. The skill exhibited in 'Pettin'' does not emanate from the performers it could be almost anyone acting out the parts in this surreal sequence calculated to just barely pass the censors' pencil – Berkeley's imagination is again the star of the show.

Subsequently, *Gold Diggers* follows a plotline concerning Powell's family, a Boston blueblood clan unhappy with his activity in the supposed impropriety of the musical theatre world. They threaten the loss of his inheritance unless he abandons his performing and songwriting, and are particularly unhappy that he wishes to marry the character played by Keeler. To his relatives, showgirls are 'little parasites, gold diggers'. Powell refuses to relent, so his brother and uncle go to the chorus girls' apartment to offer Keeler money to back off from the marriage. But Powell's brother and the family lawyer uncle are taken in by Keeler's roommates and fellow actresses played by Joan Blondell, who is mistaken for Keeler by the two bluebloods, and Aline MacMahon. Together, affronted by the rich socialites' insulting of them and their profession, they seduce and trick the rich socialites into buying them expensive clothing and accessories. In a preposterous premise, Powell's brother believes he can make Blondell/Keeler transfer her affections from Powell to him, thereby breaking up the potential marriage. While Blondell and Keeler are not excited by the gifts that the bluebloods' money can buy, MacMahon's character is quite smitten, fulfilling the gold digger stereotype. Various games and charades ensue, and, rather unrealistically, the Blondell character and Powell's brother fall in love, despite their initial disrespect for each other. Blondell proves she is not a gold digger when she refuses a cheque for $10,000 that the brother pays when tricked into thinking he has taken sexual advantage of her while drunk. An unseemly plot miraculously works out in the end – everyone is happily married, and redeemed without rancour.

While some have condemned Warners' *Gold Diggers* films for their portrayal of women as money-grasping millionaire-chasers, the overall portrait in this film suggests a less mercenary interpretation. As film historian Molly Haskell has remarked, such films marked 'one of the few genres and occasions where there is a real feeling of solidarity among women. Although theoretically in competition, they also realise that the cards are stacked against them, that they have this in common, and that they stand a much greater chance of succeeding if they unite.'[28] The solidarity they demonstrate in the opening scenes in their shared apartment, sharing what little food they have and the tips they hear of possible stage work, demonstrate this quality, as does the quick and witty intelligence of their dialogue and their ease with and caring for each other. But such qualities unfortunately were not used to sell these films, and so are less remarked upon then and now.

Relief from the ridiculous blueblood scenario is finally provided by Berkeley. He takes one of Warren and Dubin's less appealing and more saccharine songs, 'The Shadow Waltz', and transforms it into rapturous cinema. Women dressed in diaphanous white skirts with undulating hoops that seem to magically float on air play violins and dance alongside 40-foot-tall art deco staircases with a reflecting pool. When the lighting is extinguished, the women's violins and bows are lit with neon, creating a singular ghostly image. Gimmick, yes, but a beautiful and dreamy gimmick, especially when medium close-ups reveal the chorus girls attractively bathed in chiaroscuro from the neon light of their violins. Berkeley's traditional overhead shots follow, showing the assembled women forming attractive flower shapes with their dresses. Berkeley once again redefines the visual and dance elements of the movie musical.

In the film's final moments, with no warning or connection to the plot, the Great Depression returns. Hopkins' vision for a musical focusing on 'the big parade of tears' is finally realised in the 'Remember My Forgotten Man' sequence, which opens with Blondell watching a man down on his luck pick a cigarette butt off the street. He has no matches to relight it, so Blondell lights a new cigarette in her lips, and places it in his lips, demonstrating an affection towards him that the lyric implies society has not shown. Blondell starts singing as she leans plaintively against the same lamppost that the man was leaning on as the scene began, once again putting herself in his place. The lyrics are soon echoed, with New Orleans jazz-styled brass counterpoint, by the African American vocalist Ella Moten sitting in a window; one year later she became the first black artist to perform at the White House. Her appearance in *Gold Diggers* represents a rare non-stereotyped vision of an African American from a major studio during the decade, and led to the black press referring to her as 'The New Negro Woman' in Hollywood films.[29] She is portrayed juxtaposed, as an equal, with other (non-black) despondent women waiting for their forgotten men, and she shares the lead vocal with Blondell. Her singing is sincere, not accompanied by the minstrel buffoonery often marring black performances in 1930s Hollywood studio films. She is dressed similarly to the other women in the scene. Berkeley's dance sequences from this period included surprisingly progressive portrayals of black Americans; the final scene in this 'Forgotten Man' sequence features an African American man right next to Blondell, wearing the same kind of respectable suit and hat as the rest of the male chorus. The point appears to be made subtly that African Americans are citizens and war heroes, and that they too are suffering in the Depression; their humanity is recognised, an unfortunately rare occurrence in Hollywood product during this period.

The next segment in the 'Forgotten Man' sequence spotlights returning veterans in an intriguing way: it begins with soldiers parading in triumph to the beat of patriotic music after coming home from the war, pelted by ticker tape and kisses from strangers (as actually occurred after World War I). Following that, we see the struggles it took to get to that point in counter-chronological order, as they march in the rain, and then are seen bloody, blind and limping in the aftermath of a battle. The initial celebratory mood of soldiers returning to society has been altered, yet the patriotic marching music continues – the effect is moving. Next, we see the men in Depression bread lines, looking cold, weary and lost, sharing cigarettes as they wait for food.

According to film writer Michael Freedland, Harry Warner worried that audiences would not want to see 'dirty poor faces' when going out to the movies. The betrayal of these returning veterans served as the focus of the song's lyric: 'Remember my forgotten man, you put a rifle in his hand, you sent him far away, you shouted "hip-hooray!", but look at him today'. Perhaps Harry should have remembered that a few months before the release of *Gold Diggers*, Bing Crosby enjoyed the top-selling record in the country with Jay

Gorney and Yip Harburg's song 'Brother, Can You Spare A Dime?', which painted similar word pictures of veterans 'slogging through hell', and 'destitute and forgotten' Americans during the Great Depression. Crosby biographer Gary Giddins referred to the composition as 'the one Tin Pan Alley hit [during the period] that addressed the darkness in American life', perhaps unique in the same way as the 'Forgotten Man' sequence was among American films when it came out. Crosby, the most popular vocalist in the nation, covered three of the Great Depression Musicals numbers and two of them topped the sales charts during 1933.[30]

The Al Jolson-starring hit musical *Hallelujah, I'm a Bum*, which reached theatres a month before *42nd Street*, also referenced the current suffering in the United States, but in a whimsical rather than a tragic way. The beautifully

Figure 2.4 Al Jolson starred as a hobo named Bumper in the beautiful and bitter-sweet *Hallelujah, I'm a Bum* (1933), with songs by Richard Rodgers and Lorenz Hart. It was one of the few non-Warner films of the period that directly referenced the economic suffering of millions of Americans during the Great Depression. (United Artists/The Kobal Collection)

shot and bitter-sweet film follows the activities of a hobo and his compatriots living in New York City's Central Park. Witty and conversational songs by Rodgers and Hart forward the plot skilfully. Much of the dialogue is delivered in verse in a style Shakespeare might have employed had he been alive during the 1930s. Like the Warner Bros. Great Depression Musicals, the film's characters share an ambivalent relationship with money and riches. 'You got the grass, you got the trees', declares one lyric. 'What do you want with money?' As millions of Americans were themselves homeless and suffering, this film made such a lifestyle seem attractive and honourable, while still acknowledging the difficulties such a life entails. It's a musical that deserves more notice; like the three 1933 Warners musicals, its influence was unfortunately mostly ignored by the more fanciful movie musicals that later defined the genre. Some evidence indicates that, contrary to Harry Warner's concerns, audiences appreciated seeing the difficult circumstances of their times envisaged on film. 'Every patron [was] well-pleased', according to a theatre owner in Oxford, NC. 'The last scene, "The Forgotten Man" scene, seemed to impress patrons more than the others.'[31]

In the final scene of the 'Forgotten Man' sequence, Berkeley again uses silhouettes to dramatic effect, only this time they trace the figures of World War I soldiers, not nude chorus girls changing after a rainstorm. The soldiers are elevated to the top of a gigantic set in what probably was meant as purposeful symbolism, marching behind and over the massed vocalists and 'forgotten men' in suits. A female chorus on-stage, stretching their hands skyward as if they were in church, provide the 'wailing' that Barney wished for when he first visualised this number. The music in this section contains more than a hint of Jewish cantorial minor-key singing, and the song as a whole may be Warren and Dubin's most famous and emotionally moving composition. One wonders if it is significant that at the end of the number, the men and the women are separated, especially considering the solidarity between the sexes that the sequence opened with. Could this have served as symbolism for the increased incidence of divorce and the drop in childbirths that occurred during the Great Depression?

The 'Forgotten Man' sequence was doubtless inspired by the Bonus Army episode that occurred scant months before the completion of the first draft of *Gold Diggers*.[32] During the spring and summer of 1932, thousands (accounts claim anywhere from 11,000 to 25,000) of unemployed World War I vets travelled to Washington, DC, residing in a makeshift camp near the Anacostia River, squatting in unused government buildings on Pennsylvania Avenue (the same street the White House resides on), and demanding early instatement of the bonuses due to them from the federal government in 1945. The signs they carried and slogans they recited, such as 'Cheered in '17, Jeered in '32', could have been incorporated into the 'Forgotten Man' sequence. Certain themes from *I Am a Fugitive from a Chain Gang* and *Heroes for Sale* were probably inspired by the Bonus Army as well.

Sadly, the government generally ignored the so-called Bonus Army, and worse. The Senate refused to pass a bill allowing early bonus disbursement, and many of the disgusted veterans decided to stay on in protest. On 28 July, President Herbert Hoover, then engaged in a tough presidential re-election race with Franklin D. Roosevelt, in a White House surrounded by chains and cleared of nearby pedestrians because of a fear of the protesters, issued orders for the US Army to evict the protesting veterans. Led by future World War II General Douglas MacArthur, 'four troops of cavalry with drawn sabres, six tanks and a column of steel-helmeted infantry with fixed bayonets entered downtown Washington', according to historian William E. Leuchtenberg. 'After clearing the buildings on Pennsylvania Avenue, they crossed the Anacostia Bridge, thousands of veterans and their wives and children fleeing before them, routed the veterans from their crude homes, hurling tear gas bombs into the colony, and set the shacks afire with their torches.' In addition, the District of Columbia police shot and killed two veterans squatting in government buildings on Pennsylvania Avenue. Hoover had not ordered such an excess of confrontation, particularly the tear gas attacks and fatal shootings, but nonetheless he refused to condemn his general and the local police force afterwards, making it appear that he condoned the incident. This fuelled the impression of Hoover as callous and out of touch with the suffering of the nation, and likely pulled even more supporters away from his flagging campaign.

In addition to leading attacks against American war veterans, the Hoover administration weakened its image further by 'vilifying the Bonus Army as a rabble of communists and criminals', in Leuchtenberg's words. MacArthur publicly referred to the marchers as 'a mob . . . animated by the essence of revolution'. Such accusations were laughable, belied by public statements and goals issued by the veterans. The men, patriots not traitors, were poverty-stricken and under-appreciated – there existed little if any talk about overthrowing the government. But such loose talk by government figures fell comfortably within a growing tradition of Communist baiting that had escalated since the rise of Soviet Russia and the Red Scare in Washington, DC during the 1917–20 period. As was discussed in the previous chapter, the American Communist Party grew by meagre numbers during the Depression. Events occurring during the filming of *Footlight Parade* during the summer and fall of 1933 would mark the first appearance of a drive against perceived Communist leanings in the film business by Congress and film industry executives.

The phrase 'forgotten man' apparently originated from a Roosevelt 1932 campaign radio speech that stressed a connection between WWI vets and the Depression, mentioning 'the forgotten man at the bottom of the economic pyramid'. When Roosevelt was in Los Angeles for the September 1932 motion picture industry-sponsored pageant, he proclaimed in one of his speeches that his administration would be interested in the 'forgotten people' of the United States. The reprise of the Bonus Army sentiment in *Gold Diggers of 1933*, particularly as part of a stirring and patriotic conclusion to the film, represented another important on-screen indication of the pro-Roosevelt bias of the Warner brothers in early 1933, just as the Administration took office. These various associations help to explain why 'Remember My Forgotten Man' proved controversial in some circles. 'A few years later, the song still being popular, the censors refused to allow the song to be performed via the airwaves, contending that the lyrics were not in the best interests of the country's morale and were "subversive"', according to Patricia Dubin McGuire, Al Dubin's daughter. 'Al loved that; he took it as a real compliment and it promptly became one of his favorite lyrics.'

The marketing for *Gold Diggers* surpassed the campaign for *42nd Street*, representing a new, more aggressive promotional strategy for Warner Bros.[33] No individual film during 1933 was the subject of more full-page and multi-page ads in *Motion Picture Herald*, including three full pages of ads devoted to the film during its premiere week. One of those ads spotlighted the pressbook for the film, something no other studio emphasised in its film marketing. Eight life-size standees of characters were available to exhibitors for $5.95 apiece. The studio provided drama scripts based on the film for radio stations. Cartoon shorts were commissioned by Warners and released for three of the film's songs, including 'We're in the Money', which in the decades that followed became a staple of the studio's cartoon soundtracks, particularly those starring Bugs Bunny. No doubt this ubiquity was at least partly due to the song being owned by Warner Bros.' music publishing arm. The pressbook and ads in film trade magazines featured advertising for the film's sheet music (the same would be true a few months later for *Footlight Parade*). A Dick Powell dress shirt was made and promoted in tandem with the film, and displayed in 'over 12,000 stores' nationwide. The studio even tried to negotiate a deal with Roosevelt's Treasury Secretary to borrow a collection of rare 'gold coins of all denominations' from the government for display in the New York theatre that premiered the film. In informing exhibitors how to sell *Gold Diggers*, the pressbook instructed them to emphasise its identity as a Warner Bros. film, and that it was not one of the many imitations in production around Hollywood, but a film made by the same creative team that did *42nd*. 'It's bigger and better', brags the copy. 'The show backs you up in this absolutely.' For newspapers too strapped to send a reviewer, Warners provided ready-made reviews, including one that immodestly referred to the film as the 'Super Spectacle of All Time'.

Sexier elements of the film were stressed in the marketing. The studio made available to newspapers a ten-part serialisation of the film, the titles emphasising the more prurient moments: 'All Show Girls Are Gold Diggers', 'Sleeping in Strange Beds'. One of the pre-prepared stories for newspapers reported how 'Diners at the Warner Bros. studio café in North Hollywood got the shock of their lives when 200 pretty gold digger chorus girls romped in for lunch clad in next to nothing during the production'. The theme continued in photos and drawings promoting the film, most of which featured women from the film with little clothing, and many of which featured tableaux not included in the film. One picture of actress Muriel Gordon depicts her nude with a sheer cloth held to her middle. Another features a trio of women holding hoops with cloth which barely covers their nipples and displays some of their breasts. Perhaps the most famous of these images features Joan Blondell stuffing money into her panty hose at mid-thigh. The caption reads 'Blondell uses her own First National bank in *Gold Diggers of 1933*', even though not only is her character in the film never shown doing this, but she fights being defined as a gold digger, and ultimately refuses to cash a $10,000 cheque offered by a rich suitor. Such prurient marketing was forbidden by the Advertising Code, an adjunct policy of the Production Code, 'that mandated decent copy and demure illustrations', according to Thomas Doherty. Yet the studios knew from years of experience that the 'sex angle . . . led audiences in a straight line to the box office'.[34] In 1933, the Advertising Code had as much power of enforcement as the Production Code and was routinely ignored.

Simultaneously, the publicity materials attempted to build an entirely different image for the ingénue film star Ruby Keeler. The prepared stories concerning her feature the headlines 'Keeler Just an Old Fashioned Sweet Girl: She's the Type Old Timers Love to Refer to When Lamenting Scarcity of "Gals of Mother's Time"' and 'Keeler, Millionairess, Is as Timid as an Extra', with a subhead of 'Unusually Modest'. Such themes coalesced with the personalities of the characters Keeler tended to portray. While the showgirls that Keeler's character lives with tend to harbour a realistic attitude towards romance during the Great Depression, placing their emphasis on finding a provider for a mate, Keeler plays a dreamer who still believes true love will lead her to where she will be happiest. One can sense the Warner marketing team trying to reach for as many audiences as possible, the ones who wanted to view some flesh and the more family-minded demographic. Tellingly, the promotional materials almost completely ignore the segments in the film focusing on the Great Depression. Perhaps such themes did not represent the mood of escapism that the public relations department thought would sell best. In the initial 1933 trio of Great Depression Musicals, the showgirls are not so much mercenary as realistic as they try to survive within a harsh environment, and for most of them, love and career trump money as their priorities – starting in 1934, the girls in the Warner musicals become more money-obsessed and calculating, one of many reasons the films don't work nearly as well, and perhaps a reason why box-office returns dwindled.

The reviews for *Gold Diggers* in the New York, Los Angeles and Denver papers (where the film was previewed) were uniformly positive, usually more positive for Berkeley than for the film as a whole.[35] The reviews were often so good that they often sounded like publicity, but they did not quote the ghosted stories Warners provided. *Variety* declared it 'superior' to *42nd*. In Los Angeles, at the film's premiere at Grauman's Chinese theatre, the studio arranged a parade down Hollywood Boulevard, set up a live radio broadcast that announced the arrival of various Hollywood stars (including Joan Crawford, Clark Gable and the Marx Brothers), and funded an elaborate series of five 'prologues' before the main feature began featuring a cast of 100 choreographed by Larry Ceballos, a Warner employee who went on to design one of the major dance sequences in *Footlight Parade*. Prologues were short live theatre pieces, usually of a musical or comedy variety, staged before films at the more prestigious first-run theatres in major cities; in the age of sound films they were fading away, but they serve as a major plot point in *Footlight Parade*. While Warner publicity mostly ignored the Depression-related themes featured in *Gold Diggers*, critics did not. Denver reviewers called 'Forgotten Man' 'as moving a song as I can remember' and 'the most timely, strong heartappealing song we have ever heard'. New York papers tended to ignore the first and last musical numbers of the film, which registered the Great Depression most strongly, and one New York critic took the filmmakers to task on this issue. Lucius Beebe, the famed author and journalist, writing in the *New York Herald Tribune*, viewed the film as

> a combination of very satisfactory film revue and as annoying an essay in national legislative propaganda as may well be imagined. As entertainment, up to the last fifteen minutes of the film, the pieces [*sic*] is an adroit, amusing well filmed and at time hilarious screen farce, after which it descends to depths of bathetic sentimentality which, for sheer and gratuitous offensive, would be hard to rival . . . [the Forgotten Man sequence], apparently inserted in the script of the film as an afterthought, tends to diminish in a very emphatic manner its effectiveness and its qualities as entertainment . . . 'Gold Diggers of 1933' is a film strictly on the gold standard. It is only a pity that its producers had to diminish its effectiveness by the introduction of a shabby theme of bogus sentimentality in general favoring a legislative action [the early payment of veterans' bonuses] which should be no concern of a photoplay designed primarily as amusement fare.

Beebe correctly noted that the 'Forgotten Man' sequence essentially represented 'an afterthought'. No mention of it exists in surviving scripts, and according to the daily progress reports for the production, the sequence was filmed last, from roughly 7 to 13 April 1933.[36] It is testament to the speed and efficiency of the Hollywood system that the completed film previewed in Denver on 26 May 1933, roughly six weeks later. It is almost impossible to imagine a film today taking as little time from the cessation of filming to release. This situation occurred not only because the Hollywood studios consolidated and vertically integrated production, distribution and exhibition, but also because they employed year-round the experts and technicians needed to complete a film. The much more atomised studios of today can't afford to retain thousands of people full-time on the payroll; each film's crew is usually assembled for that film and that film alone, a far less efficient system. The studio employees of the Golden Age were used to working together, and the force of their actions was carefully organised by studio management. If Warners wanted a film like *Gold Diggers* rush-released, they possessed the manpower and expertise to make it happen.

Other critics, and certainly audiences, did not share in Beebe's critique; the film, which premiered on 27 May 1933, became a huge box-office success, with initial returns easily surpassing those of *42nd Street*.[37] First-week receipts for *Gold Diggers* were 42 per cent higher than for *42nd* in New York and Denver, 48 per cent higher in San Antonio, and anywhere from 16 to 32 per cent higher in Charlotte, Cleveland and Memphis, despite a national heat wave. Like *42nd Street*, it was the top-grossing film in its first full month of release (June), but, unlike its antecedent, also held that title for the month following, and was the third-highest-grossing film in August. By late August, three months after its original release, *Gold Diggers* had surpassed the runs for *42nd* in major cities, running for eleven weeks at Grauman's Chinese theatre in Hollywood, nine weeks in New York City, six weeks in Portland, OR, five weeks in Seattle, and six and four weeks respectively at two different theatres in Chicago. The engagements for other films of the period did not last anywhere close to as long or profitably in theatres. One example of the competition, the Universal Studios musical *Be Mine Tonight*, played for seventeen weeks in Los Angeles, but averaged $1,000–2,000 per week, a far cry from the roughly $18,000 weekly that *Gold Diggers* pulled in at the Chinese during its eleven-week run.

Once again, theatre owners mostly raved about the business the film did: 'For the first time in five years, my house [theatre] was not large enough' (Montpelier, ID); 'we enjoyed the best business in the past five years' (Oxford, NC); 'Biggest business in two years and the picture pleased' (Frankfort, KS); 'it drew for 30 miles in every direction and we had more paid admissions on this than on any one show in the history of this theatre, which runs ten years back' (Selma, LA). *Gold Diggers* earned more for Warners than *42nd Street*; in *Motion Picture Herald*'s chart of the top movie earners from October 1932 to September 1933, it ranked as the top draw of the season, with *42nd Street* in third place.[38] The two films together doubtless evinced an impact on the good financial news at the end of August when Warners' fiscal year ended. The studio had lost $6.29 million for that past year, less than half of their loss for the year previous, and September and October 1933 saw the company earn its first 'small net profit' in three years.[39]

Gold Diggers of 1933 also became immediately influential in the industry, as especially witnessed in MGM's *Dancing Lady*, released in November 1933, which features various Berkeley-like devices and images, such as chorus girls revolving upon Lazy Susans, unorthodox camera angles including from directly above the performers, silhouettes of nude women behind scrims, and close-ups of its chorus girls. Though it is a quite entertaining film that stands on its own, particularly because of winning performances by Joan Crawford and Clark Gable, this backstage musical is the kind of imitative film that Albert Warner was complaining about when the Warner Great Depression Musicals became immensely popular. It's a better looking, more technically accomplished film than its Warner Bros. competition (MGM films almost always were), but it

Figure 2.5   Albert Warner, treasurer and head of distribution at Warner Bros., publicly complained after the massive success of *42nd Street* and *Gold Diggers of 1933*, rueing that rival studios were quickly producing a 'flood of imitations' glutting the market. Here is a behind-the-scenes shot from the one of the best of such replications, MGM's *Dancing Lady*, released a few months later, which featured various devices and angles seemingly cribbed from Warner Bros. choreographer Busby Berkeley's signature style. (Getty Photos)

contains little of the spirit of innovation seen in the Warner films, none of the grime and desperation that marks those films as singular within their genre. While the dance sequences feature many imaginative shots, and better hoofing from Crawford than one sees from Keeler, they don't boast the sustained level of abandon and imagination that are found in Berkeley's work.

With the 'Forgotten Man' segment over, *Gold Diggers of 1933* abruptly concludes, and one can feel its divided nature – about a third of it represents the most poignant portrayal of the economic dislocation of the period in musical form, and another third comprises clichéd, dubious rags-to-riches plot and dialogue. One can almost feel the two disparate parts grafted together Frankenstein-style by the studio's writers and producers in the wake of the success of *42nd* and the election of President Franklin Roosevelt, the man who vowed to directly confront the problems of the desperately poor as his predecessor, Herbert Hoover, had mostly refused to do. One of the many reasons *Footlight Parade* proves the best of the Warner Bros. Great Depression Musicals is that it keeps the theme of struggle against calamity and exploitive forces at the centre of its existence. *42nd Street* and *Gold Diggers* pointed the way, but their successor *Footlight Parade* carried the idea of the series to its perfection. Back in the real world, during the production of *Footlight*, the Hollywood film industry was simultaneously fully engaged in an all-consuming brawl concerning the very issues the film embodied.

NOTES

1. This section on how Hollywood endured the Great Depression is based on the following sources: Tino Balio, 'A Mature Oligopoly: 1930–1948', in Balio, ed., *The American Film Industry* (Madison, WI: University of Wisconsin Press, 1976): 213–16; John Kobal, *Gotta Dance Gotta Sing: A Pictorial History of Film Musicals* (London: Hamlyn, 1971): 24–5; Iwan Morgan, 'Introduction', from Iwan Morgan and Philip John Davies, eds, *Hollywood and the Great Depression: American Film, Politics and Society in the 1930s* (Edinburgh: Edinburgh University Press, 2016): 4–7; Nick Roddick, *A New Deal In Entertainment: Warner Brothers in the 1930s* (London: British Film Institute, 1983): 19–21; Thomas Schatz, *The Genius of the System: Hollywood Filmmaking in the Studio Era* (New York: Henry Holt, 1988): 69, 86–97, 98–9, 119, 136, 159–61; Robert Sklar, *Movie-Made America: A Cultural History of American Movies* (New York: Vintage, 1994): 161–6; [uncited author], 'Warner Bros.', *Fortune* (December 1937). The Warren quotation is from: Tony Thomas, *Harry Warren and the Hollywood Musical* (Secaucus, NJ: The Citadel Press, 1975): 21.

2. Lary May with the assistance of Stephen Lassonde, 'Making the American Way: Moderne Theatres, Audiences, and the Film Industry 1929–1945', *Ramparts* (May 1987). The numbers publicised by the MPPDA (the Motion Picture Producers and Distributors of America), the powerful trade association representing the major film companies, were usually registered as more than twice this figure, but May and Lassonde's research has debunked those estimates.

3. Brad Tuttle, 'Thumbs Down: 2011 Saw Least Movie Tickers Sold Since 1995', *Time Magazine Moneyland* site available at: http://moneyland.time.com/2011/12/28/thumbs-down-2011-saw-least-movie-tickets-sold-since-1995/ (last accessed 12 December 2013).

4. 1930 Warner Bros. musicals in order of release: *Sally, No No Nanette, Spring is Here, Showgirl in Hollywood, Mammy, Top Speed, Golden Dawn, Dancing Sweeties, Bright Lights, Big Boy, Sunny* (*Mammy* and *No No Nanette* were hits). 1931: *The Hot Heiress, Men of the Sky, Children of Dreams, Her Majesty Love*. 1932: *Central Park, Crooner, Big City Blues*. For more on these films, consult: Clive Hirschhorn, *The Warner Bros. Story* (London: Octopus, 1979): 84–123. For a list of 1929–30 musicals from studios other than Warners, see Kobal, 36.

5. This section on the 1929–30 Hollywood musicals is based on the following sources: A. Scott Berg, *Goldwyn: A Biography* (London: Penguin, 1989): 198–200; Mel Gussow, *Zanuck: Don't Say Yes Until I Finish Talking* (London: W. H. Allen, 1971): 46; Kobal, 24–46; Leo Rosten, *Hollywood: The Movie Colony, The Movie Makers* (New York: Harcourt, Brace & Co., 1941): 169, 313–15.

   As Rosten reports, a similar dynamic to that concerning Hollywood's new musicals occurred with screenwriting during this period. Broadway playwrights could write skilled dialogue and plots, but mostly could not deliver what was needed for successful screenwriting. Most of the initial New York playwrights hired in this period were back in Manhattan relatively quickly.

6. Anthony W. Hodgkinson, '*42nd Street* New Deal: Some Thoughts About Early Film Musicals', *Journal of Popular Film* 4:1 (1975); May/Lassonde, 92–106.

7. This capsule biography of Darryl F. Zanuck is based on the following sources: Rudy Behlmer, *Inside Warner Bros. (1935–1951)* (New York: Viking, 1985): 12–14; Michael Freedland, *The Warner Brothers* (London: Harrap. 1983): 38, 48, 58–9; Gussow, *Zanuck*, Chapters 1–5, 8; Leonard Mosley, *Zanuck: The Rise and Fall of Hollywood's Last Tycoon* (London: Granada, 1984): 60–111; Schatz, 58–63, Ch. 9; David Thomson, *The New Biographical Dictionary of Film* (London: Little, Brown, 2003): 959–60.

   Sources in this footnote vary as to whether Zanuck was making $4,000 or $5,000 per week when he became head of production at Warner's. I am relying on Schatz's figure of $5,000, since he made a thorough investigation of the files. The figure is also duplicated in Gussow and Mosley, although it should be noted that a memo by Harry Warner quoted in the Behlmer book (p. 12) has it at $4,000.

8. This capsule biography of Busby Berkeley is based on the following sources: Freedland, 67–9; Martin Rubin, *Showstoppers: Busby Berkeley and the Tradition of Spectacle* (New York: Columbia University Press, 1993), Chapters 1, 3 and 4; Schatz, 148–53; Thomas, 46; Tony Thomas and Jim Terry, with Busby Berkeley, *The Busby Berkeley Book* (New York: New York Graphic Society, 1973): 15–27; Thomson, 76; *Busby Berkeley's Kaleidoscopic Eyes* documentary, on *Dames* DVD (Warner Bros., 2006).

   The Ziegfeld Follies actually started in 1907, not in the nineteenth century, although Ziegfeld had done similar revues previously. Rubin mentioned other earlier antecedents for Berkeley tropes, many heralding back to the nineteenth century: glow-in-the-dark effects, musical instruments as props, gigantic props, placards, vast scale, water spectacles, female dancers as objects like flowers or cigarettes, geometric kaleidoscopic patterns, dancers on steps, etc.

9. This section on the making of *42nd Street* is based on the following sources: Patrick Brion and Rene Gilson, 'A Style of Spectacle: Interview with Busby Berkeley', *Cahiers du Cinéma in English* 2 (1966): 32; Gussow, *Zanuck*, 54–8; Kobal, 112; Mosley, 185–6; Roddick, *New Deal*,18; Bradford Ropes, *42nd Street* (1932),

retyped by Warner Bros. studio, from the '42nd Street Book' file (1890), Warner Bros. Archives, University of Southern California, Los Angeles [henceforth WBA/ USC]; Schatz, 140–53; [uncited author], 'Directors, Like Cooks, Can't Agree on Recipes for Films: "Make Them Simply", Says Frank Borzage; "Make 'Em Hot!" Says Mervyn LeRoy', *Los Angeles Times* (3 December 1933).

10. Thomas, Terry, Berkeley, 51–4.

11. Brion and Gilson, 27–32; William Meyer, *Warner Brothers Directors: The Hard-Boiled, the Comic and the Weepers* (New Rochelle, NY: Arlington House, 1978): 32.

12. John Landis and John Waters interviews from *Busby Berkeley: A Study in Style*, documentary featured on the *Gold Diggers of 1935* DVD (Warner Bros., 2006).

13. Patrick Brion and Rene Gilson, 'A Style of Spectacle: Interview with Busby Berkeley', *Cahiers du Cinéma in English* 2 (1966): 28.

14. Thomas hints in his book about Harry Warren that Keeler mainly received the *42nd Street* assignment over others because of her status as the wife of Warner star Al Jolson: 21.

15. This section on Al Dubin and Harry Warren is based on the following sources: Jack Burton, *The Blue Book of Hollywood Musicals* (Watkins Glen, NY: Century House, 1953): 43–51; Roy Hemming, *The Melody Lingers On: The Great Songwriters and Their Movie Musicals* (New York: Newmarket Press, 1986), Chapter 9; Hodgkinson, 34–6; Patricia Dubin McGuire, *Lullaby of Broadway: Life and Times of Al Dubin* (Secaucus, NJ: Citadel Press, 1983): 10–17, 59–63, 94–112; Thomas, 1–53; *Footlight Parade: Music For The Decades* short documentary available on the *Footlight Parade* DVD (Warner Bros., 2006).

16. Meyer, 29.

17. 'Chick', 'Selling "42nd Street"', *Motion Picture Herald* (11 March 1933); *42nd Street* advertisement, file 679 (1933), WBA/USC.

18. *Crooner* Pressbook, *Crooner* publicity file 679A (1932); *Dancing Sweeties* Pressbook, *Dancing Sweeties* publicity file (un-numbered). WBA/USC.

19. Sources for this section on the development of the Production Code Administration: Balio, 220–2; Berg, 106–7; Thomas Doherty, *Pre-Code Hollywood: Sex, Immorality, and Insurrection in American Cinema 1930–1934* (New York: Columbia University Press, 1999), Chapter 1, 125; Scott Eyman, *Empire of Dreams: The Epic Life of Cecil B. DeMille* (New York: Simon & Schuster, 2010): 294–7; Father Daniel Lord and Martin Quigley, 'The Motion Picture Production Code of 1930', included as an appendix in Doherty, 347–67; Sklar, 82–5, 173–4; A. E. Hancock in 'What the Picture Did for Me' [column], *Motion Picture Herald* (30 September 1933).

   Examples of the sociological research done on motion pictures in this period: Henry James Forman, *Our Movie-Made Children* (New York: Motion Picture Research Council, 1933); [uncited authors], 'The Researchers – and Reactions: Film Disquieting to the Children, Researchers Hold' and 'Save the Screen from Degeneracy, Is Hearst's Plea', *Motion Picture Herald* (10 June 1933); 'Scientists Answer Forman's Charges', *Motion Picture Herald* (7 October 1933).

20. Sources for this paragraph: Jason Joy/Production Code Administration to Darryl Zanuck, 28 September 1932; Wingate/PCA to Darryl Zanuck, 27 December 1932; Joseph Breen/PCA to Jack Warner, 26 August 1936; PCA Files for *42nd Street*, microfilm, Margaret Herrick Library, Department of Special Collections, Academy of Motion Picture Arts and Sciences.

21. Ads for *Today We Live*, *The Story of Temple Drake* and *Gold Diggers of 1933*, *Los Angeles Times* (1 June 1933): 9.

22. Mordaunt Hall, 'Putting on a Show', *New York Times* (10 March 1933); Edwin

Schallert, '"Forty-Second Street" Lively, Tuneful Film', *Los Angeles Times* (18 March 1933).

23. [Uncited author], 'Special Train Carries "42d Street" To Record', *Motion Picture Herald* (18 March 1933); Warner Bros. advertisement, 'These Days Other Companies . . .', *Motion Picture Herald* (8 April 1933); 'The Box Office Champions For March' and 'What the Picture Did for Me' [columns], *Motion Picture Herald* (22 April 1933); 'Theatre Receipts', 'What the Picture Did for Me' and 'Asides and Interludes' [columns], *Motion Picture Herald* (29 April 1933); 'What the Picture Did for Me' [column], *Motion Picture Herald* (13 and 20 May, 17 June 1933); 'The Box Office Champions for March' [column], *Motion Picture Herald* (20 May 1933); [uncited author], '84 Features with Music Available for Booking in the Next Few Months', *Motion Picture Herald* (20 May 1933).

While the great majority of theatre owners praised *42nd Street* in *Motion Picture Herald*, not all did. A theatre owner in Geneseo, IL complained that *42nd* featured 'No outstanding stars, no beautiful sets, no singing of any account and dancing numbers far short of wonderful': 'What the Picture Did for Me' [column], *Motion Picture Herald* (13 May 1933).

24. Sources for the background information on *Gold Diggers of 1933*: *Gold Diggers of 1933* Story Outline file (1920) (25 November 1932); *Gold Diggers of 1933* Revised Temporary Script file (1920) (18 January 1933); *Gold Diggers of 1933* Story – Coverage file (1920) (7 February 1933); *Gold Diggers of 1933* Story – Revised Final Script file (1920) (8 February 1933); *Gold Diggers of 1933* Cutter's Scripts file (1920) (11 February 1933). WBA/USC. [Uncited author], *Gold Diggers of 1933* review article, *c.* May 1933, *Variety Film Reviews* database. In the latter Warner script, 'Money' was included, but as the closer for the film, not the opening number. In the 8 February script, 'Money' opens and closes the film. There are no scripts in this file that reference the 'Forgotten Man' number – as will be noted later in the chapter, this sequence seems to have been written and produced at the last minute in the production.

Information about the 1919 'Gold Diggers' play is from: Martin Rubin in *Gold Diggers of 1933: FDR's New Deal Broadway Bound*, short documentary feature included on *Gold Diggers of 1933* (Warner Bros. DVD, 2006).

25. *Gold Diggers of 1933* Publicity – Pressbook – 'Advertising Section', file 681 [probably May or June 1933]; Jack L. Warner to Jerome Kingston, 25 April 1933, from *Footlight Parade* Story File 2872; James Wingate/Production Code Administration to Jack L. Warner, 8 June 1933. WBA/USC. The latter letter shows that the PCA was already worried about the *Footlight* script by 8 June 1933, one day after the *Gold Diggers* New York premiere, five months before the *Footlight* premiere.

[Uncited authors], '84 Features', and 'Pictures to Be Released with Music', *Motion Picture Herald* (20 May 1933).

Albert Warner's moaning represented a typical Warner complaint. The year before, Jack Warner had publicly berated other studios for copying their successful *I Am a Fugitive from a Chain Gang*: [uncited author], 'Jack Warner Burns at Cycles', *Variety* (4 October 1932).

The 1933 Hollywood rush to make more musicals after the massive success of *42nd Street* will apparently be duplicated in 2017–18 after the worldwide box-office profits of *La La Land* (2016): Clarisse Loughrey, 'La La Land Is Opening the Door for a New Era of Movie Musicals', *The Independent* (17 January 2017).

26. Richard Dyer, 'Entertainment and Utopia', in Rick Altman, ed., *Genre: The Musical: A Reader* (London: Routledge & Kegan Paul, 1981): 186.

27. Hemming, 260.

28. Molly Haskell, *From Reverence to Rape: The Treatment of Women in the Movies* (Chicago: University of Chicago Press, 1987): 145.

29. John Troesser, 'Ten Things You Should Know about Ella Moten Barnett', *Texas Escapes* [online magazine], available at http://www.texasescapes.com/TexasPersonalities/Etta-Moten-Barnett-2 (last accessed 22 February 2012). For more on the history of black performers on film, particularly musicians, see Harvey G. Cohen, *Duke Ellington's America* (Chicago: University of Chicago Press, 2010), Chapter 3; Thomas Cripps, *Slow Fade to Black: The Negro in American Film* (Oxford: Oxford University Press, 1993).

30. Gary Giddins, *Bing Crosby: A Pocketful of Dreams, The Early Years 1903–1940* (Boston: Thorndike Press, 2001): 305, 308, 598–9.

31. J. J. Medford in 'What the Picture Did for Me' [column], *Motion Picture Herald* (21 October 1933). The 'Forgotten Man' theme remained in Hollywood during the 1930s, perhaps most famously in the silly yet poignant *My Man Godfrey* (1936).

32. This account of the 1932 Bonus Army is based on the following sources: Frank Friedel, *Franklin D. Roosevelt: A Rendezvous with Destiny* (New York: Little, Brown, 1990): 75; David Kennedy, *Freedom from Fear: The American People in Depression and War, 1929–1945* (Oxford: Oxford University Press, 1999): 92–3, 138 William E. Leuchtenburg, *Franklin Roosevelt and the New Deal, 1932–1940* (New York: Harper & Row 1963): 13–16; Kyle D. Palmer, 'Campaign Issues Are Ignored by Roosevelt; Large Crowds Hear Candidate's Appeal but Learn Little of Where He Stands', *Los Angeles Times* (25 September 1932); *Gold Diggers of 1933: FDR's New Deal Broadway Bound.*

In one of his actions during his first month in office, Roosevelt actually cut the pay of veterans by almost 50% as an austerity measure, at a time when veteran benefits made up about a quarter of the entire federal budget. The March 1933 bill similarly slashed the salaries of all government and military personnel, including Congressmen – see Kennedy, 138. In 1936, Congress finally passed a 'bonus bill, awarding the World War I vets their bonuses nine years early' – over Roosevelt's veto – see Kennedy, 279. Despite benefiting politically from Hoover's mishandling of the Bonus Army, Roosevelt also never capitulated on early bonuses for them as part of his New Deal.

33. Sources concerning the marketing of *Gold Diggers of 1933*: Gold *Diggers of 1933* serialisation, in *Gold Diggers of 1933* Publicity – Clips file (681); *Gold Diggers of 1933* Publicity – Pressbook, file (681); WBA/USC. 'Asides and Interludes' [column], *Motion Picture Herald* (27 May 1933).

'We're in the Money', 'Pettin' in the Park', and 'Torch Song' cartoons featured on *Gold Diggers of 1933* (Warner Bros. DVD, 2006).

34. Doherty, 107–13. For more information concerning the 1933 introduction of the Advertising Code, see: [uncited author], 'Hays' 12 Commandments to P.A.'s Just About Takes in Everything', *Variety* (26 December 1933).

35. Reviews referenced in chronological, then alphabetical order: [uncited author], 'Orpheum, Aladdin Get "Gold Diggers of 33"', *Denver Post* (23 May 1933); Betty Craig, '"Gold Diggers Is Lavish Picture of Theater Life"', *Denver Post* (27 May 1933); Alberta Pike, '"Gold Diggers" Put Reviewer in Raving Mood', *Rocky Mountain News* [Denver] (27 May 1933); 'Premiere Attracts Notables', *Los Angeles Times* (1 June 1933); '"Gold Diggers" Premiere Will Be Gala Event', *Los Angeles Times* (2 June 1933); Eleanor Barnes, '"Gold Diggers" Glamorous at Grauman's Chinese: Prologue? Silly Question!', *Daily News* [Los Angeles] (3 June 1933); Relman Morin, '"Gold-Diggers", Dazzling Musical, Opens at Chinese', *Los Angeles Record's Cinematters Section* (3 June 1933); Edwin Schallert, '"Gold Diggers of 1933" Arrives with Elaborate Premiere Fanfare at Grauman's Chinese',

Los Angeles Times (3 June 1933); Lucius Beebe, 'On the Screen [column]', *NY Herald-Tribune* (8 June 1933). These reviews, and numerous others, particularly from New York papers (except for most of the articles from the *Los Angeles Times*), are found in the *Gold Diggers of 1933* Publicity – Clips file (681), WBA/USC.

36. *Gold Diggers of 1933* Story Production – Daily Progress Reports file (1448), WBA/USC.

37. See multi-page ads for *Gold Diggers of 1933* in *Motion Picture Herald* (10, 17 and 24 June 1933); 'The Box Office Champions for June' [column], *Motion Picture Herald* (22 July 1933); 'Box Office Champions for July' [column], *Motion Picture Herald* (19 August 1933); 'The Box Office Champions for August' [column], *Motion Picture Herald* (16 September 1933); See also *Motion Picture Herald*'s 'Theatre Receipts' columns for July, August and September.

In this period, films didn't roll out nationally on hundreds or thousands of screens on the same day as happens today in the United States. A release of even a major film such as *Gold Diggers* often took months to work its way around the country. This is why there are only box-office reports listed from selected cities concerning the opening weeks of the film's release.

38. 'What the Picture Did for Me' [columns], *Motion Picture Herald* (1 July, 5 August, 2 September, 7 October, 4 November 1933); 'The Box Office Champions of 1932–33' [column], *Motion Picture Herald* (21 October 1933).

39. Financial information on Warner Bros.: [uncited authors], 'Warners Now on Profitable Basis; '32–'33 Losses Reduced Eight Millions', and 'Highlights of Warner Finances', *Motion Picture Herald* (18 November 1933); 'Warner Profit for Quarter $100,000', *Motion Picture Herald* (16 December 1933).

3. FOOTLIGHT PARADE

Genre movies have been commonly understood as particularly good barometers of what we might call cultural 'temperature' ... Whether they are set in the past or in the future, on the mean streets of contemporary New York or long ago in a galaxy far away, genre movies are always about the time and place in which they are made. Inevitably, they are expressions of the cultural zeitgeist, instances of society engaging in dialogue with itself. Genre movies may reflect, reinforce, question or subvert accepted ideology, but viewers enjoy them as genre movies whether they fulfil, violate or thwart conventions and expectations ... In the past, myths were narratives that helped society explain religious beliefs and seemingly inexplicable natural phenomena. Similarly, in modern times genre movies are secular stories that seek to resolve the basic problems and dilemmas of contemporary life.[1]

– Barry Keith Grant, 2003

Grant's definition of the significance of genre films proves particularly to the point in respect of *Footlight Parade*. The Great Depression, the New Deal, the rising labour struggle, the changing role of women, censorship, the changes necessitated by the introduction of sound movies – these are themes that resonate within this film. But it's not a history lesson, not by a long shot – it's a full throttle example of 1930s Hollywood (and Warner Bros.) at its best, replete with a crackling script, memorable songs and indelible performances.

With *Footlight*, filmed in the summer of 1933, the Warner Bros. Great

Depression Musicals welcomed, for the first time in the series, a real movie star. Propelled by James Cagney, *Footlight* sports a modern, breakneck pace, as the characters fight for artistic and financial survival in the midst of economic and cultural dislocation. Also, in the months since they had gained fame by starring (and spooning) together in *42nd Street* and *Gold Diggers of 1933*, Ruby Keeler and Dick Powell had paid some dues and gained on-screen experience as stars. They were more seasoned, less amateurish; they still played ingénues, but they were no longer ones themselves.

Furthermore, *Footlight Parade* echoed the optimism and energy stemming from the initial months of President Roosevelt's administration. Immediately upon attaining office, he and the US Congress attacked the problems underlying the Great Depression by passing a record amount of bills during its first one hundred days. The President called his programme the New Deal; it bolted to an auspicious start, and hopes were high. In Mark Roth's article about the Great Depression Musicals, he likened musicals to 'a religious service or ritual. Once we understand this, the repetition of the plots and much else becomes self-evident.'[2] In terms of providing inspiration, an apt comparison for *Footlight Parade* might be a religious service, but part of what makes the film so powerful and singular is its resistance to the usual conventions not only for its time, but also for decades afterwards. Very little in *Footlight* is done by rote, and not only does it viscerally reflect the mood of many during the Depression, it also epitomises the Warner Bros. film ethos of championing the underdog, fiercely struggling to achieve and prove him- or herself in the face of amassed power, as the Warners had had to do in the 1920s during their ultimately successful quest to become a major studio. *Footlight* is grimy, more realistic and quicker-paced than the typical musical, and the Warners musicals that preceded it. The people who populate it are often desperate, and sometimes profane (at least by Hollywood standards). In terms of breaking convention, most of the best numbers are saved for the end of the film, instead of being doled out steadily throughout. Nobody sings unless it's part of a real stage number; in the world of *Footlight*, no orchestra arises dreamily out of nowhere to accompany a character in a romantic moment.

In this time of economic ruin and crushed hopes for millions, *Footlight Parade* offered reassurance and hope, without climbing upon a soapbox and without sacrificing laughs or entertainment. It is the musical that most encapsulates the struggles of the period, and most represented the Warner brothers' support of the Roosevelt administration during its nascent months. *Footlight* became successful even though Darryl F. Zanuck, the progenitor of the Warner Bros. Great Depression Musicals, had left the studio before filming began, and even though concurrent New Deal reforms inspired the worst labour stress Hollywood had yet experienced (which echoed plot points in *Footlight*). These events and convergences make the production of the film, as well as the film itself, even more of an emblematic story.

For years, the major Hollywood studios fended off proper union representation for actors, writers and directors. The International Alliance of Theatrical Stage Employees (IATSE) and the International Brotherhood of Electrical Workers (IBEW) (which included grips, electricians, soundmen, projectionists and other manual labourers) and the musicians had their unions, but these were tolerated by the studio moguls because they were long-standing unions with national memberships. The moguls were not about to allow their creatives to follow suit. In addition to escaping the prying eyes of Edison's trust, they also came to Los Angeles during the 1910s because of its reputation as an anti-union town, and they brooked no intention of giving up that economic advantage. The Academy of Motion Picture Arts and Sciences (AMPAS) began in 1927 as an organisation supposedly representing creative film workers, but it enjoyed little independence from studio executives and owners. AMPAS supervised arbitration between studio employees and the studios, but except for an occasional sop to the former (often the more famous actors who possessed some pull), the Academy generally sided with the film companies. It functioned more as a company union than an independent union, unlikely to disturb the system or its owners, and keeping more militant unions from arising. The fact that the MPPDA paid the Academy's annual $50,000 running costs demonstrated how beholden they were to the major studios. At almost the exact moment *42nd Street* became a huge hit, the beginning of the end of the non-union era for higher-status employees such as writers and actors was arriving, and the Academy's function would soon be relegated mainly to administering the Oscars. As biographer Leonard Mosley wrote, 'all might have been well for the studio chiefs had not some of the greedier ones among them decided to push too hard'.[3]

The principal impetus for the shift that changed forever how Hollywood employees, elite and non-elite, viewed their livelihoods was the studios' insistence that temporary eight-week wage cuts for all employees were necessary for the industry's economic survival, beginning on 7 March 1933.[4] Such cuts were not unprecedented, but had never previously been applied to the entire industry. Fox Movietone and Hearst Metrotone newsreels had cut 25–50 per cent of employee salaries, and Warners announced a 'salary moratorium' for one week during the previous summer. Warners had already asked its contract players to take a salary cut before the industry as a whole acted, and one month before the new edict Cagney agreed to a $500 weekly salary 'slice' and fellow Warners star Ruth Chatterton volunteered to star in a film gratis.

This new, more universal and urgent call for radical salary adjustment was delivered at a time of extraordinary action aimed at averting catastrophe in the United States, just as Roosevelt took his oath of office. Immediately upon becoming President he closed every bank in the country between 5 and 13 March 1933 to allow time for his cabinet to deal with the problems of those institutions. This 'bank holiday' marked one of the more important of his administration's initial moves as it embarked upon a legislative agenda featuring many unprecedented and arguably radical government-sponsored relief programmes. During that week, Roosevelt also outlined Federal government budget cuts, particularly salary cuts, of half a billion dollars, including 15 per cent pay reductions for Senators and Congressmen.

For a business so dependent on lending to finance productions, Roosevelt's 'bank holiday' hit the film industry harder than most; most studios claimed they could not meet their payroll that week. The studio moguls felt they needed a similarly aggressive approach to what Roosevelt imposed in order to ensure their continued viability, and saw their opening. If the nation's highest representatives needed to tighten their belts to help their country, why couldn't movie stars and most others in the film industry take a hit as well? As Jack Warner wrote in a 9 March letter to Warner Bros. star Edward G. Robinson that was probably sent to many other studio employees:

> FOR THE PAST THREE DAYS AND NIGHTS MOTION PICTURE PRODUCERS HAVE BEEN MEETING FOR THE PURPOSE OF TRYING TO DEVISE PLANS TO KEEP STUDIOS OPEN, AND LAST NIGHT THEY MET WITH BOARD OF DIRECTORS OF THE ACADEMY OF MOTION PICTURE ARTS AND SCIENCES WHO ADOPTED ... FOR THE ENTIRE INDUSTRY ... A PLAN WHICH MUST BE SUCCESSFUL, AND IF NOT WILL RESULT IN THE IMMEDIATE DISCONTINUANCE OF ALL MOTION PICTURE PRODUCTION. AS YOU KNOW, THIS CONDITION IS CAUSED BY NATIONAL EMERGENCY, AND BUSINESS AT THE THEATRES [UPON] WHICH WE DEPEND FOR COMPLETE SOURCE OF INCOME HAS BEEN DEMORALIZED, MAKING IT IMPOSSIBLE TO TRANSFER MONIES TO LOS ANGELES.[5]

The studios' initial plan mandated a 50 per cent pay cut for all non-union employees, including 'all stars, executives, directors, writers and free-lance players, and all branches of mechanics', for eight weeks. As Jack Warner put it in his letter, the 'situation [is] so serious [that] unless drastic action on our part is carried to its fulfilment, we cannot carry on'. Other studios followed a similar line. A Paramount executive revealed that receipts had dropped 41 per cent during the previous two months and were 'two-thirds off in ... nine key cities', hinting that such numbers necessitated drastic measures. Fox employees were already enduring a four-week 'pay holiday'. The *Los Angeles Times* chimed in with the chorus during its first article on the cuts, insisting that they were 'the only way of keeping the studios open at all'. AMPAS did not challenge or question the salary cuts, demonstrating its uselessness as a force representing actors and other creatives. The wage cuts revealed, even to elite well-paid actors, how tenuous their economic position could be.

Were such desperate measures necessary? Or did this situation represent the exploitation of an opportunity to cut costs that the notoriously skinflint movie moguls (particularly the Warners) could not resist? Labour proved an intrinsic issue within Hollywood during 1933, as *Footlight* was written, produced and released. The year 1932 marked the worst year Hollywood had ever faced up until that time; jobs were threatened, receipts significantly down, talk of bankruptcy and receivership reverberated in trade newspapers.

Yet, an examination of film industry statistics of the period does not elicit much sympathy for the moguls and their methods of business organisation and compensation. Their vertically integrated control over every major aspect of the business, particularly the restrictive block-booking contracts limiting non-studio-owned or -supplied theatres to showing only one or two company films over long periods of time, enabled the studios to financially dominate the industry.[6] According to scholar Douglas Gomery, Hollywood film companies 'controlled [80%] of all first-run movie palaces in the 92 largest cities in the United States'. These theatres, the most prestigious, charged premium prices and featured the best of a particular studio's films as well as the best from its competition, if the competition did not own their own first-run theatre nearby. The studios often did not abide by their own block-booking policies for their first-run theatres, but usually forced small exhibitors to do so when they ran the same films weeks or months later in second-run, third-run, and in bigger cities like New York even twelfth-run, venues. Such policies allowed the 'Big 5' studios (Fox, MGM, RKO, Paramount, Warner) to not only deny major first-run showings to almost all independent theatres, but also to claim 75 per cent of American box-office proceeds, even though their studio-owned venues comprised just 15 per cent of American theatres. These are oligopoly numbers. Block booking allowed the studios a protected guaranteed market, even for their worst products, ensuring steady revenues and saving the studios money since they didn't have to strike thousands of prints at one time as modern-day film companies do; the same prints were used for each run, sometimes for as long as two years. Using a practice known as full-line forcing, the block-booking system even controlled the shorts, cartoons and newsreels shown before features, enhancing studio production and profits while often allowing little local control of a local theatre's programme. The inherent unfairness and rigidity of this system proved a controversial recurring theme in NRA motion picture industry negotiations, both before and after the code was passed, as will be seen in subsequent chapters.

Moreover, rewards were unevenly distributed, with studio moguls and executives receiving an especially large share. In 1931, for example, screenwriters earned only 1.5 per cent of the total payroll of the film industry, directors received 5 per cent, and actors on average received less money than screenwriters. Leo Rosten's highly researched study of Hollywood, which especially focused on the years 1936–41, found the film industry 'paid its executives (officers and directors of the corporations) remuneration which amounted to 1.59 per cent of its total volume of business – [a figure] second [in the United States] only to cement manufacturing, which paid its executives 1.61% of the total volume of business'. Rosten demonstrated that the motion picture industry ranked fourteenth among the top eighteen American businesses in volume of business, and eleventh in total assets, but it paid 18.96 per cent of net profits to its executives. Once again, only one industry paid a higher percentage to their executives – department stores. In 1937, fourteen of the leading twenty salaries in the United States went to movie industry figures, and Louis B. Mayer boasted the highest salary in the country. These figures do not include bonuses or stock awards. As William DeMille, brother of director Cecil and a writer and director for three decades in Hollywood, argued in his 1939 memoir:

> when times are hard . . . everyone is asked to show his loyalty by accepting a salary cut . . . I have heard one of the biggest [producer/executives] speaking with tears in his eyes to a mass meeting of the studio personnel, begging them to help him tide the company over a financial stringency, and nobly offering to cut his own immense salary drastically . . . When money was lopped off [the employees'] salaries it was gone forever, but when it was taken from the producer's weekly check . . . it finally came home to roost in the shape of profits and bonuses. In fact, if the producer had been able to achieve a fifty percent cut among the loyal comrades, he could have easily cut his own salary to zero and, by so doing, very probably have tripled his yearly income. Still, his speech on loyalty was extremely moving and, in its climax particularly, suggested the Gettysburg [Address].[7]

Rosten also documented how shareholders complained during the 1930s about a lack of dividends from the profit of the major studios. Evidently, Hollywood executives were loath to pay out money to people who did not directly contribute to the creative success of their films; in executives' minds, stockholders deserved only a modest profit for bankrolling studio facilities and film budgets (this represented one of the issues in the 1937 Warner stockholder revolt reported in the previous chapter). While these figures derive from a slightly later period than 1933, Rosten reported: 'The Big Money is not a recent phenomenon for movie producers and executives.' The stakes in the

1933 wage cut fight were different for executives from how they were for other studio employees. As would be the case later in the year when the Roosevelt administration forced the film industry (as well as all other major industries) to assemble a universal code for complying with New Deal employment policies, the movie mogul executives tried wherever possible to ensure that artists and regular studio employees would suffer the economic pain of the Great Depression, not executives. Even when national box-office receipts swung noticeably upward less than three weeks into the eight-week period of cuts, including, as reported by *Motion Picture Herald*, 'a 10 per cent increase over the weekend at theatres of the Warner circuit' (probably due in large part to the success of *42nd Street*) and a 40 per cent rise in eleven major cities, most major studios, including Warner's, did not rescind the cuts (Columbia Pictures did).

Because of these circumstances, it is difficult to muster much sympathy for the studios' pursuit of wage cuts. While it is true that much filming in Hollywood stopped during Roosevelt's 'bank holiday', the companies enjoyed excellent financing even in the wake of recent losses. Anonymous film executives told the *Motion Picture Herald* that the current 'tightness of cash and the inability to transport currency to Hollywood' led to the cuts, but with the banks open again roughly a week later, it seems conceivable that the studios could have begun filming again even without such draconian reductions. It is hard to imagine that the financial interests which put up the money for the movies whose production was interrupted by the bank holiday would countenance an abandoning of projects. Not only that, but in 1933 MGM stockholders received their 'highest dividend in years', according to scholar Nancy Lynn Schwartz, which might explain why Mayer, alone among his peers, instituted a full repayment of the austerity cuts to employees. The *Los Angeles Times*'s March 1933 front-page cries of 'Will the movies fold up entirely?' seemed alarmist and unrealistic, perhaps in keeping with its generally industry-friendly right-wing-slanted coverage.

By June 1933, the film studios' stock market valuation had risen $140 million since Roosevelt's inauguration, nearly doubling in value, its highest showing in two years. Warner Bros. common stock value during that period went from $3.8 to $23.7 million, easily covering its $1.58 million operating loss for the second quarter of 1933. An even higher overall price rise in industrial stocks during the same period demonstrated that the upward market movement doubtless reflected national confidence in Roosevelt's new approaches to economic stewardship more than Hollywood studio performance, but the figures demonstrated further evidence of the studios' relative economic health in the weeks after the salary cuts.[8]

Employees with signed and guaranteed studio contracts needed to approve the slashing of their pay cheques. And not all were compliant. Within two days of the announcement of the cuts, the *Times* headlines on the issue went from 'Film Workers Accept Pay Cut' to 'Film Pay Cut May Hit Snag'. Perhaps part of the resistance came from the justified fear that the moguls were using the economic crisis to do something about their long-seated complaint that actors, particularly stars, were paid too much; the *Motion Picture Herald* quoted a Fox executive who claimed that 'Hollywood's unfathomable salary demands were ... the reason for the reduction order'. Walter Pidgeon, Warner Bros. employee and later president of the Screen Actors Guild, refused to comply with the cuts. Jack Warner threatened Pidgeon's career if he did not take the cut, then gave him demeaning assignments to demonstrate how miserable life could become if he continued to defy management: Pidgeon was asked to report more than once as an extra, and then as an off-screen narrator of a short nature documentary, hardly the tasks an ambitious young actor would wish for. Jack 'Warner, disgusted, paid off Pidgeon's contract', reported Laurence Beilenson. 'Whereupon Pidgeon sold Warner Bros. stock short at a large profit. No one laughed louder at the story than the Warner Bros. lawyer.'

In the end, across Hollywood, most actors, writers, cinematographers and directors accepted the temporary reductions; 97 per cent of non-union motion picture employees had signed agreements acquiescing to the cuts two days after they were announced. 'Everybody got very pious and scared about the possibility that the studio might close down. So we took the pay cut', according to MGM screenwriter Frances Goodrich, co-writer of *It's a Wonderful Life*, among other films. 'Most of us had never had so much money anyway, and we preferred a few tough weeks rather than coming to the end of pastures of plenty.' Lowly extras, however, far from the media spotlight with wages far below those of contracted creatives and who typically suffered through sporadic employment, found their pay rates slashed during the period of the cuts, according to labour historian Murray Ross: 'Minimum daily rates for extras declined drastically. Fewer extras were used and a larger proportion were hired at reduced rates. Similarly, the studio craftsmen were suffering from curtailed production schedules and impaired wage standards.'[9]

The 'mechanics', mostly represented by IATSE, took a strong stand against wage cuts, and their national muscle helped them prevail, despite the studios' closing down production on 13 March 1933 in an attempt to try to intimidate them with the seriousness of the industry's economic plight. IATSE did not back down, and in fact further insisted that all lower-paid studio employees not be included in the wage cut scheme, another fight they eventually won. They could get away with such boldness because a strike by IATSE would shut down not only most Hollywood production but also film screenings nationwide, since most projectionists were members of the union.

In light of the unionised employees' relatively easy victory in avoiding the sweeping cuts, it represented no accident that the first serious Hollywood craft unions, particularly the Screen Writers Guild (SWG) and Screen Actors Guild (SAG), began forming in the weeks and months after the 50 per cent wage cuts. At this point, Jack and Harry Warner did not make it easier for their mogul brethren or the public image of their industry by announcing that they would not reduce their own personal salaries, even while insisting that their creative talent did. Mayer did the same.[10] This served as yet another reason, perhaps the most powerful one, why the cuts appeared less than necessary. Roosevelt tended to frame the massive New Deal cuts he favoured as a unifying call for all to sacrifice for the greater good of the country. The Warners' motives were transparently not as honourable.

Furthermore, news coverage in *Variety* indicated other reasons for the cuts besides temporary economic dislocation.[11] The cuts fitted snugly into the major film companies' recent efforts to pare down production expenses in the wake of their significant capital outlay for new theatres, music companies and sound systems in their studios and theatres. Lowering talent expenses represented a way for executives to keep film quality high and pay back these outlays without affecting their own compensation. In an article appearing during the first week of cuts, 'Break for New Talent: If Stars Walk, OK, Say Execs', unnamed industry sources practically dared actors 'disgruntled' by the cuts to walk out, noting that plenty of 'new talent' existed to take their places. 'So far as the bankers are concerned, the more walkouts of high-salaried people, the better, under existing conditions, as that may be one of the few ways studio overhead will get a material cut', according to the article. 'The new attitude is an official ban on temperament and without much say-so it applies to the biggest and smallest [film industry workers].' As will be detailed in the next chapter, some movie stars, particularly Cagney, were already challenging the restrictive terms of studio contracts, withholding their labour when management refused to negotiate, and eventually winning raises on the basis of their box-office performance, ensuring they shared in the large financial proceeds they helped create. The design of the wage cuts seemed intended as a way to curb such rebellious 'temperaments', and make actors and other well-paid creatives thankful to have jobs, even as their pay was cut in half. Perhaps this strategy was inspired by the studio's success in a similar strategy in the 1927–8 period when 'talkies' were introduced. 'Producers used the [sound] crisis as an opportunity to cut the escalating salaries of stars', reported film historian Danae Young. Older movie stars were thus pressured at that time to take salary cuts or resign, but the motion picture industry workers, particularly actors, were not going to easily fall for such tactics in 1933.

The next week, under a banner headline, *Variety* reported that yearly studio payroll costs had dropped 67 per cent in two years from $156 million to $50 million. 'The announced eight weeks [cut] was just a publicity move designed by the leaders for the hoped-for psychological effect of stringent economy', the paper argued. 'There is little chance of any of the slashed salary percentages being returned until the country's box offices reflect a decided up movement.' The article indicated, or perhaps more accurately gloated, that average costs for a 'first run quality' film decreased from $250,000 to $200,000 as a result of the cuts. These cuts weren't about survival or the industry banding together in unity during a crisis; they sought to intimidate employees and bring down payroll costs so that executives could still draw enormous pay cheques in spite of the Depression's lowering of box-office receipts.

By 15 March, supposedly aided by the economic relief the cuts afforded, 'work was in progress in practically all pictures previously suspended'. Lower-paid employees were mostly spared the rod, with only those making more than $50 per week (about $925 in today's dollars) taking a cut, and those making between $50 and $100 taking less of a cut than the 50 per cent mandated by those employees making $100 per week or more. The *Times*, obviously reading from a script prepared by the major studios, reported that 'higher sala-ried contract employees of the studios . . . will bear the brunt of the reduction'.

Another resistor of the 50 per cent cut, not just for himself but for all Warner employees, was Darryl F. Zanuck. Harry and Jack instituted the 50 per cent cut in his salary without notice, and did not consult with him, the head of produc-tion, on how the cuts should be implemented for creative employees. Zanuck couldn't believe the lack of gratitude Harry and Jack demonstrated towards their workers; he had also recently joined the Republican Party and may not have been pleased about the public support the brothers gave to Roosevelt's programmes in their films and advertisements. Without soliciting the brothers' approval, he issued a statement on 10 April 1933 that instituted a new pay policy similar to that recently announced by Sam Goldwyn at his independent studio in the wake of the pushback by IATSE and other non-unionised studio employees: all wage cuts would be rescinded, and bonuses awarded in some cases for above average service during the Depression. Jack Warner would not be dictated to by one of his own employees, and, as a notoriously obsessed cost-cutter, he certainly would not give up a hard-won reduction in employee salaries. He issued his own public statement reinstituting the cuts for Warner employees and for good measure, added an additional week of the cuts.

Zanuck's frustration over this issue was also doubtless related to a lack of respect he had long felt from his fraternal bosses. According to his biographers, Zanuck thought he had received signals from Jack over the years that, with the enormous success he brought to Warners, he would someday share in company ownership. By 1933, he realised this represented a lost cause. If he wanted to enjoy the full benefit of his sizeable contributions, he needed to leave. One could make a convincing argument that Zanuck saved the studio during the Depression and, with the brothers, created a house style that would be fol-lowed past World War II, but Jack and Harry Warner would never relinquish

Figure 3.1 (L to R): Film/stage star and writer George Arliss, with Darryl F. Zanuck, Warner Bros. head of production from 1930 to 1933, the architect of their 'social realism' film style. The two were close, with Arliss leaving Warner Bros. for Twentieth Century Pictures at the same time as Zanuck in April 1933. (The Kobal Collection)

ownership to a non-family member, particularly during the studio's halcyon years. On 15 April, Zanuck tendered his resignation, effective immediately.

It proved easy for Zanuck to jump ship. Within the industry, he was viewed as the 'hottest young man in Hollywood', according to biographer Mel Gussow. Other studios were gunning for his talents, including industry-leading MGM as well as Columbia. Instead, perhaps informed by his experience at Warner, he created his own opportunity, assembling and running his own new studio Twentieth Century, and amalgamating it with Fox two years later, forming Twentieth Century Fox in 1935, which became one of the major Hollywood studios. For over two decades as Vice President in charge at Twentieth Century Fox, he added to his reputation as a champion of social realist Hollywood films by producing and releasing such works as *The Grapes of Wrath* (1939), *Gentleman's Agreement* (1947), *All About Eve* (1950), and dozens more. Between 1933 and 1942 Zanuck's place as Warner's head of production was taken by Hal Wallis, but Wallis never wielded the same authority, and was viewed within the Warner hierarchy as Jack Warner's assistant, rather than as his own man.

The wage cuts, and the resulting fallout, proved the first major harbinger of tensions that would roil the industry as *Footlight Parade* went before the cameras. As Ceplair and Englund reported, the wage cuts 'finally shattered the Academy's moral and professional stature in the eyes of Hollywood artists'. In May 1933, AMPAS offered a new constitution to its members in a bid to remain a relevant force in Hollywood, but it was too little, too late. The proposed revisions to the organisation's remit offered no new protections for the film workers it supposedly represented and did little to establish independence from the major studios which largely controlled the organisation. The animus that led to the establishment of the SAG and SWG was understandable, especially among creatives: with the March 1933 wage cuts, a bond of trust between owners/executives and artists, which even in the past had been shaky, had irreparably broken. The festering wound of betrayal and the increasing trend towards employee organisation would only increase as the year and decade went forward.

Ten days after Zanuck's sudden exit from Warners, Jack Warner bought the rights to the stories that would become *Footlight Parade*.[12] The stories, 'The Footlight Parade' and 'Prologues', were written by Jerome Kingston, who wrote stories for films during the 1920s and 1930s. He should have received screen credit for *Footlight*, but due to an oversight by Warners did not – he did receive $10,000 for the rights, almost as much as the three screenwriters and script supervisor combined earned for their weeks of work on the film.

Though Zanuck vacated his Warners post six months before the release of *Footlight Parade*, his aesthetic informed it, and people he had chosen served in principal roles making the film. Files in the Warner archives indicate that he had worked on the film before he left, and probably greenlighted it. The two main stars of the film, James Cagney and Joan Blondell, were, according to Zanuck, 'my complete discovery'. In one week during the late 1920s or early 1930s, so he claimed, he signed Blondell, Cagney and Bette Davis.[13] All three were classic Warner stars representing the difference of the Warner studio, made to order for the more realistic productions Zanuck aimed for. They were not the usual glamorous generic film actors; they were energetic performers specialising in playing characters ensconced in the struggle, roles projecting an inner strength, perhaps because they possessed an inner strength in real life. With Cagney's pug nose and attitude, Blondell's 'chipmunk cheeks' (her own description) and Davis's intense gaze and haughty manner, they did not sport smooth perfected looks. They were not the relaxed or easy kind of actors who faded into the background; they fit within Zanuck's cinema of realism. The characters they played were usually desperately trying to better themselves and liable to take big risks to do so, as in *Footlight*. Then and now, their difference from the norm captured screengoers' attention.

For Cagney, *Footlight Parade* represented an especially risky and important project in his career. After a rough childhood in various insalubrious New York City neighbourhoods, and a decade-long vaudeville and stage career including a stint starting up a dance school with his wife Billie, Cagney began acting for Warners at the age of 31 in 1930. His roles as working-class toughs with occasional sociopathic streaks in films such as *The Public Enemy* (1931) and *Taxi!* (1932) earned him instant fame. And as was usually the case within the Hollywood star-making machinery, Warners placed their exclusively signed star Cagney into similar roles repeatedly. Between 1930 and 1933, Cagney starred in fifteen films for them.

Under the restrictive multi-year contracts most actors signed, repetitive typecasting formed the studio's prerogative and economic strategy. Cagney's first Warner contract spanned five years. These contracts not only attempted to freeze film actors' compensation for years before anyone knew whether or not they would win favour with the public – they also did not allow actors latitude in choosing roles. The studio, at least on paper and in the great majority of cases, possessed ultimate autonomy and placed actors in the productions they thought would be the most profitable, not the ones that expanded or challenged an actor's ability. If an actor struck box-office gold with a certain kind of role, that kind of role was usually repeated until audiences burned out on the typecast actor. The long-term career of an actor usually did not connote an issue considered by the studios, since most film actors did not enjoy long careers, and long-term stars exacted higher salaries. In 1933, Warners issued an edict barring their screenwriters from showing scripts to actors while still in the writing stage 'because of actor interference on yarns which resulted in numerous stories being botched up', according to *Variety*.[14] Writers sometimes consulted with actors in their movies, hoping that including more of the actor's feel or interpretation of the part would improve their scripts. James Cagney and his relationship with hard-left-leaning John Bright, who worked on several Cagney films, may have served as the source of this action by the studio.

Within the Hollywood labour system, it made economic sense to lock actors into supposedly iron-clad low-paying contracts at the start of their careers. Film is often seen as an art in the present day, but studio executives rarely countenanced such perspectives during this period. With such high fixed costs, profit had to come first. But yet, well-crafted, well-acted artistic pictures brought in audiences; a balance needed to be struck. In the 1930s media world, where no one knew the longevity of the appeal of Hollywood studio product or that performances by stars like Cagney would be viewed and bought for decades to come, actors' careers were generally thought to be evanescent, an asset taken full advantage of before the juice ran out, and another newer actor won public favour. As artists who wished to enjoy lengthy lucrative careers, actors did not want to be relegated to such a limited fate. By making his screen dancing and singing debut in *Footlight Parade*, Cagney was testing whether he could propel himself out of the snarling straitjacket in which Warners had previously constrained him. He was making a bid to be viewed as a rare figure in the studio system by succeeding in two different genres, attempting to secure a long-term, multi-faceted career. Warners seemed cautious while rolling out Cagney's singing and dancing debut. 'There is some secrecy surrounding the event insofar as the timbre of Cagney's crooning voice [is concerned]', *Daily Variety* reported concerning a live radio preview of Cagney's main vocal performance from *Footlight*: 'Nobody knows whether the toughster is a basso or a tenor.'[15]

Screenwriter James Seymour, chosen by Zanuck to work on the earlier Great Depression Musicals, continued doing so with *Footlight*. Seymour wrote *Footlight*, aided by Manual Seff. They carried on the tone already set by previous incarnations in the series, and improved upon it. Five days before he left the studio, Zanuck indicated that he approved of their approach: Seymour 'has all the characterizations set down perfectly and all the changes he made I am greatly in favor of'. In an introductory note to the shooting script, Seymour and Seff outlined their modus operandi, which helps explain much of the success and continuing relevance of *Footlight Parade*. The attitude was decidedly Zanuckian:

> THIS PICTURE DEPENDS ON TEMPO! SCENES HAVE BEEN MADE INTENTIONALLY BRIEF AND STACCATO ... THERE MUST BE NO SLOW FADE AWAY SCENES ... QUICK CUTS AND WIPE-OFFS MUST GIVE THE EFFECT ACHIEVED ON THE STAGE BY BLACK OUTS ... THE DIALOGUE MUST BE RAPID FIRE ... EXCEPT, OF COURSE, IN CONTRASTING QUIET SCENES OF ROMANCE. IF ANY SCENE LACKS INCIDENT OR DRAGS IT MUST BE CUT. THE PICTURE MUST HAVE THE PACE OF A PRODUCTION DANCE NUMBER PUNCHED UP WITH A MINIMUM OF DIALOGUE.

The script's title was originally *Prologue*, but this changed early in the process. Various drafts in the Warner archive reveal some effective pruning, by Seymour and Seff, as well as by uncredited screenwriter Sheridan Gibney and script supervisor Robert Lord, the latter of which made some particularly important changes. One could argue that Lord was just earning his keep, as he was paid more than the two credited screenwriters made together (as script supervisor he also attended most filming days). The parts of the script that should have been excised, including portions that did not live up to the directive on 'tempo', were thrown out, clearly improving the work.[16] In this case, the studio's system of assigning multiple writers to one script, sometimes unknown to each other and uncredited, bore fruit. This practice would later become one of the rallying cries behind the formation of the Screen Writers Guild.

Lloyd Bacon, whom Zanuck chose to direct *42nd Street* when Mervyn LeRoy took sick, also helmed the non-musical majority of *Footlight Parade*. The fast 'tempo' called for in *Footlight* matched Bacon's aesthetic. 'I see that the public gets action', commented Bacon decades later. 'Some others may use motion pictures as a vehicle for psychological study. I haven't that patience.' Bacon, like LeRoy, was a company stalwart, directing 98 films between 1926 and 1954, including 73 for Warners.[17] The filming of *Footlight* took place between 19 June and 5 August 1933. As happened with the production schedule for *Gold Diggers of 1933*, an ambitious concluding musical sequence for *Footlight* went before the cameras at the last minute, after all other principal photography had ceased, between 31 August and 15 September.[18] Less than three weeks later, the film premiered in New York.

Footlight Parade opens with musical theatre producer Chester Kent (portrayed by Cagney) being informed by his producers Frazer and Gould that his musicals are no longer supported by the public: 'People aren't paying for shows anymore. Talking pictures, that's what they want.' Gould is pleased with this new economic situation and buys up movie houses because 'they deliver the show in tin cans and we got nothing to worry about'. Kent mentions that some movie theatres still feature 'prologues', short live musical numbers before the main screening, but Frazer and Gould insist they're too expensive and also on the way out. But Kent sells them on the idea that if they produce musical prologues and tour them around the country instead of just playing them in one Manhattan theatre, they'll create an economy of scale, and make money with the enhanced market for prologues. And Kent will be able to keep doing the job he loves, creating musicals, but now on a national level.

In 1933, prologues still existed in the film industry but, as the film argues, were on the way towards extinction, mostly occurring in large cities, often for premiere runs of big budget studio pictures. As recently as 1928, according to research by Douglas Gomery, prologue 'minispectacles' could tour the Publix theatre chain, the most successful in the world at that time, 'for 33 weeks plus four weeks of guaranteed vacation. Then the cycle began again.' This roughly represented the business model Kent 'invented' in *Footlight*. Ironically, a 1932 article in *Variety* outlined how, in reality, Warner Bros. were trying to supplant prologues with less expensive Warner film shorts.

According to scholar Linda Mizjewski, the character of Chester Kent in *Footlight* was almost certainly inspired by Chester Hale, producer of musical prologues for the Capitol Theater in New York City between 1925 and 1938. Busby Berkeley worked alongside Hale choreographing producer Lew Leslie's *International Revue* on Broadway in 1930 – could Berkeley have provided some of the details that fleshed out the character of Chester Kent, based on the real-life Chester Hale? No evidence was found to support this. 'Kent also more than slightly resembles the public persona of [legendary producer Florenz] Ziegfeld', Mizjewski added. Additional inspiration was doubtless provided by Fanchon & Marco, Inc., a company with offices in Hollywood, New York, San Francisco, Seattle and Milwaukee that created, produced and distributed prologues for theatres around the country just as Frazer and Gould did in *Footlight*. *Variety* claimed Frazer and Gould's offices in the film 'were almost a replica' of those housing Fanchon & Marco, and that 'Some of the characters are familiar as F. & M. workers'. In addition, two of the sixteen prologues advertised in a November 1932 Fanchon & Marco ad were either mentioned or used in *Footlight*: 'Ubangi', which seems similar to an idea broached by the character Viv, and 'Shanghai', which seems at least a close cousin of 'Shanghai Lil', *Footlight*'s closing number.[19]

As his scheme of touring national prologue companies becomes reality, Kent/Cagney charges through the frame, a blur of kinetic energy and machine gun dialogue, dispatching quick solutions for problems that emerge on a minute-by-minute basis, hoping that the sleepless pace he maintains doesn't land him in 'the laughing academy'. One can feel the effort of the cinematographer tracking him as Cagney bolts quickly through room after room, the camera going through walls to match his lead, an example of the 'action' filmmaking Bacon specialised in. Cagney plays a workaholic obsessed with creating original and exciting prologues, pulling an all-nighter thinking up new routines, since Frazer and Gould's purchasing of new movie houses forces him to initiate three new prologues per week for his ever-expanding company. It's a classic case of doing more with less during a time of economic uncertainty. But his competitor, Gladstone Prologues, keeps stealing his concepts for routines: 'I slave day and night, worry about ideas, and Gladstone steals them, he's been doing it for months.' Kent and his loyal personal secretary and confidante Nan, played by Joan Blondell, are slowly realising they harbour a Gladstone spy in their company.

But even worse for Kent, he's also being cheated by his own company. Frazer and Gould, his supposed partners, fashion a separate phony earnings statement for him so that he won't know that 'profits are going up all the time'. They draw out $20,000 in profits for themselves, instructing their accountant to 'charge it to production costs, as usual' and hide the gains from Kent. Even the accountant netted a 'century note' in this clandestine deal, but Kent, the one whose ideas have brought in the profits, supposedly a full partner, sees no profits. *Footlight Parade* is a film about labour, and the lack of respect and profit accruing to those who do the main intellectual and creative work. It probably represented no accident that it was written and shot during a year when that issue flared up in Hollywood like never before.

Events in the film come to a head when Kent's company is offered 'the chance of a lifetime', competing with Gladstone for a contract with George

Apolinaris, who owns forty de luxe movie houses. Gladstone will preview three of their new longer prologues for audiences in Apolinaris' theatres the next Sunday; if Kent will preview three new prologues the night before, the company that wins the most audience approval will score the contract.

Kent wants the contract, but is not sure if Frazer and Gould can provide the support he needs to win it. 'So you're going to hire detectives? A fine pair of quarter-wits I teamed up with', Kent loudly complains to Gould. 'Every time I get a great idea, you let Gladstone steal it!' Kent comes up with a radical idea to solve his spy problem: he'll miraculously assemble three prologues with just three days' preparation that 'will stand [Apolinaris] on his ear', and will foil Gladstone's espionage by locking all his employees in the building until the premiere of the new prologues. 'It can't be done', declares Gould. 'Give me absolute authority until Saturday night and I'll do it', hotly replies Kent. 'You got it', his partners chirp in return. 'It's done!' Kent shouts, stalking off with his usual speedy brio, raring to start work immediately.

In the next scene, Kent outlines the situation to his dancers and singers, belting out words with urgency, a general rallying his troops during a time of crisis. It's a speech reminiscent of Warner Baxter's emphatic rant to the ingénue unexpectedly promoted to the star role, played by Ruby Keeler in *42nd Street*, but Kent's speech is more directly evocative of the Great Depression and Roosevelt's approach to selling Americans on the New Deal:

> Now this is the way we're going to do it. Nobody leaves here until Saturday night. You'll eat here and sleep here. Live three whole days right here in the studio . . . this is war, a blockade. Anybody comes in, stays in. Now this is your last chance to get out. Well? Anybody wanna go? [The company say 'No' in unison.] All right, thanks. This is a large order, three prologues in three nights. We're gonna work your heads off. Curse you and break your hearts. But by Saturday night we'll have what we want. All right, hop to it.

In the following montage, everyone in the company is shown working hard with a purpose, many dancing and sweating, while others try to catch some shut-eye during the three-day marathon. We see the chorus girls excitedly sitting down to a meal together and witness their ravenous appetites, a common motif in films of the Great Depression. Unsurprisingly, this blockade situation also provides an excuse for chorus girls to be seen in diaphanous nightgowns as they prepare for bed.

Many characters in *Footlight Parade*, including his partners and employees, tell Kent that his audacious three-day plan is doomed to fail; as Roosevelt took office, he heard similar sentiments from some quarters of the country. Many felt that the economic problems had gone on for too long, and were too deeply ingrained to solve. Roosevelt provided a steady charge from the opposite direction, emphasising optimism and government solutions. During the famous first 100 days of his administration, the Congress passed more than a dozen major pieces of Roosevelt-designed legislation which redefined the responsibility and relationship between the federal government and its citizens. This unequalled (then or now) onslaught of laws reformed banking on a national basis, providing additional security by insuring depositors against most losses; it reformed the stock market; it provided millions of government-funded jobs improving the country, giving millions a steady if small pay cheque and some dignity; it provided government refinancing for the many underwater home and farm mortgages; it repealed the prohibition of alcohol, providing a valuable new source of taxes and some relief from stress for US citizens. *Footlight* implicitly makes the same kind of argument: that a strong, visionary and outspoken leader armed with new ideas, who insists that problems can be solved, goals achieved, money earned and jobs saved, can and will succeed – if people will follow his well-considered plan and work hard.

When Kent's personal secretary Nan employs a clever ruse to reveal Frazer and Gould's embezzlement of Kent's share of the profits, Kent tells off his partners and storms out, breaking the blockade, insisting the show is over and putting the Apolinaris contract in jeopardy. After he drives around town with Nan in a cab, cools down a bit and gets a new inspiration for a waterfall-themed number, he returns to the building and informs the exiting players that the show is back on. He then has a spirited exchange with Frazer and Gould, which serves as yet another example of how Kent's character resembles President Roosevelt's:

> GOULD: What about that 'accounting mistake'?
> KENT: Mistake, your Aunt Fannie.
> FRAZER: We're giving you a new deal.
> KENT [with a combination of threat and triumph]: Yeah, and I'm the dealer!

It's an irresistibly well-acted moment from Cagney, providing another example of how the Great Depression is even more of a central character in *Footlight Parade* than in previous Warner Great Depression musicals. The trio of musical numbers that close the film, mostly directed and created by Berkeley, also symbolise an optimistic strain of the New Deal, as dancers mesh together to create something larger and more impressive than themselves. Berkeley's routines contain 'a New Deal spirit: deemphasis of star power, [a] certain melting pot idea', argued scholar Martin Rubin. In another example, one of the prologue units rehearsing in the film is preparing a prosperity-themed number. Kent accuses the dancers of 'dying on your feet', and the dancers retort by blaming the sulky yet humorous choreographer played by Warner stock player Frank McHugh: 'How can we look prosperity when he's got depression all over that pan of his?'

Finally, the frenzied period of lockdown and preparation comes to a close, and the three new prologues are premiered in one night for Apolinaris. They are shown consecutively in the film, with short interludes during which we see the chorus girls running in scanty costumes towards stage doors and changing their clothes on a bus accompanied by wailing police escort so they can make it to all three theatres on time.

The first of three prologues on deck is 'Honeymoon Hotel'. For decades, this was believed to be a Berkeley-designed number, but when the Warner Bros. archives were opened in the 1970s, scholars discovered that Warner employee Larry Ceballos choreographed it. Perhaps more alert filmgoers could have guessed this beforehand. While entertaining, 'Honeymoon Hotel' doesn't feature the sparkle and singularity of a Berkeley sequence. According to film editor Robert S. Birchard, Ceballos was assigned to choreograph *Footlight* when Berkeley's contractual commitments to Samuel Goldwyn made Berkeley's participation in the film impossible. But Ceballos' work did not prove as effective as Berkeley's, so Berkeley was brought back for the final two numbers.[20] This could be part of the reason why the last number for *Footlight* went before the cameras so long after the rest of the principal photography had ceased.

In 'Honeymoon Hotel', Ceballos's framing and editing are more traditional than Berkeley's. Little flair is present; most of this sequence could have been shot by any journeyman 1930s director. Also, the sequence, despite being about honeymooners and featuring plenty of negligée-clad chorus girls, is rather tame, tweaking tired romantic clichés with none of the trademark Berkeley sexual eccentricity. Stereotyped prim older women in an elevator look askance at the honeymoon couple played by Keeler and Powell, embarrassing them and making them retreat to a stairwell to find their honeymoon suite. In the suite, the couple are unexpectedly greeted by the bride's hectoring family, shaming the eloping couple in song for keeping their marriage secret from them. The best bits, such as when a dozen brides who have been at the Honeymoon Hotel for a week advise the neophyte bride played by Keeler in song, are provided more by the songwriters Al Dubin and Harry Warren than by Ceballos. The brides are photographed unimaginatively, and all they do is sway side by side in a direct frontal shot; the unexpected Berkeley camera angles are missing in action. It's the situation, more than the visuals, that carries the sequence. In another repeat of Berkeley hallmarks, dwarf Billy Barty returns, mistakenly ending up in bed with Powell.

Another key difference from the Berkeley sequences is a brief capitulation to racial stereotyping. In one scene, an African American porter performs a lyric of the 'Honeymoon Hotel' song in a cringing minstrel stereotyped style, echoing the usual degrading way in which blacks were depicted in Hollywood. *Footlight* sequences directed by Bacon also featured the usual racial stereotypes of the period. A glum-looking minstrel performer is featured in one of the earliest shots of the Frazer and Gould company. And in a scene with Nan's roommate who mentions a history book about slavery, Kent comes up with an ultimately rejected idea for a prologue: 'I can see it now – pretty girls in blackface, slaves of old Africa, white men capture them.'

The next number, 'By a Waterfall', remains, 85 years later, the most famous of all Berkeley sequences – stills deriving from it frequently pop up in film books. As often the case with Berkeley, it begins with a theatre curtain opening, an audience watching and a conductor eagerly turning his gaze to the stage, but from the first shot, it is obvious that there is no way this production could have existed as a live performance, especially staged as a short prologue before a feature film. It's too sumptuous and over the top for such a humble setting. But that quality embodies the fun of the piece, as Berkeley delights himself and us in his deliberate veering away from reality.

The prologue opens with Dick Powell's character resting (in a suit and tie!) on the grass in a sylvan glen, with a creek trickling over rocks beside him. The music and lyrics he sings, written by Sammy Fain and Irving Kahal instead of the usual Warner team of Dubin and Warren, yearn for 'love in a natural setting . . . just a winding stream where I can drift and dream'. Suddenly, from behind ferns, Ruby Keeler, in a costume resembling bridal clothing, emerges vocalising with Powell. Keeler proceeds to lull him to sleep with her singing, leaving him to snooze as she waves at water nymphs who appear in the distance sitting amid a gigantic waterfall. Soon, behind some greenery, Keeler changes into a similar bathing suit as the nymphs and joins them in the water.

The camera pans back to reveal a huge set, one of the most elaborate movie musical settings ever staged. According to the budget in Warner Bros. files, sets and construction for the 'Waterfall' number cost a shade over $32,000 (about $600,000 in today's money), about 30 per cent more than the cost of *Footlight*'s other two major sequences put together.[21] At least fifty chorus girls cavort upon a rock-strewn hillside surrounded by trees and vegetation, wearing tight nylon body stockings over their torsos with costumes over those stockings that look like leaves and vines. Rushing water cascades upon the rocks and down three smooth water slides, down which the chorus girls glide before making splash-landings into the water.

Nothing like this had ever been constructed on a Hollywood soundstage, and predictably, Berkeley ran into resistance from the Warner brass before being allowed to mount such a spectacle. 'The day I had the idea, I let Jack Warner know about it and he told me I would ruin even the Bank of

America', he recalled decades afterwards. Perhaps this is why in some of the Daily Production Reports issued by the studio, 'By a Waterfall' is listed as 'GLORIFIED POOL NUMBER'. According to Berkeley, Jack 'blanched at the probable cost, but our pictures had been doing so well financially that he pretty well agreed to let me do whatever I wanted . . . The mountain wilderness and the pool covered almost an entire soundstage . . . I had [the stagehands] build me plate-glass corridors underneath the pool so I could light and shoot it from the bottom.' Studio publicity bragged that Berkeley's pool held 80,000 gallons of water, and '400 men working 6 days in three shifts' enabled water to be 'pumped up from the gleaming pool and poured over the waterfall' at a rate of 7,500 gallons per minute.[22]

Berkeley created a magical effect, an on-screen environment that feels as though the viewer has come upon a secret forest hideaway full of frolicking laughing women. They smile radiantly as they paddle and loiter around the pool, wave and splash water at each other. The absence of men and the feeling of joy radiating from these women represents an attractive melding of both innocence and sexuality. While the character Powell plays sings about experiencing a romantic life amid nature, these pool nymphs have already created such a world unto themselves, and it appears that he can have no part in it, except in his dreams.

According to studio files, five days of rehearsal and eight days of filming were required for the 'Waterfall' number.[23] The women are viewed from every conceivable angle, above and below, but not usually in overtly sexual poses; they enjoy the impact of the waterfall on their backs and being soothed in close-up by the current's flow. Berkeley's adventurous approach to perspective in the Great Depression Musicals continues as a shot of one of the nymphs diving from a low angle ends up being only her reflection in the water taken from underneath the surface, the image broken by her splash, and then replaced by her body quickly gliding by the camera, the impact evident in her speeding form. Underwater, women are seen darting underneath and over each other, as well as female duos linking their legs around each other's necks, spinning themselves in and out of the water. During the number's most sensual moment, at least thirty chorus girls float closely side by side in the water, with each woman's feet resting near her neighbour's head, each floating woman propped up in the water by another woman behind her. Another woman makes a high dive, landing near them, then swims right through the middle of the floating women, their bodies drawing back as the swimmer's strokes touch them. Then, at the end of the row of floating women, the swimmer doubles back executing a backstroke, and the women slowly knit their bodies back together again in her wake. If a lesbian subtext exists here, it is subtly and artistically drawn.

During the final moments of the sequence, sixteen women at a time repeatedly dive into the pool, quickly filling it with swimmers and creating a fireworks-like effect with their splashes in shots taken from above, as a flute-led 'Swan Lake'-like orchestration plays on the soundtrack. Berkeley's trademark shot taken between many pairs of legs is completed underwater this time out, as a beaming female swimmer glides underneath a series of spread and spangled female crotches for a few seconds. The most otherworldly impression Berkeley creates occurs when the chorus girls float on the water linking their hands and feet while moving in concentric circular motions, with underwater lighting bestowing a ghostly effect when shot from above.

The women are then shown out of the water attired in diamond-shaped scanty bathing suits, holding hands, moving on a rotating platform of multiple Lazy Susans moving in opposite directions, as water sprays from hidden jet streams near their feet. This vision is also viewed in a reflecting pool. According to publicity materials, the revolving fountain consisted of 'more

Figure 3.2   Perhaps the most famous image devised by musical film choreographer Busby Berkeley: tiers of kaleidoscopically arranged beaming women with their legs spread and water jets spraying out from beneath them, photographed from an angle that could never be viewed by an audience in a live musical theatre setting. From the 'By a Waterfall' number in *Footlight Parade* (1933). (Warner Bros./The Kobal Collection)

than thirty tons of steel', as well as 'eleven powerful motors and pumps, pulsing dynamos and huge water mains'.[24] Next, the women sit down on their platforms and are viewed from above making geometric kaleidoscopic patterns with their outstretched legs, an indelibly beautiful and sexy image. Soon, the audience is transported back to Powell asleep, with Keeler, dressed in the outfit she first had on, splashing water onto his shoes in order to wake him, making the audience wonder if the vision before our eyes constituted a dream. As if to simultaneously counteract and vindicate the glistening sensuality unveiled during the preceding eleven minutes, the sequence ends with a last shot of a bird in a tree as four of its chicks pop up out of its nest – images of marriage and ensuing children were often used in Hollywood films as the best justification for presenting sensual images. Film historian Martin Rubin unleashed a stream of adjectives embodying the Berkeley aesthetic, and the 'Waterfall' sequence epitomises them more than any other: spectacle, gratuitousness, uselessness, extravagance, rampant excess, over-indulgence, flaunting, conspicuous consumption.[25] It's no wonder such qualities particularly entranced poverty-stricken Americans during the Great Depression.

Berkeley called 'By a Waterfall' 'the most difficult number of my career to film because of the shots underwater and because of the physical efforts that the girls had to make in the water'. This is not only evident in the many physically demanding acts they perform; also, when, if one looks closely, one can sometimes spot one of the water-borne performers grimacing at efforts made, or the cold temperature of the unheated pool. Just like in *Footlight Parade*, Warner Bros. posted guards at the soundstage doors where the number was filmed, making sure no other studios could pirate Berkeley's ideas.[26]

The mass of performers Berkeley carefully controlled during his musical sequences led to accusations of fascist themes in his work.[27] 'It was fashionable during the 30s to describe Berkeley's choreography as "fascist"', according to film historian Arthur Knight. 'The girls were dehumanized . . . mere integers in an abstract design.' Film historian Gerald Mast reported that the 'Waterfall' sequence was 'a great favorite of Hitler'. Critic and intellectual Susan Sontag, in her essay 'Fascinating Fascism', compared the work of Nazi house director and propagandist Leni Riefenstahl to Berkeley, although it's surprising that the Berkeley film she cites is *The Gang's All Here* (1943), instead of the three Warner Great Depression Musicals he made in 1933, all released before key Riefenstahl Nazi-era films such as *Triumph of the Will* (1935) and *Olympia* (1938). Regardless, Sontag's list of 'fascist aesthetics' does bear a resemblance at times to the Berkeley style:

> a preoccupation with situations of control, submissive behavior, extravagant effort, and the endurance of pain . . . two seemingly opposite states, egomania and servitude. The relations of domination and enslavement

take the form of a characteristic pageantry: the massing of groups of people; the turning of people into things; the multiplication or replication of things; and the grouping of people/things around an all-powerful, hypnotic leader-figure or force . . . the orgiastic transactions between mighty forces and their puppets, uniformly garbed and shown in ever swelling numbers. Its choreography alternates between ceaseless motion and a congealed, static, 'virile' posing. Fascist art glorifies surrender, it exalts mindlessness, it glamorizes death.

Comparisons that Sontag did not mention, but that are also shared between Berkeley and Riefenstahl, also include the athleticism and racial homogeneity of the on-screen performers. While discussing a film so obviously enmeshed in the New Deal, it is also worth mentioning that historian Lawrence W. Levine listed numerous political commentators of the 1930s, particularly between 1933 and 1935, either equating Roosevelt's programme with fascism or wondering if it might be true, particularly when discussing the government–industry partnership embodied in the National Recovery Administration. As president, former New Deal supporter Ronald Reagan repeated the charge. Levine also lists many films from the 1930s that reflect fascist themes.

However, even to the casual observer, large differences of vision exist between Berkeley and Riefenstahl. Most of the large groups captured by Riefenstahl's lens are essentially faceless, devoid of individuality, displayed not as individuals but as massed converts to Nazi fascism who will not be diverted from Third Reich beliefs. They conform to a viewpoint of themselves as a uniform, blindly loyal movement that the film attempts to encourage others to join. The athletes depicted in *Olympia*, for example, are idealised, consistently performing perfectly, as seen in the diving sequence. Berkeley's *Footlight Parade* divers are not displayed to perfection. They hit the water at slightly different times; they cavort informally in the pool; not every moment on-screen is animated by an overarching force or belief. Alongside Berkeley's more choreographed settings are shots of the women playing, laughing and swimming at random, their personalities plainly shown on screen. Berkeley is in control, and is as usual the star of the show in many ways, but these women, the so-called 'chorus girls', usually anonymous in other Hollywood musicals, are not mere 'puppets'. They are spotlighted in close-up (a device Berkeley brought to the movie musical), allowed to express themselves more than was the case for other contemporary film choreographers. Along with the Roosevelt imagery and racial diversity attending the last number in *Footlight Parade*, these filmed sequences make any argument for Berkeleyian fascism dubious to say the least. Nonetheless, as film journalist Dave Kehr points out in a short essay comparing similarities between Berkeley and Riefenstahl: 'Certainly there was something in the air, and not just in Nazi Germany, that drove people to find a sense of strength

Figure 3.3 Choreographer Busby Berkeley and stars Ruby Keeler and James Cagney conferring on the set of the 'Shanghai Lil' sequence in *Footlight Parade* (1933). (Warner Bros./The Kobal Collection)

and safety in numbers, after the economic individualism of the 1920's culminated in the stock market crash and the Depression.' But like Roosevelt's New Deal legislation and programmes, many of Berkeley's routines made a point of lifting the individual from the mass, celebrating individuality in the midst of organisation. His choreography glamorised life, personality and sensuality, certainly not death.

Berkeley's final *Footlight* number is 'Shanghai Lil', a madcap *mélange* of both progressive and stereotypical sensibilities, a sequence that could only have passed muster before the Production Code went into full effect in 1934. In the minutes before showtime for the third prologue, the male lead is drunk, his alcohol provided by Gladstone's spy. He reveals to Kent his lack of professional acting experience, and refuses to go on. In the tussle that follows as Kent attempts to force him on-stage, Kent falls onto the stage in front of an

Figure 3.4   During the Pre-Code era, the major studios amped up the sex and
              violence in their films and marketing because they found it brought in
              bigger audiences, particularly during the Great Depression. With the
              Warner Bros. Great Depression Musicals, risqué images were used in ads
              that went far beyond what appeared in the films, as seen in this press
              photo from *Footlight Parade* (1933), which features star James Cagney in
              the centre. This picture, not from the film but based on its 'Shanghai Lil'
              scene, also serves as an example of the 'yellowface' depiction of Asians,
              where whites were made up to portray Asians, usually in demeaning
              ways, in Hollywood films of the period, and afterwards. (Warner Bros./
              The Kobal Collection)

SRO crowd as the curtain rises and decides on the spur of the moment to play
the lead himself. The scene takes place in a dissolute bar in China where an
international crowd of barflies, flappers in net stockings and garters, prostitutes, and US Navy sailors like the one Kent plays coexist in an alcoholic and
nicotine haze. Kent's tuxedo-clad character surveys the bar's patrons searching
for his Shanghai Lil, aggressively fending off the advances of other women who
show interest in him by crushing an offered flower under his foot, and cruelly
pushing another woman's face away.

Soon after, the camera pans across a gallery of diverse characters discussing the relationship between Kent's character and Shanghai Lil. The characters include a French Foreign Legion officer, a black African soldier, a British regular and a Jew from Palestine. There's a worldliness to these personages seldom seen in 1930s Hollywood: two white women surround the black African and one speaks to him as an equal and touches him – an action rare and respectful for the period. Elegantly and sexily dressed women surround these men and at least one if not more of them is a glamorous prostitute. 'That Oriental dame [Shanghai Lil] is detrimental to our industry', she complains in song. A Chinese couple at the end of the bar is also portrayed more respectfully than usual for a Hollywood production. Some of the ideas for this 'Shanghai' setting probably derived at least in part from the hit film *Shanghai Express* the year before, which also featured a surprisingly international cast amid hints of immorality, including prostitution. The scenes described above, with their flaunting of American racial codes and aura of foreign exoticism, could be viewed as an embryonic version of that other memorable venue for equalitarian multiculturalism in the Warner Bros. canon, Rick's Café Americain in *Casablanca* (1942).

But despite some progressive portrayals of the races alongside images of a diverse set of women enjoying nightlife in a sexually alluring and liberating atmosphere, most imagery of the Chinese patrons is offensive, or close to it. Several white women, including Ruby Keeler as Shanghai Lil, are made up to look Chinese, and use pidgin English accents ('I miss you velly much a long time') that amount to a Chinese minstrelsy, or 'yellowface', as modern scholars term it.[28] In the same scene, an older Chinese woman runs an adjoining 'joss house' dispensing opium to gorgeous white women in gowns, another familiar stereotype. But interestingly, the Chinese men in the sequence are recognisably Asian, not made-up 'yellowface' whites. The assuming of an Asian identity perhaps allowed white actresses like Keeler to temporarily adopt a less savoury and more sexual persona than usual, encouraging an image of Asians as decadent. Film scholar Karla Rae Fuller has focused on the practice of Hollywood substituting white actors for Asian characters, maintaining that such depictions exist 'to ridicule . . . and demonize . . . a parody and caricature of race'. The practice occurred frequently in pre-Code Hollywood, and historian Thomas Doherty has argued that one of the reasons for this was that when 'white actors romanced white actors in yellowface, the yellow peril was also an erotic possibility', since the Production Code forbade interracial romance on-screen. The Code also prohibited 'derogatory portrayals of foreign peoples'. Warner Bros. knew this to be the case, and when the Chinese Embassy heard about the sequence and made enquiries, the studio kept details of the sequence from them before the film's release. In a memo written three days after photography on 'Shanghai Lil' had wrapped, Warner head of production Hal Wallis made the decision to stonewall:

I would hesitate to show the 'SHANGHAI LIL' number to the Chinese Consul in view of the fact that we do just exactly what he thinks we are doing. It would probably be difficult to make him understand that this is a musical comedy and that we have musical comedy license on such matters. I think we are better off in not looking for trouble. Tell him that the sequence is not yet ready to be shown, by explaining to him that the sequence isn't objectionable and will not be harmful to his people.[29]

The 'Shanghai Lil' sequence's use of white actors as non-white characters falls into a Hollywood tradition concerning the portrayal of not just Asians, but also African Americans, Latinos and Native Americans during the first half of the twentieth century and beyond. Caucasian Hollywood stars appearing in 'yellowface' included Fred Astaire, Ingrid Bergman, Katharine Hepburn, John Wayne and many more, particularly during and directly after World War II. Fuller notes that 'certain [instances of Hollywood Asian] stereotypes rely even more on exaggerated mannerisms and physical cues' than other examples. 'Whether portrayed as fantasy figures, nightmarish monstrosities or inscrutable mystics, these [Asian] figures of the imagination embody elements both strongly seductive and deeply threatening.' *Footlight Parade*'s 'Shanghai' number includes elements of all these qualities, combining both offensive and more enlightened portrayals of Asians on-screen.

When a drunk and dishevelled sailor pronounces Shanghai Lil 'anybody's gal', Kent's character socks him on the jaw and a bar-wide mêlée results. When the brawl clears, Kent's character has somehow changed back into his sailor suit and finally finds his Shanghai Lil and they dance with gusto on the bar-top and a table-top. While Keeler again seems to retain a stand-in for the close-up of her dance solo, Cagney handles his steps with an impressive grace and fluidity, his whole body from his shoulders to his feet swinging with the beat. Berkeley was impressed, though, considering Cagney's years of hoofing on Manhattan stages during the 1920s, perhaps he shouldn't have been. 'He could learn whatever you gave him very quickly', Berkeley remarked. 'You could count on him to be prepared. And expert mimic that he was, he could pick up on the most subtle inflections of movement.'[30] Before Cagney and Keeler can finish their dancing, a trumpet sounds and Kent's character's unit is called to vacate the area. The American sailors march outside the bar, allowing Berkeley to show off his military choreography experience as Cagney and his fellow Navy brethren parade in formation, twirling their guns with drill team precision. They also incongruously mix ranks and do a marching routine with a group of Asian-looking women (most if not all of them 'yellowfaces') wearing Asian peasant hats and Western-style short dresses.

At this point, a loud patriotic horn-led fanfare plays for the first and only time in *Footlight Parade*. The US Navy personnel and 'Asian' women hold up small flash cards to the camera perched directly above them. When aligned together, these cards generate a graphic of the American flag. Immediately thereafter, those in the centre of the flag turn their signs over to reveal a large portrait of the new US president, Franklin Delano Roosevelt, superimposed upon the flag. The sailors and women then fold up their flash cards, and, with the camera still providing an overview from the ceiling, quickly rearrange themselves into the Blue Eagle, the central symbol of Roosevelt's New Deal programme. When the eagle pattern is achieved, including the trademark lightning bolts in its claw, rifles are fired in salute. A theatre owner in Dante, VA informed the *Motion Picture Herald* that 'when they formed President Roosevelt's picture the audience applauded'.[31]

The Blue Eagle served as the emblem of Roosevelt's NRA, probably the New Deal's most significant response to the Great Depression, entailing an almost complete reorganisation of the American economy.[32] With the NRA, Roosevelt attempted to prime the pump of consumer spending and jobs on a nationwide scale. Through voluntary national action, the NRA sought to compel all businesses to set maximum weekly hours for employees (usually 30–40) so that more Americans could earn pay cheques, and it also set a minimum wage ($12–13 per week). For hundreds of major industries, including the motion picture industry, the NRA helped its leaders draw up an NRA code that set prices, production quotas and other rules. These voluntary regulations aimed to stop 'unfair competition and disastrous overproduction', according to Roosevelt, and ensure that as many companies and employees as possible remained active and working. The hope was that, by workers and bosses both giving up something, they could guarantee their continued jobs and raise the overall economic health of the country by working together. It also abolished child labour, one of Roosevelt's favourite accomplishments. Section 7(a) of the code became probably the most controversial provision of every NRA code. It provided a federally guaranteed right for workers to organise themselves and bargain collectively with management, utilising representatives that they, and not the companies they worked for, chose. Previously, the federal government had not supported unions in any fashion. Section 7(a) inaugurated a Golden Age for the American labour movement, but as will be seen in future chapters, led to problems and resistance from American industries, especially the notoriously anti-union Hollywood movie moguls.

In order to compel Americans to support this legislation, which imposed an unprecedented amount of federal control upon the affairs of private enterprise (a controversial concept to many Americans then and now), the NRA mounted an intensive national publicity campaign. President Roosevelt explained the concept during his popular 'fireside chats' on the radio, pamphlets and pins promoting the policy were manufactured, parades and brass bands were employed, and businesses were encouraged to place NRA Blue Eagle emblems, usually with the slogan 'We Do Our Part' printed beneath them, in the front window of their shops, at factory entrances and even on company station-ery. The Blue Eagle, based on a Native American thunderbird design, was deemed necessary by Roosevelt because he felt that 'those who cooperate in this program must know each other at a glance'. According to historian Arthur Schlesinger, over 2 million employers signed up to support the NRA, and a march promoting it in New York City drew 1.75 million participants and spec-tators. 'When every American housewife understands that the Blue Eagle on everything that she permits to come into her home is a symbol of its restoration to security', remarked General Hugh S. Johnson, head of the NRA, 'may God have mercy on the man or group of men who attempt to trifle with this bird.'

The Blue Eagle formation accompanied by patriotic music in *Footlight Parade* served as an extraordinarily public banner placed in the Warner Bros. shop window, seen by millions around the country and the globe. Other Warner feature films, such as the aforementioned *Wild Boys of the Road* (1933), featured the insignia in subtle ways in the background of key scenes. Most if not all Warner Bros. films from March 1933 and throughout the year featured the Blue Eagle at the start or close of the film or both. During spring 1933, as the *Footlight* script was being written, the Warner brothers were basking in the victory of their chosen presidential candidate Roosevelt and his legislative agenda. The scene of Roosevelt's face and policies being so baldly celebrated in a feature film during the *Footlight* dance routine is unprecedented in Hollywood films then and now.

The end of *Footlight Parade* features requited love onstage and backstage. By the close of the number, Keeler as Shanghai Lil has donned a US Navy uniform so she can join Kent's character on the 'great big steamboat across the sea'. In the theatre after the 'Shanghai Lil' finale, the crowd cheers loud and long, and Apolinaris happily signs the contract with Frazer and Gould. The last scene with Kent and Nan, his indomitable personal secretary, is particularly moving because it takes place backstage in quick segments, in between Kent's curtain calls as the audience applauds wildly:

NAN: 'You did it, boss.'
KENT: 'You mean *we* did it.'
   [Kent goes off for a curtain call and rushes back to her.]
KENT: 'I've got a great idea.'
   [Kent is called for yet another curtain call and rushes back to her.]
KENT: 'This idea's for a wedding.'
NAN: 'For the [Frazer and Gould] unit?'
KENT: 'No, for you and me.'
DANCE DIRECTOR: 'Come on, take another bow!'

KENT: 'Take it yourself!'
[He pushes the dance director onto the stage, shuts off the backstage lights, leaving Kent and Nan in silhouette.]
KENT: 'You like it?'
NAN: 'Whatever you say, boss.'
[The curtain closes, leaving them in complete darkness.]
KENT: [laughs] 'I'll make you love it!'
[He gives her a loud kiss as the film ends.]

The last lines are particularly powerful because they are spoken with the actors in shadow and then with a completely dark screen, their faces unseen, leaving the film audience to imagine their excitement. Even though the screen goes dark during the last seconds of the film (much as it did in *I Am a Fugitive from a Chain Gang*, but for completely opposite reasons), the way in which Cagney and Blondell read their lines leaves us in no doubt as to their happiness in what they have achieved together for the company, and their recognition of their feelings for each other. Subtle hints throughout the film indicated that they harboured romantic feelings for each other (more on this later), and the open revelation of their love finally surfacing in this manner proves dramatic and affecting.

Both Roosevelt and *Footlight Parade* made the case that by following a smart plan from a charismatic visionary leader, it is possible to avert crisis and realise success. The Depression can be dealt with, the movie seems to intimate, but it will entail much hard work with no guarantee of success. In its eccentric Berkeleyesque way, the military imagery at the end of the film fits, not only in its rededication to the American dream (a similar patriotic aura also infuses the concluding 'Forgotten Man' number in *Gold Diggers of 1933*), but also in the sense that what Kent and his loyal associates underwent was a kind of war, or at least an intense struggle. They fought against dishonest management and disloyal employees, on behalf of those who work within musical theatre and who provide its craft, those who know how to attract and thrill an audience. And of course, they were engaged in the struggle against the Depression itself, both in the film and thematically, for the film audience. *Footlight* focuses on labour, supplying good and bad examples of its practice. As the film went before the cameras, no one could be certain if Roosevelt's New Deal programme would deliver on its ambitious initial promise, but the public was evidently ready for a film that could deliver a story skilfully combining fun and realism while echoing a Rooseveltian approach in attempting to save a theatre company; *Footlight Parade* became a hit, earning over $2.4 million internationally (over $44 million in today's dollars), with a production budget of $459,760, according to studio files.[33]

These same principal attributes of *Footlight Parade* make it align with much popular culture of the 1930s. The insightful historian Lawrence W. Levine outlined how, during the Great Depression, Americans tended not to blame outside forces for their economic plight, even though plausible arguments could be made against, for example, banks that too hastily foreclosed on farms. Instead, Levine documented how Americans held a 'tendency to internalize the responsibility for one's position which often led to feelings of shame'. They blamed and excoriated themselves for their misfortunes, often apologising when forced by circumstances to seek aid. Levine argues that this philosophy made cultural works depicting 'personal responsibility' and a refusal to fail under dire circumstances a principal motif in many popular cultural productions. As evidence, he points to Margaret Mitchell's *Gone with the Wind* (1936), which dominated fiction sales for two years and became the film box-office champion of the decade. The main character, Scarlet O'Hara, as well as the country during the Civil War, faced a situation of scary upheaval not unlike the Depression, and no one knew how life would continue when the crisis passed, or if it would pass at all. 'O'Hara emerges as the individual who refuses to give in to these irrational processes', Levine observed. 'She survives the war, the siege of Atlanta, the destruction of her society . . . [and] on the very last page she loses her man, Rhett Butler, [but] she remains unbowed.' Her attitude, though certainly self-obsessed at times, enables her to survive harrowing times, and we do not doubt her future ability to succeed, or her possibly getting Butler back some day.

Levine found similar currents of 'enduring values' enabling 'triumph over adversity' across a wide spectrum of Depression-era American culture. His brief list includes radio shows starring Will Rogers and the fictional characters Amos 'n' Andy, Disney's Oscar-winning 1933 *Three Little Pigs* cartoon short ('Who's afraid of the big bad wolf?') and the perennial non-fiction bestseller *How To Win Friends and Influence People* (1937), which stressed personal conduct as a key tenet of business success.[34] To that list of 1930s culture could also be added the bitter-sweet yet swinging music of Duke Ellington, John Steinbeck's brutalised yet relentlessly forward-moving Joad family in *The Grapes of Wrath*, and of course Chester Kent and his stage company in *Footlight Parade* (as well as many other Warner social realist films). These various productions supplied entertainment, but did not deliver a simple escapism. They provided inspiration and wisdom, and even though their realism arrived in sometimes disturbing form, audiences embraced them, probably because they related to the public's situation without insulting them, and because these cultural works represented the kind of character audiences hoped they would exhibit themselves when placed in the path of such catastrophe.

As shooting wrapped and the post-production process went into full swing, Warner executives felt confident they had a major hit on their hands. After a preview screening for Warner's public relations team nine days after filming wrapped, Jack Warner sent a congratulatory telegram to Wallis:

> Can only say it is everything you said it would be everyone wildly enthusiastic about its possibilities ... everyone to man says footlight parade is greatest musical of all time stop you were right in lobby that night in saying don't touch foot of it stop that's consensus of opinion here stop ... am sorry you cannot be here with me to enjoy with [Warner Bros. PR] men here the thrill they are getting out of exploiting and selling this picture.[35]

This enthusiasm found expression in the wide-ranging juggernaut for *Footlight* that the Warner publicity department assembled, even more elaborate than campaigns undertaken for the previous Great Depression Musicals.[36] The large-format 56-page *Footlight* pressbook comprised dozens of stories, matrixes and photos that newspapers and magazines could include in their pages. Film reviews were supplied, adorned with heavily biased headlines such as '*Footlight Parade* the Greatest Ever: Its Equal Has Never Been Seen'. For a price, theatre owners were offered a wide variety of official *Footlight* merchandise that they could sell or display in their lobbies and around town: chewing gum, balloons, postcards (with the waterfall scene on the front), tyre covers for taxi advertising, banners, art posters, life-size standees of the characters and chorus girls, sheet music (published by a Warner subsidiary), even an official *Footlight Parade* bottle-opener in the shape of a 'youthful-looking girl's leg'. 'With the return of beer and the impending repeal of the 18th amendment [which prohibited drinking in the United States], this [bottle] cap remover will be in great demand in every home in the country', the copy predicted. Diana Corsets advertised their promotional tie-in with the film in the pressbook, noting that Macy's department stores around the country showcased coloured cut-outs of *Footlight* chorus girls and the waterfall scene as a backdrop in shop windows and in their 'Corset Department'.

Promoters stressed the sexier portions of the film, with content often going beyond what the film featured. A nine-part radio drama script based on the film served as part of the pressbook package, as did a written serialisation encompassing 'ten tense instalments'. In an attempt to attract Depression-era audiences during a slump in the movie market, the previews provided for each chapter (including one entitled 'A New Dealer') played up and exaggerated the film's prurient aspects: 'A producer turned dictator ... the gripping story ... of chorus girls imprisoned so the show can go on ... of a blonde-loving boss, of the blondes who are willing to play with him, of a blackmailing secretary in love with her boss'. A four-page 'pictorial review' for distributors and exhibitors featured shots of the scantily clothed women around the waterfall, in even more revealing costumes than they donned for the film. A story about the 'By a Waterfall' number describes the chorus girls as 'nymphs' performing 'nude', which they clearly were not in the film. In a photo that did not derive from the film, co-star Guy Kibbee observes a young blonde woman with a $10 bill emerging from the slit in her dress, hiked up well above her knee. The caption: 'Kibbee watches his investments carefully in *Footlight Parade*.' One of the ads displays an enthusiastically smiling young woman lying upon the ground, her feet against a wall spread into a V, breasts sprouting out of her strapless top. She's also holding a string tied to the wall that's inside her legs duplicating the shape of the V of her legs. No similar image occurs in the film. Underneath is written for exhibitors: 'here's the "leg angle" for your poster campaign!' There existed no doubt which angle Warner exploited in selling the film; the Great Depression Musicals is how film enthusiasts and scholars often label these films now, and Depression-related themes are present and repetitive within them, but these themes were not used as a sales point for these films when released.

As in the marketing for *Gold Diggers*, the young star Ruby Keeler remained the one female exception to this general overtly sexual trend. Even as *Footlight Parade* ramped up the sexuality in its imagery supporting the film, the clean-scrubbed Keeler image remained intact. She is described in *Footlight* publicity with terms like 'wide-eyed and innocent' and 'refreshingly naïve', even though she was married to Warner star Al Jolson, displayed as much as skin as any of the chorus girls in the waterfall scene, and appeared to dispute such characterisations. 'I can't help the way I look', she protested in one story from the pressbook, to little avail. 'I'm really just as sophisticated as can be. I've been around!' At roughly the same time as *Footlight* came out, *Broadway Through a Keyhole*, scripted by the nation's top gossip columnist Walter Winchell, was also released. *Keyhole* was apparently based on the true story of Keeler's romantic involvement with a gangster before she met and married Jolson, who felt so aggrieved about the film and presumably its potential effect on his wife's image and reputation that he reportedly 'decked' Winchell.[37] Perhaps the Warner publicity slant concerning Keeler also meant to counteract these kinds of reports about the past personal life of their innocent-looking new star.

Advertisements and posters for *Footlight* also particularly stressed musicals as a key part of the Warner brand. Some sample captions: 'Only Warner Bros. could make it!'; 'Warner Bros., master makers of musical films!'; 'So magnificent you'll wonder that even Warner Bros. can make it!' Every poster but one in the Warner archives mentions the company, usually in bold lettering, sometimes bigger than the fonts that the star's names were printed in. Most of them also mention previous successes *42nd Street* and *Gold Diggers*. As previously discussed, every major Hollywood studio possessed its own recognisable screen identity. Establishing a strong studio brand denoted a much more important priority during this period than today, when most film fans are probably unaware of which studio presents their favourite films. By Warners stressing their studio's distinctiveness and prowess in their ads for *Footlight*, they were encouraging audiences to patronise the theatres nationwide that played Warner movies and tried to make visits to their theatres an ingrained habit, enhancing box-office take for the studio and its preferred exhibitors. It represented good business all around.

While the marketing of *Footlight Parade* concentrated mainly on women as barely clad silent nymphs rather than as multi-faceted female characters and personalities, the film presented a different portrait. The political angle and Berkeley's elaborate fantasies did not represent the only ways in which *Footlight* differed from usual Hollywood product; it also offered a unique vision of women's roles. While Berkeley's routines focused on chorus girls (objectifying them or paying tribute to them, depending on your perspective), the film's script proved more enlightened than most in its portrayal of women, work and romance. While plenty of female flesh appears on display along with various examples of men checking out women in tight and clinging chorus girl attire as they walk by, Kent refuses to countenance the usual male interest in women's legs when they audition for roles. When they lift their skirts to show their legs as they are apparently asked to do in other companies, Kent orders them to cease such activity: 'This is an audition, not an exhibition.' In assembling his cast, the issue for Kent centres on a performer's talent, whether they can do the job at a high level. As he says with admiration in another scene, 'There's a girl for you. [She's got] Brains. You can buy beautiful women a dime a dozen.' In another sequence, Kent passes right by a group of rehearsing chorus girls spreading their legs in the air repeatedly with hardly a glance; he has a job to do and is not ogling them like other men usually do in the film.

But it's the relationship between Nan, played by Blondell, and Kent that really illustrates the difference embodied by *Footlight Parade*. She wins her man in the film's concluding scene not for the usual reasons offered in 1930s Hollywood films, such as her looks, some elaborate scheme, or by sacrificing her own ambitions. She succeeds through her political skill, her knowledge of business, her astute sense of how much to trust various personalities, and her dedication to Kent's welfare. Competing against a wily, more conventionally attractive and sleekly dressed opponent, Nan ends up as Kent's paramour by looking out for and brilliantly covering his blind spots. He clearly would not succeed if not for her skills.

Both Nan and Kent prove resourceful in ways that complement each other. Part of what makes *Footlight Parade* so fun and romantic is how this principal relationship builds slowly, based on trust and mutual aid. It's not obvious as the film begins, but it dawns upon the audience slowly that this relationship could blossom into a romance. These two people are together because they respect and need each other; it is not a relationship based on blind, lustful love. An earned camaraderie exists between them; their partnership is forged in the heat of the battle to assemble the prologues needed each week. Kent falls for Nan because of her intelligence, because she proves so insightful about his life and his business, because she can get things done, protect him, and will stay up all night with him hammering out a script. They share a lovely chemistry, and truly listen to each other. One feels an ease in their manner together. On a night when a prologue has to be finished so the company can rehearse it in the morning, Nan volunteers to stay late to help Kent get it done:

> NAN: 'If the little girl is not too bold, how's for me sticking with you til we get [an idea for a new prologue], you can think out loud.'
> KENT: 'Like we used to?'
> NAN: 'It might help. Keep throwing ideas at me.'
> [She says this as they're forehead to forehead.]
> KENT: 'You throw the poor ones right back. Sold. We'll give Apolinaris a show if it takes all night. We'll have dinner, think and walk.'

At the end of a night brainstorming together, Kent and Nan fall asleep innocently on a couch, a few inches apart, with their clothes on; they smile sweetly and chastely at each other before they close their eyes to sleep. They've obviously formed a partnership. Kent finally realises this at the end of the film and asks her to marry him. While the musical sections of the film portray romance with the sniggering images of 'Honeymoon Hotel' or as the embodiment of a howling, sexy cat sitting on a fence, a much more mature and equal vision of love is privileged in the story of Kent and Nan. Such behaviour from a character depicted by James Cagney might have startled 1933 audiences, who were far more used to Cagney portraying violent misogynists such Tom Powers, who rubs a half-grapefruit into the startled face of actress Mae Clarke in *The Public Enemy* (1931), the film that made him a star. Cagney probably relished participating in a more equal, less volatile romance than was usual on-screen; he resented Warner's relentless typecasting of him in gangster roles.

But not all the women in *Footlight Parade* rise to the level of Nan. Kent endures turmoil before he realises Nan's worth, some of it due to his own blindness. At the beginning of the film, Kent's wife demands a divorce and leaves him when he tells her that Frazer and Gould want to phase out the kind of musical theatre Kent specialises in; all she cares about is money and fine possessions. She comes back into the picture at the end demanding $25,000 for their divorce when she learns Frazer and Gould are making significant profits on Kent's prologues. Nan's old roommate, the more conventionally attractive and sleekly outfitted Viv, also sets her sights on the upwardly mobile

Kent. Viv also affects a faked cultivated air, pretending she's conversant with intellectual books. Kent gets hooked by her surprisingly easily, proposing marriage to her almost immediately and offering her a job and office at his company. Nan sees through Viv's façade, correctly labelling her a 'chiseller' who irresponsibly gets Kent drunk on a night when he has important work to do. Viv complains about her lack of mobility during the studio blockade, as Nan retorts: 'I wouldn't beef about being locked up with the man I love.' When Kent's wife makes her return appearance, Viv shows her true colours, brooking no sympathy and tearing into Kent with ferocity: 'you promised to marry me and you're going to marry [me] . . . listen, you silly looking baboon, who do you think you're running around with, some punk from the sticks? . . . I know the book and I know all the answers . . . [I'm] smart enough to sue and attach everything but your garters.' Kent, chastened, replies: 'I'd rather have you sue me than marry me.'

In *Footlight Parade*, in distinction from other films of the period, a woman doesn't have to descend to the depths for love or rise to the top ruthlessly without love. As film scholar Jeanine Basinger wrote in her history of women's films, most females in 1930s Hollywood cinema who do intelligent work or engage in some activity or adventure outside of the home do not fare nearly as well as Nan:

> No one ever suggests how unintentionally liberating a form the women's film actually was . . . Women in the audience could watch while their favourite female stars wore great clothes, sat on great furniture, loved bad men, had lots of sex, told the world off for restricting them, destroyed their enemies, even gave their children away . . . When the end of the movie came around, the surrogate woman was usually dead, punished or back in the fold, aware of the error of her ways . . . a perfectly safe form of pseudo liberation for women to enjoy . . . The women's film was successful because it . . . both held women in social bondage and released them into a dream of potency and freedom.[38]

While Basinger's research[39] repeatedly demonstrates that women in women's films usually 'cannot challenge power', Nan exposes, without punishment or comeuppance, the embezzlement of Kent's share of his profits by his partners, ensuring a happy ending for her and her boss. Unlike most active screen women, she doesn't succeed by manipulating men or 'putting out'; she succeeds by her own volition. While most women received 'two minutes of joy' in what Basinger termed the 'Happy Interlude', a quick montage of romantic happiness often featured in women's films, and subsequently suffer a denial of what they have achieved by the end of the film, Nan enjoys a movie full of drama, intrigue, fun and joy, and at the end has marriage proposed to her by a man who loves and respects her. In the context of the time, it's an almost shocking ending, particularly for a musical – some witty and smart women existed in 1930s screwball comedies and married (or remarried) successful men who recognised their non-physical as well as physical gifts, but most of these examples came after *Footlight Parade*.

As Joan Crawford's character lamented in *Possessed* (1931), in the typical women's film 'a woman can do anything, be anything, as long as she doesn't fall in love'. Basinger offers the reader dozens of examples of how women in Hollywood movies of this period found themselves 'entrapped' if they stepped outside of traditional home-bound roles, with themes of single motherhood, suicide and alcoholic abuse recurring throughout. Film writer Molly Haskell similarly demonstrated how 'the film industry maneuvered to keep women in their place'. Yet, Nan in *Footlight* breaks free of these usual restraints in a manner rarely seen at the time, except in Mae West's similarly empowered (and self-written) female portrayals of the 1933–4 period when she briefly reigned as a top-ten Hollywood star. Not only that, but in *Footlight*, Nan triumphs while lazy and false women like Viv and Kent's ex-wife are thwarted and cast to the side. We can't be sure of what transpires after Kent and Nan get married, but it seems unlikely that a character as colourful and resourceful as Nan will stay strictly relegated at home making babies – and as the next chapter will demonstrate, that's not how Blondell conducted herself in real life.

Basinger remarked that 'it's an interesting fact of life in the woman's film that it is almost always true that good women pick bad men, and bad women pick good men', but this is not how the plot resolves in *Footlight*. The film cast a somewhat liberated eye on men as well. According to Basinger's extensive examples concerning this subject, most 1930s and 1940s women's films cast men as hopelessly selfish and neglectful, or unappreciative of women's efforts on their behalf, or purposely stripping away women's freedom or independence – *Footlight Parade* offers a completely different vision of the male/female romantic dynamic in Nan and Kent's evolving relationship. While Haskell maintained that heterosexual relationships 'proceeding from deep, mutual respect' only arrived on Hollywood movie screens with the justly acclaimed Katherine Hepburn–Spencer Tracy films of the 1940s and 1950s such as *Adam's Rib* (1949) and *Pat and Mike* (1952), *Footlight* illustrated such concepts and emotions more than a decade previously.

Haskell convincingly argued that more positive roles for women existed in the 1930s and 1940s than during the supposedly more liberated 1960s and 1970s, especially when considering such films as *Klute* (1971) and *Love Story* (1970). Basinger seemed to agree. Concerning the earlier period, she wrote:

> Viewers were asked to enjoy looking at feminine beauty and to consider a woman as a companion, an equal, a challenging opposite who wore

great clothes and always had a comeback for any remark or a suggestion for how to get out of any pitfall. These were the women who had no fear of leopards and who willingly donned disguises and dove off the sides of ships.

Though ignored by most if not all writers focusing on women during the Golden Age of Hollywood (including Basinger and Haskell), Nan and *Footlight Parade* belong in this category. Some latter-day observers have characterised movie musicals of this period as exclusively and hopelessly misogynist. In their analysis of 'male chauvinist musicals', Robert Patrick and William Haislip argued that the 'common denominators' of musicals from this period were 'clear': 'Women are objects, idiots, infants – but they look great, are desirable for sex, and can dance . . . women's only sensible goal is marriage.' Warners star Edward G. Robinson, in his autobiography, felt that Hollywood in this period tended to treat women as 'second class citizens, rarely having any function beyond basting turkeys or bearing children'.[40] The time has come for a reappraisal of *Footlight Parade* as an exception to this usual rule.

Once again, Studio Relations Committee (SRC) censors objected to adult humour and situations in the *Footlight* script, and once again the studio tended not to follow their advice. The cuts that Warner Bros. consistently made, however, were those that SRC official Dr James Wingate felt made the dance director Francis look like a homosexual 'pansy'. The original script featured Francis talking about knitting 'doilies'; the line was dropped. But it should be noted that one of the funniest scenes in the finished film, and a more subtle and classy hint as to Francis's sexual identity, occurs when Francis and Dick Powell's character rehearse a new love song together to show the mostly female company how it goes, with both of them spooning and swaying, and Francis sporting a large cigar in his teeth. Although the original Production Code objected to homosexuality being portrayed on-screen at all (particularly in an 'attractive or beautiful way'), its authors could not find the fortitude to name the practice, referring to it coyly and disturbingly as 'impure love'. On the basis of SRC advice, Warner also excised *Footlight*'s references to 'brassieres' and 'drawers' and getting to 'first base'. Other key salty lines remained intact. Yet, when Wingate viewed the finished product in late September 1933, he informed Jack Warner that 'this production struck us not only as being satisfactory under the Code and free from any danger of censorship difficulty, but also as being one of the most colorful and entertaining pictures we have had the pleasure of reviewing recently'.[41] Perhaps he realised that the SRC received some of what it wanted, and could not legally insist on more in 1933. In 1934, when the Production Code was fully enforced and a $25,000 fine punished studios that did not remove transgressions to the code, more strict compliance would ensue.

Individual states and cities demanded and apparently received cuts to *Footlight Parade*.[42] The states of Ohio and Maryland, as well as the city of Chicago, insisted that Nan's insult to Viv – 'As long as they've got sidewalks, you've got a job!' – be excised. The state of Massachusetts asked for certain cuts only to be instituted for Sunday screenings! Kansas requested the elimination of the 'entire scene of Dick Powell in bed with Ruby Keeler' during the 'Honeymoon Hotel' sequence. This incision seems particularly cruel as this scene was one of the highlights of the often leering number – it constitutes a sweet and rare moment within Hollywood musicals seeing two lovers singing together romantically in bed, and it is fairly chaste as well since they both have a full set of pyjamas on underneath the covers. Kansas requested the elimination of the picture of the baby at the end of the sequence that suggested the product of Keeler and Powell's wedding bed. Surely, such a cute product of lovemaking by a married couple should have been approved by these religious-based authorities. As was the case with the previous Great Depression Musicals, the 1936 rerelease of *Footlight* occasioned even more cuts – not only for the racy language and visuals, but also for its embracing of imagery of President Roosevelt and his New Deal programme – the post-1933 strict enforcement of the Production Code sought to keep Hollywood films away from any politics, which were seen as 'bad for business'.[43] A *Footlight* reissue in 1970 earned a G (all ages admitted) rating. Production Code Authority files from the mid-1930s also show that *Footlight*, *Gold Diggers of 1933*, *I Am a Fugitive from a Chain Gang* and dozens more Warner pictures were summarily 'rejected by the nationalist authorities in Spain'.

Footlight Parade also openly tweaked SRC censors. Warner stock player Hugh Herbert played Bowers, the censor for Frazer and Gould. His authority is already compromised when we learn that he is the brother of Gould's wife. It is clear that nepotism forms the only reason he retains his job, and that he contributes little if anything to the enterprise other than weakly attempting to squelch some of the production's better ideas. Bowers informs Kent that a cat-themed prologue will not pass moral muster:

> BOWERS: 'I got bad news for you, Chester. You can't use the cat idea.'
> KENT: 'Oh, you're gonna start to tell me what I can and what I can't use.'
> BOWERS: 'It's my job to see that our prologues fit in with the censor's regulations. I'm only doing my duty.'
> KENT: 'Oh, I see, the tomcats and the pussycats are all right. But the kittens are illegitimate.'
> BOWERS: 'They certainly are.'

KENT: 'Unless they're married by a preacher cat. No preacher cat, no kittens. You can't use it in 39 cities. Well, I've got some bad news for you. You're fired.'

BOWERS: 'You can't fire me, Mrs. Gould's my sister!'

Later on, Mrs Gould cajoles her husband into rehiring the censor, but Kent warns him to keep clear, or he'll sock him on his 'blue nose'. Near the end of the film, in a further insult to his profession, Bowers is caught with Kent's (soon to be ex-) fiancée Viv drinking, giggling and commingling together on an office couch. His feeble response to being discovered *in flagrante delicto*? 'I was just showing her what cannot be done in Kalamazoo.' The quotation could have been lifted from one of the Production Code representatives' lengthy and hectoring letters in real life to the studio. Unsurprisingly, several states requested this last scene excised, and Wingate threatened Jack Warner about the 'preacher cat' scene: 'If the censors feel that they are being ridiculed in this scene . . . it is possible that you will lose some of this dialogue.'

One wonders if Zanuck, famous in Hollywood for his intolerance of censors, had been behind the idea for the scenes with the simpering Bowers. Zanuck and Warners had a reputation for paying as little attention as possible to the Production Code and its representatives. Other studios were more concerned about staying on the good side of the SRC, or at least wanted to preserve a family-friendly aesthetic in a difficult declining market. Over at Paramount the previous year, Josef von Sternberg's *Blonde Venus* (1932) featured 'a script so heavily bowdlerized' by Production Code concerns 'that it hardly made sense at all' by the time it went before the cameras, according to biographer Steven Bach. Admittedly, the original script 'seemed to tolerate, if not condone, adultery, prostitution and kidnapping',[44] a far cry from the less heated antics of the Great Depression Musicals, but one couldn't imagine Zanuck or the Warners knuckling under to the SRC so completely unless absolutely forced to do so. In any case, the censor-ribbing scene remained in *Footlight*, a last act of rebellion before a more formal censorship descended upon Hollywood creatives the year after.

Reviews for *Footlight Parade* following its New York City premiere on 5 October 1933 usually landed on one end of the scale or the other, extremely good or extremely bad, a historically typical reaction for a film that pushed at the borders of mainstream filmmaking.[45] The *New York Times*, perhaps in keeping with its Grey Lady image, pronounced it 'dull and turgid . . . an awkward rewrite of the backstage romances of three years ago'. The *New York Sun* found the film, aside from Berkeley's contributions, 'confusingly plotted, suspenseless and rather humorless', with the *Brooklyn Daily Eagle* also terming it 'pretty much a bore . . . We warn you, it's not another *42nd*

Street.' Los Angeles Times and *Variety* correspondents at the New York premiere complained that it took an hour before the main musical sequences commenced. *Daily Variety*, utilising showbiz argot, proclaimed it 'the best piece of musicker screen entertainment' and praised the 'story' quality of the film, arguing: 'None of the hoke usually injected into stage pictures has been allowed to creep in.' The *Los Angeles Times'* main cinema reporter Edwin Schallert called the 'By a Waterfall' sequence 'the most exceptional created so far for the talking and musical screen', which he said put the audience at the West Coast premiere 'under a spell', probably a difficult feat for a jaded company town audience. 'For fast talk with a punch [Cagney and Blondell] almost seem to have no rivals', he proclaimed. Richard Watts, Jr, critic for the *New York Herald-Tribune*, raved about the film, thought it better than its predecessors, and was the only New York critic besides *Variety* to mention the New Deal imagery:

> The new Warner musical show is elaborate, fantastically elegant in its musical numbers, slightly less tuneful and considerably more disrobed than its predecessors, well acted and pretty certain to be a smashing economic success . . . Marching marines somehow or other turn into N.R.A. emblems, and a picture of President Roosevelt flashes on the screen. For a combination of imaginative extravagance and less than impeccable taste I recommend 'Shanghai Lil' to you . . . 'Footlight Parade' is a lively cinema pipe dream.

The strongly negative reviews are surprising, given how the film is viewed today. Perhaps certain critics were surprised by the sharper satire and dialogue as well as the brisker pace of *Footlight* compared to previous Great Depression Musicals, or perhaps they were taken aback by the sight of James Cagney dancing and singing, which the *Los Angeles Times* pronounced a 'novelty of no slight merit'. Perhaps some felt that too much realism had been inserted into a musical, a complaint regularly levelled at Stephen Sondheim's musicals for the last half-century.

In any case, as reported by *Variety*, *Footlight Parade* did excellent business nationwide.[46] 'Exhibs [exhibitors] all over the country are in a hubbub of hey-hey over prosperity biz pulled in by "Footlight" . . . Latest Warner song-and-dance has key city slickers and small town yokels reaching deep into the jeans proving that depresh or no depresh, the dough is there if the attraction is.' In its first week at the Strand in New York, proceeds were $55,190 (over a million dollars in today's money), 20.4 per cent higher than for the first week of *Gold Diggers* and the most lucrative week the theatre enjoyed all year. This was at least partly due to an all-out marketing assault carried out by Warner: dozens of showgirls performed at the premiere, changing into their costumes on a bus just like in *Footlight*; thousands of four-page ads were distributed at the Polo Grounds and World Series games; 'animated marionettes' of the film's stars were perched on the theatre's marquee; and Busby Berkeley and Ruby Keeler attended, all of which 'packed the house and jammed the sidewalks with waiting lines'. An October 1933 Warners ad aimed at exhibitors noting the initial success of *Footlight Parade* was labelled 'Sizing Up The New Deal', yet another connection between the studio and the Roosevelt administration. In Newark, Jersey City, Pittsburgh, New Haven, Memphis, Brooklyn, Denver and Los Angeles, proceeds were 10–45 per cent higher than for previous Warner Great Depression Musicals. In Hollywood, the film's West Coast premiere inspired a Warner-sponsored parade from its Sunset Boulevard studio to its flagship cinema on Hollywood Boulevard, featuring an orchestra conducted by famous bandleaders accompanied by 'Hollywood beauties'. The major stars in the film attended, with Dick Powell serving as master of ceremonies.

However, even though *Footlight* brought back about a million in profit for Warner Bros. on the domestic box-office front alone and represented a solid hit, it almost certainly did not make as much money as its two musical predecessors.[47] While its first week set records in New York, it often underperformed against the first weeks of *42nd* and *Gold* in major US cities. The longest run it enjoyed in major cities was four weeks in Seattle, while its predecessors posted runs of nine and eleven weeks. It did not top the box-office chart for November, as *42nd* and *Gold* did, but it did make second place following Mae West's *I'm No Angel*, which ended up the top moneymaker of 1933, with *Gold* and *42nd* in second and third place respectively, and *Footlight* not even listed on the year-end chart, which listed nineteen films in all. Still, thanks no doubt in large part to *Footlight* and its two predecessors, Warner Bros. posted its first quarterly profit in three years during the last three months of 1933. True, the profit was a relatively measly $100,000 after amortisation, much less than Cagney or Jack Warner earned in a year, but the quarter proved another firm sign, along with the fivefold increase in the company's stock price, that the studio was starting to return to normalcy and profit after three years of net losses. *Footlight* and the two previous Great Depression Musicals played a huge role in that turnaround, and were constantly used in advertisements during 1933 that argued for the artistic and financial strength of the company. A month after *Footlight*'s release, Warner Bros. advertised their new Paul Muni film *The World Changes* by bragging, in tall bold letters, '"Footlight Parade's" success duplicated in drama by Warner Bros.'.

Perhaps an overfamiliarity with the Warner musicals provided some of the reason for *Footlight*'s relative box-office drop, and the fact that the studio released the first three Great Depression Musicals in a span of just seven months. As previously documented, other studios were also jumping on the trend. Though most theatre owners writing to *Motion Picture Herald* praised

Footlight and its financial performance, some also stressed such points, including this report from Greenville, MI:

> This picture is so big and good, you have got to see it to appreciate it. Wonderful entertainment. We have had too many of these good musical pictures in past months to make any money on them. Now we are back to where we were when they killed them before [in the early 1930s] before people could get too much of a good thing.

Though a couple of complaints emerged concerning the higher than usual 50 per cent of receipts that Warners took from theatres for their first two 1933 musicals, more complaints about the policy were aired in connection with *Footlight*, particularly since its grosses were usually less and did not offset the percentages as much as previous Warner musicals. An Ellenwood, KS theatre owner warned his compatriots:

> If you have not bought this one [yet], better take it easy. As good as any of the musicals but will not get the dough that 'Gold Diggers' got. Better think a long time before you give Warners a fat percentage for this. The cast is fine, the musical numbers are okay, but all come in a bunch. Should have strung them out all through the picture instead of right at the last.[48]

But, as will be seen in Chapter 6, Warners did not heed the advice of those who counselled making fewer musicals, and kept putting out even more of them per year with a similar formula and less verve throughout 1934 and 1935, inspiring steadily diminishing box-office returns.

In his book on pre-Code cinema, Thomas Doherty devotes a chapter to the 'preachment yarns' issued by Hollywood during this period, films such as *Chain Gang* and *Cabin in the Cotton* (1932) that portrayed how society supposedly was drifting tragically in the wrong direction. These films 'express the anguish of the dispossessed and fearful, but they have no idea how to alleviate the symptoms of what seems a terminal case', observed Doherty. 'Despite their billing, the preachment yarns do not so much administer a cure as watch helplessly while the patient howls in pain.'[49]

But *Footlight Parade* represented an anti-preachment yarn. Though one can sense the howling wind of the Depression outside the Frazer and Gould studios, and see it in the threadbare surroundings in which the movie usually resides, the film offers a plan and a solution to predicaments presented. The main characters succeed in their mission to do the work they love and defeat the scheming and immoral forces standing in their way. It is a more political film than previous observers have given it credit for. Also, while numerous other 1930s Warner Bros. releases, many listed in this book, reflect a great cynicism, *Footlight Parade* does not – it combines hard-won optimism with a surprising realism in a striking, and, I would argue, inspiring, balance.

A historical category that Doherty finds among pre-Code films that accurately fits *Footlight Parade* is the 'dictator craze' that surfaced during 1933 as Roosevelt began his presidency. Films such as *The Power and the Glory*, *Employee's Entrance* and *Gabriel Over the White House* showcased Hollywood visions of 'benevolent dictatorship' in the fields of business and politics, as fascism took hold in Germany and Italy.[50] With his blockade of the Frazer and Gould studio to foil Gladstone's company spies, Chester Kent also could fit within Doherty's rubric. As Lawrence Levine's survey of film images of national politics during the Great Depression indicates, there existed

> a quiet but pervasive sense of despair concerning the future of both the individual and democracy. This despair can be seen in how often those who champion the cause of the people and the cause of democracy are forced to go beyond the democratic method ... in the early 30s most political films emphasized the need for forms of extraordinary action.

The disappointment over the perceived lack of action taken by Roosevelt's predecessor Herbert Hoover and the depths of misery caused by the Depression probably were at least somewhat behind the rash of movies with this theme. But as Levine demonstrates, this theme also surfaced in other aspects of popular culture, including the rise of private detectives in literature and superheroes in comic books during the decade; the actions of characters in each of these genres frequently went beyond the law, browbeating witnesses and ignoring habeas corpus rights with no penalty in pursuit of wrongdoing.[51] Many felt at the time that the system was not working to protect citizens, so such extralegal measures were justified, at least by fictional characters, if not in the real world.

Yet, Kent's brief totalitarian manoeuvre has far different ramifications from those portrayed in other 'dictator' movies. Kent's stint of martial law is fixed at just 72 hours, harms no one except through exhaustion, and provides beds and plenty of food and coffee for the entrapped dancers and singers, ultimately saving the company and dozens of jobs. The dictators in the other films behave quite differently: in *Power*, hundreds are killed in a labour massacre, and in *Gabriel*, a divinely inspired president arrogantly bypasses the US Constitution in declaring himself an unchallengeable Mussolini-like dictator to pass the laws he feels are needed to resurrect the country. Kent's transgressions are nowhere near as serious or significant. *Footlight Parade* makes the case that seemingly intractable problems can be solved if the right people are in charge, while

Gabriel depicts the political process as too hopelessly hidebound and corrupt to solve the world's problems unless God or a similar voice of Providence steps in to influence events. *Footlight*'s idealistic Rooseveltian perspective is miles away from the cynical almost fascistic mindset of *Gabriel*. Both illustrated significant strains of thought during the Great Depression, and Levine expressed surprise that the fascistic prescriptions offered in *Gabriel* were often described as sensible in contemporary film reviews. Perhaps he should not have been. As scholar Martin Rubin has pointed out, well-known 'numerous fascistically inclined organizations and demagogues proliferated in the United States in the 1930s', including the German American Bund, the Christian Front, Father Coughlin, Gerald L.K. Smith and many more. William Randolph Hearst, the multi-millionaire media mogul whose film studio produced *Gabriel*, and according to biographer David Nasaw exerted creative influence upon the project, also exhibited fascist sympathies during this period. Reporter Walter Lippmann described *Gabriel* as 'A dramatization of Mr Hearst's editorials'. Nasaw documented that Hearst had communication with Roosevelt and the White House before and after the film to ensure nothing insulting or threatening was implied towards Republicans or Democrats.[52]

Perhaps these kinds of differences from its contemporary competition, musical and otherwise, represent one reason for the mostly forgotten status accorded to *Footlight Parade* in the twenty-first century, despite its financial success and the fact that its crackling modern pace and subject matter still excite audiences. Probably the most immediate comparison to the Warner Bros. Great Depression Musicals, as a series of musicals that captured public attention during the 1930s, was provided by the nine RKO musicals starring Fred Astaire and Ginger Rogers between 1933 and 1939, which, according to Peter Williams Evans, 'did much to rescue the financially troubled RKO studio from the bankruptcy it had declared in the depths of the Great Depression',[53] just as the success of the 1933 Berkeley musicals saved Warner from potential bankruptcy.

The Astaire–Rogers musicals prove an intriguing contrast. They unfold in various glamorous international spots, sporting immaculately designed high-ceilinged art deco sets. The films' characters usually exist in upper-class environments far from any reference to economic calamities of the day. Astaire's characters are almost always outfitted in formal evening wear. The music backing the films' songs often arrives out of thin air with no orchestra visible on-screen, and an appealing privacy sans audience between Fred and Ginger's characters reigns in many of the best dance sequences in the series. Such sequences provide romantic interludes of courtship, a way for the characters to express the intimacy that many of us in the everyday world feel, yet cannot manage to say or act out as poetically as Fred and Ginger do.

Astaire and Rogers usually preside over a dream world, while the 1933 Great

Depression Musicals are situated in the real world, even if Berkeley's dance sequences test metaphysical bounds of on-stage reality. Dirty backstage areas form *Footlight Parade*'s milieu, adorned with sweaty performers and shouting staff, people looking for their break and hoping to earn a meagre crust from their talent during difficult times. Love is earned by Kent and Nan with perseverance, trust and respect, whereas in the Astaire/Rogers films, the romances were difficult to feel or understand emotionally, especially since the convoluted and preposterous plots kept placing various obstacles and epic misunderstandings in their path instead of providing the blueprint for a believable, mutually supportive relationship. The Rogers-played female characters are nowhere near as smart or capable as Nan in *Footlight* or the struggling actresses (including Rogers) in *Gold Diggers of 1933*. At the end of the RKO films, Rogers' characters were often either just married or about to be hitched, with Astaire having to convince them to switch their affections to him at the (supposedly suspenseful, more often irritating and predictable) last moment. Sometimes it feels frustrating enduring the dialogue sections of these films, waiting for Astaire and Rogers' immaculate and joyous dance routines to return, which consistently showed Keeler and Powell for the second rate, although highly likeable, musical performers they were. Whereas Astaire's characters often had to decide between romantic and economic success, Kent and Nan enjoy both, because they put in the hard work. One often does not quite understand the attraction between the lovers in the Astaire/Rogers romances, until we view the perfect way they mesh together on the dance floor. In *Footlight*, we feel Kent and Nan's bond throughout, within their conversations and how they treat each other, long before they acknowledge their relationship and kiss backstage as an audience roars at the film's conclusion.

Although shades of darkness and reality exist in a very few Hollywood musicals released before 1960, the dominant movie musical model followed the Astaire/Rogers dream-world example, particularly the later Arthur Freed-helmed classic MGM musicals that defined the genre. The model was decidedly not the Warner Bros. Great Depression Musicals. As the worst years of the Depression faded, perhaps escapism trumped Zanuckian realism. Perhaps the market moved on, just as Zanuck had. Or perhaps the Warners' dissatisfaction with the Roosevelt administration and its left-wing policies during the second half of 1933 soured them towards musicals reflecting Rooseveltian idealism and the overt referencing of tough realities and current politics. As will be discussed in Chapter 6, after 1933 the Great Depression Musicals changed significantly in tone and theme, and did less well financially.

This chapter has documented *Footlight Parade* as a film and a production, and how it reflected the national mood and history of 1933. But the various political and labour back stories unfolding as filming and post-production occurred are just as interesting and further define the impact and context of the film, within Hollywood and beyond.

NOTES

1. Barry Keith Grant, 'Genre Films and Cultural Myths', *Film International* (2003): 30.
2. Mark Roth, 'Some Warner Musicals and the Spirit of the New Deal', *The Velvet Light Trap* No. 17 (Winter 1977): 2.
3. Laurence W. Beilenson, 'NRA: Blue Eagles, Sick Chickens', *Variety* (25 Oct. 1983); Larry Ceplair and Steven Englund, *The Inquisition in Hollywood: Politics in the Film Community 1930–1960* (Garden City, NY: Doubleday, 1980): 19–20; Danae Clark 'Acting in Hollywood's Best Interest: Representations of Actors' Labor During the National Recovery Administration', *Journal of Film and Video* 17:4 (Winter 1990); Leonard Mosley, *Zanuck: The Rise and Fall of Hollywood's Last Tycoon* (London: Granada, 1984): 166–78, 257–8; Murray Ross, *Stars and Strikes: Unionization of Hollywood* (New York: Columbia University Press, 1941): 101–3.
4. This account of the 1933 wage cuts at the studios and Zanuck's ensuing departure from Warner Bros. is based on the following sources: Rudy Behlmer, *Inside Warner Bros. (1935–1951)* (New York: Viking, 1985): 10–11, 53; Beilenson, ibid.; Ceplair and Englund, 1–3, Chapter 2; Clark, ibid.; James P. Cunningham, 'Theatre Receipts Swing Upward as Public's Confidence Returns', *Motion Picture Herald* (25 March 1933); Michael Freedland, *The Warner Brothers* (London: Harrap, 1983): 58–9; Mosley, ibid.; Neal Gabler, *Walt Disney: The Triumph of American Imagination* (New York: Vintage, 2006): 184–6; Leo Rosten, *Hollywood: The Movie Colony, The Movie Makers* (New York: Harcourt, Brace & Co., 1941): 65, Chapter 4; Edwin Schallert, 'Studios Taking It Standing Up', *Los Angeles Times* (9 March 1933); Edwin Schallert, 'Will the Money Crisis Make or Break Hollywood?', *Los Angeles Times* (12 March 1933) [front page top story of the day]; Nancy Lynn Schwartz, *The Hollywood Writers' Wars* (New York: Knopf, 1982): 10–13; [uncited authors], 'Cagney Takes WB Cut; Chatterton Gives Free Film', *Variety* (7 February 1933); 'Film Workers Accept Pay Cut', *Los Angeles Times* (8 March 1933); 'Film Pay Cut May Hit Snag', *Los Angeles Times* [front page article] (10 March 1933); 'Industry Meets Dollar Crisis With 25 And 50% Salary Cuts', *Motion Picture Herald* (11 March 1933); 'President Maps Cuts: Reduction Set at $500,000,000', *Los Angeles Times* (11 March 1933); '"New Deal" for Films Predicted as Certain', *Los Angeles Times* [front page article, top story of the day] (12 March 1933); 'Attendance at Theatres Rising' and 'Roosevelt Action Aids Business; Film Industry Revises Pay Cuts', *Motion Picture Herald* (18 March 1933); 'Restoring Pay Begins; Theatre Receipts Rising', *Motion Picture Herald* (8 April 1933); 'Film Academy Basis Outlined', *Los Angeles Times* (29 May 1933).
    Summer 1932 events: [uncited authors], 'Fox-Hearst's 25–50% Cuts', *Variety* (5 July 1932); 'Warners' 1 Wk Moratorium August 2', *Variety* (19 July 1932).
    Just a week and a half before the cuts were to take effect, producer Samuel Goldwyn insisted that studios needed to cut production costs by 50%. Could this declaration have served to inspire the moguls to institute their 50% salary cuts for higher-paid employees?: [uncited author], 'Production Costs Not Cut, Must Be Halved, Says Samuel Goldwyn', *Motion Picture Herald* (25 February 1933).
5. Behlmer, 10–11.
6. This paragraph on block booking is based on the following sources: Cephair and

Englund, 1–3, Chapter 2; Douglas Gomery, *Shared Pleasures: A History of Movie Presentation in the US* (Madison, WI: University of Wisconsin Press, 1992): 60–8; Douglas Gomery, *The Hollywood Studio System: A History* (London: British Film Institute, 2005): 71–5; Giuliana Muscio, *Hollywood's New Deal* (Philadelphia: Temple University Press, 1997): 129–30.

7. William C. DeMille, *Hollywood Saga* (New York: E. P. Dutton & Co., 1939): 300–1.
8. The Analyst, 'Value of Film Securities Soars $140,000,000 Under "New Deal"', *Motion Picture Herald* (10 June 1933); [uncited author], '13 Weeks Warner Net Operating Loss Is Only Half of Same Period Last Year', *Motion Picture Herald* (29 July 1933).
9. Ross, *Stars*, 89, Chapter 6.
10. Tino Balio claims that Louis B. Mayer, alone among the production heads of studios, lowered his salary during the period of the 1933 cuts from $10,000 to $75 per week, but he provides no source and I could find no other primary or secondary source to corroborate this: Tino Balio, *United Artists: The Company Built by the Stars* (Madison, WI: University of Wisconsin Press, 1976): 98.
11. 'Break for New Talent; If Stars Walk, OK, Say Execs', *Variety* (7 March 1933); '50 Vs. 156 Millions in 2 Yrs.; Films Payrolls Drop Off 67%', *Variety* (14 March 1933); Danae Clark, *Negotiating Hollywood: The Cultural Politics of Actors' Labor* (Minneapolis: University of Minnesota Press, 1995): 33–5.
12. Jack L. Warner to Jerome Kingston, 25 April 1933, from Footlight Parade Story File (2872); George Cohen to Jack L. Warner, 23 September 1933, from Footlight Parade Legal file (2777). Both from Warner Bros. Archives, University of Southern California [heretofore WBA/USC].
13. Mel Gussow, *Zanuck: Don't Say Yes Until I Finish Talking* (London: W. H. Allen, 1971): 49. None of Cagney's biographies confirms this story, but Zanuck's boast is possible, however – in 1929, Cagney and Blondell were working together on Broadway and scoring rave reviews that stressed their on-stage compatibility in shows entitled *Maggie the Magnificent* and *Penny Arcade*. The latter became the source material for their first movie at Warner, *Sinner's Holiday* (1930), which they also co-starred in: Patrick McGilligan, *Cagney: The Actor as Auteur* (San Diego, CA: A. S. Barnes, 1982): 12–13.
14. [Uncited author], 'Warners Draw Line on All Actors Muddling with Scriveners at Work', *Variety* (19 December 1933).
15. [Uncited author], 'Tuffy Cagney Croons: "Shanghai Lil" Unlooses Flood of Song', *Daily Variety* (20 September 1933). Just for the record, Cagney, in a non-starring role, does about ten seconds of graceful incidental dancing while impressing a female friend in the 1930 Warner film *Other Men's Women*, just prior to his break-out role in *The Public Enemy*.
16. Darryl Zanuck to Hal Wallis, inter-office communication, 10 April 1933, in *Footlight Parade* Story – Memos & Correspondence file (2570); *Footlight Parade* Story – Temporary Script 'Last Part; Copy with Lord's Changes' file (2170); *Footlight Parade* Story – Temporary Script file (2170). All from WBA/USC. The previously cited *Footlight Parade* Weekly Production Cost and Budget documents show that Seff and Seymour made $4,900 combined for their work on the film, while Lord pulled in $5,100.
17. William Meyer, *Warner Brothers Directors: The Hard-Boiled, the Comic and the Weepers* (New Rochelle, NY: Arlington House, 1978): 15–18.
18. *Footlight Parade* Production – Daily Progress Reports file (1448), WBA/USC.
19. [Uncited author], 'Offset Stage Shows with WB Shorts', *Variety* (18 October 1932); Fanchon & Marco, Inc. [full-page] advertisement, *Variety* (8 November

1932); Gomery, *Shared*, 51–9; Linda Mizejewski, 'Beautiful White Bodies', in Steven Cohan, ed., *Hollywood Musicals: The Film Reader* (London: Routledge, 2002): 185; Martin Rubin, *Showstoppers: Busby Berkeley and the Tradition of Spectacle* (New York: Columbia University Press, 1993): 55–6.The connection between Berkeley, Hale and *Footlight Parade* has never been made before, the choreographers' 1930 collaboration is from the Rubin book. According to the IMDB website, Hale later created dance sequences for *A Night at the Opera* (starring the Marx Brothers) and *Anna Karenina* (starring Greta Garbo), both from 1935.

    Variety also felt that the *Footlight* plot was lifted from Fanchon & Marco, Inc. reality: [uncited authors], *Footlight Parade* review, *Daily Variety* (30 September 1933); *Footlight Parade* review, *Variety* (10 October 1933).

20. Robert S. Birchard, 'A Song and Dance Spectacular' *American Cinematographer* (November 2005): 3–9. For more on the Goldwyn/Berkeley labour contretemps, see Chapters 2, 4 and 5.
21. *Footlight Parade* number 824 Budget (no date), in *Footlight Parade* Story – Memos and Correspondence file (2570), WBA/USC. I'm assuming that the 'waterfall number' and 'fountain number' together comprise the 'By a Waterfall' sequence; each cost about $16,000.
22. The Berkeley quotation in the text is from: Patrick Brion and Rene Gilson, 'A Style of Spectacle: Interview with Busby Berkeley', *Cahiers du Cinéma in English* 2 (1966): 34; the Berkeley block quotation is from: Tony Thomas and Jim Terry, with Busby Berkeley, *The Busby Berkeley Book* (New York: New York Graphic Society, 1973): 70–1. 'GLORIFIED': Daily Production and Progress Reports, 7 June 1933 [and other dates], in *Footlight Parade* Production – Daily Progress Reports file (1448), WBA/USC. Studio publicity: *Footlight Parade* Publicity – Pressbook file (681), WBA/USC.
23. Daily Production and Progress Reports, in *Footlight Parade* Production – Daily Progress Reports file (1448), WBA/USC.
24. *Footlight Parade* Publicity – Pressbook file (681), WBA/USC.
25. Rubin, 41.
26. Berkeley quotation: Brion and Gilson, 34. Guards at the studio: *Footlight Parade* Publicity – Pressbook file (681), WBA/USC; [uncited author], 'In the Cutting Room: Advance Outlines of Productions Nearing Completion' [column], *Motion Picture Herald* (8 July 1933).
27. Sources for this discussion concerning the similarities between Berkeley and fascism: John Landis commentary, in the short documentary *Busby Berkeley: Study in Style* (Warner Bros. DVD, 2006); Thomas Doherty, *Hollywood and Hitler, 1933–1939* (New York: Columbia University Press, 2013), Chapter 11; Dave Kehr, 'New DVDs: Triumph of the Will', *New York Times* (28 March 2006); Arthur Knight, 'Busby Berkeley', *Action* 9:3 (May–June 1974): 15–16; Lee Lescaze, 'Reagan Still Sure Some in New Deal Espoused Fascism', *Washington Post* (24 December 1981); Lawrence W. Levine, 'Hollywood's Washington: Film Images of National Politics During the Great Depression', *Prospects* Vol. 10, 1985; Gerald Mast, *Can't Help Singin': The American Musical on Stage and Screen* (Woodstock, NY: Overlook Press, 1987): 134; Susan Sontag, 'Fascinating Fascism', *New York Review of Books* (6 February 1975). The diving sequence from Leni Riefenstahl's *Olympia* can be viewed on YouTube.
28. Sources for this discussion of Asians in Hollywood films are the following: Doherty, *Pre-Code*, 267–74; Karla Rae Fuller, *Hollywood Goes Oriental: CaucAsian Performance in American Film* (Detroit, MI: Wayne State University Press, 2010): Introduction, Chapter 1 [quotations are from pp. 10–11, 35]; Robert B. Ito, 'A Certain Slant: A Brief History of Hollywood Yellowface', *Bright Lights*

Film Journal 18 (March 1997); Eugene Franklin Wong, 'The Early Years: Asians in the American Films Prior to World War II', in Peter X. Feng, ed., *Screening Asian Americans* (New Brunswick, NJ: Rutgers University Press, 2002); Jun Xing, *Asian America Through the Lens: History, Representations and Identity* (Lanham: Rowham Altamira, 1998), Chapter 2. For other examples of 'yellowface' portrayals during the same era as *Footlight Parade* that are more sympathetic and progressive, yet not without offensive elements, see director Frank Capra's *The Bitter Tea of General Yen* (1932).

29. Inter-Office Communication, Hal Wallis to Koenig, 19 September 1933, from *Footlight Parade* Story – Memos & Correspondence file (2570), WBA/USC.
30. McGilligan, 76.
31. J. C. Daret, in 'What the Picture Did for Me' [column], *Motion Picture Herald* (7 April 1934).
32. This section on the policies and promotion of the National Recovery Administration is based on the following sources: David Kennedy, *Freedom from Fear: The American People in Depression and War, 1929–1945* (Oxford: Oxford University Press, 1999): 151–2, 177–89; Arthur Schlesinger, *The Coming of the New Deal* (Boston: Houghton-Mifflin, 1960), Chapter 7; Jean Edward Smith, *FDR* (New York: Random House, 2008): 343–4.
33. *Footlight Parade* Weekly Production Cost and Budget documents, from *Footlight Parade* Story – Memos & Correspondence file (2570), WBA/USC. International financial figures: Birchard, 10.
    The New Deal serving as an inspiration in American film apparently did not cease after the optimistic period of its rollout in 1933. For example, Yip Harburg, the lyricist who co-wrote the song 'Over the Rainbow' for *The Wizard of Oz* (1939), insisted that the Emerald City in that film symbolised the New Deal: Iwan Morgan, 'Introduction', in Iwan Morgan and Philip John Davies, eds, *Hollywood and the Great Depression: American Film, Politics and Society in the 1930s* (Edinburgh: Edinburgh University Press, 2016): 19.
34. Lawrence W. Levine, 'American Culture and the Great Depression', *Yale Review* 74:2 (January 1985).
35. Jack L. Warner to Hal B. Wallis, telegram, 25 September 1933, in *Footlight Parade* Story – Memos & Correspondence file (2570), WBA/USC.
36. All materials discussed in this section concerning publicity for *Footlight Parade* are from: *Footlight Parade* Publicity Ads file (681); *Footlight Parade* Publicity – Misc. file (681); *Footlight Parade* Publicity – Pressbooks file (681). WBA/USC.
37. Gary Giddins, *Bing Crosby: A Pocketful of Dreams, The Early Years 1903–1940*: (Boston: Thorndike Press, 2001): 539.
38. Jeanine Basinger, *A Woman's View: How Hollywood Spoke to Women, 1930–1960* (New York: Knopf, 1993): 6–8.
39. This paragraph is informed by my viewing of women's films of the period and *Footlight Parade*, as well as Basinger's research and insights: Basinger, 8, 11, 17–21, 68, 86, 108, 261–71. Also: Molly Haskell, *From Reverence to Rape: The Treatment of Women in the Movies* (Chicago: University of Chicago Press, 1987): xvi–xvii, 3.
40. Haskell, 145; Robert Patrick and William Haislip, 'Thank Heaven for Little Girls: An Examination of the Male Chauvinist Musical', *Cineaste* 6:1 (1973): 24; Edward G. Robinson with Leonard Spigelgass, *All My Yesterdays: An Autobiography* (New York: Hawthorne, 1973): 111.
41. James Wingate/Production Code Authority to Jack Warner, 6 June 1933 and 29 September 1933, Production Code Authority Collection, Academy of Motion Picture Arts and Sciences Margaret Herrick Library [hereafter: AMPASMHL].

42. Documents regarding censorship of *Footlight Parade* are found in the following microfilm roll: *Footlight Parade*, Production Code Authority files, AMPASMHL.

43. Doherty, *Hitler*, 41–3.

44. Steven Bach, *Marlene Dietrich: Life and Legend* (London: William Morrow, 1992): 154–5.

45. All press clippings referred to in this section are found in: *Footlight Parade* Publicity – Press Clippings file (681), WBA/USC. Several unidentified reviews in this folder share the same divided quality between extreme criticism and extreme praise. Also: Norbert Lusk, 'The Bowery and Footlight Parade Smash Hits of New York Show', *Los Angeles Times* (15 October 33); Edwin Schallert, '"Footlight Parade" Spectacular Picture', *Los Angeles Times* (10 November 1933).

The New York reviews for *Footlight* do not seem to correspond with the political orientation of the newspapers they emanated from, despite the pro-Roosevelt bias exhibited in the film. According to Harry Baehr on p. 375 of *The New York Tribune since the Civil War* (New York: Octagon, 1972), the New York *Tribune*, *Sun*, *Press* and *Herald* were Republican papers, while the *Times*, *World* and *American* leaned towards the Democrats. Thanks to Prof. Edmund F. Wehrle for pointing out this source.

Although most of my students have enjoyed this film when shown in class over the last few years, the ones who do not tend to agree with the *L.A. Times* and *Variety* that it takes too long for the main musical numbers to arrive.

46. [Uncited authors], 'Sock Opening for "Footlight Parade"', and *Footlight Parade* and Warner Bros. advertisements, *Motion Picture Herald* (14 October 1933); Advertisement for *The World Changes*, in *Motion Picture Herald* (4 November 1933); '"Footlight" Rates Top Musical Coin, Beater Former WB Girly-Girlies in 80% of Bookings to Date', *Variety* (21 November 1933). See also: [uncited author], 'Warner-First National in National Gross Analysis of Released New-Season Pix', *Variety* (21 November 1933). An ad for Universal Pictures in the 28 October 1933 edition of *Motion Picture Herald* calls its upcoming slate of films a 'New Deal' as well.

Sources for the West Coast premiere parade: Edwin Schallert, 'Feminine Leads Present New Film Problem; News and Gossip of Studio and Theaters', and [uncited author], 'Gala Film Event Due at Warner', both from *Los Angeles Times* (8 November 1933).

Examples of *Footlight Parade* underperforming in its first week compared to *42nd* and *Gold*: *Footlight* did a combined $35,000 in Los Angeles and Hollywood, in the same theatres, *42nd* pulled in $57,000. In Philadelphia, *42nd* won out, by $19,000 to $15,000. In Portland, OR, *Gold*'s first week drew in $12,000 vs $3,500 for *Footlight*. All numbers in this paragraph are rounded off.

47. Advertisement for *The World Changes*, in *Motion Picture Herald* (4 November 1933); [uncited authors], 'Warner Profit for Quarter $100,000', *Motion Picture Herald* (16 December 1933); 'The Box Office Champions for November', *Motion Picture Herald* (23 December 1933); 'Warners Report First Profit in Four Years', *Motion Picture Herald* (27 January 1934); 'Box Office for 1933', *Motion Picture Herald* (3 February 1934).

48. M. R. Williams and Warren L. Weber, in 'What the Picture Did for Me' [column], *Motion Picture Herald* (23 December 1933). For an alternative view of how some theatres thought the Warner percentage deal was worthwhile if the movie was as big a hit as *Gold Diggers of 1933*, and also some positive exhibitor reports concerning *Footlight*, see: 'What the Picture Did for Me' [columns], *Motion Picture Herald* (30 December 1933 and 13 January 1934).

49. Thomas Doherty, *Pre-Code Hollywood: Sex, Immorality, and Insurrection in*

American Cinema 1930–1934 (New York: Columbia University Press, 1999), Chapter 3; the quotation is from p. 53.

50. Doherty, *Pre-Code*, 70–7.
51. Lawrence W. Levine, 'Hollywood's Washington: Film Images of National Politics During the Great Depression', *Ramparts* 10 (1985): 181–6.
52. Levine, 'Washington', 175; David Nasaw, *The Chief: The Life of William Randolph Hearst* (Boston: Houghton-Mifflin, 2001): 463–7; Martin Rubin, 'The Crowd, the Collective, and the Chorus: Busby Berkeley and the New Deal', in John Belton, ed., *Movies and Mass Culture* (London: Bloomsbury, 1996): 82.
53. Peter William Evans, 'Astaire and Rogers: Carefree in *Roberta*', in Morgan and Davies, eds, *Hollywood*: 124.

4. ON THE JOB

With their visions of sweat, grime, toil, crooked producers, censorship tussles, round-the-clock rehearsals, romantic schemers of both genders and much more, the Great Depression Musicals, particularly *Footlight Parade*, attempted to bring more verisimilitude than the Hollywood backstage musical usually provided. Struggles and inequities portrayed on-screen were mirrored by struggles that ensued on the Warner Bros. lot and throughout the movie colony. As *Footlight* went before the cameras, off-screen labour struggles affected nearly all Hollywood personnel, from technicians and chorus girls to screenwriters and above-the-title stars.

Los Angeles held a hard-fought reputation as an anti-union town, years before the future film moguls settled their studios there in the 1910s.[1] The Los Angeles Police Department, in the tradition of its twentieth-century-spanning history of brutality and harassment, assembled a 'Red Squad' that, starting in the 1920s, battered and infiltrated all labour, communist and socialist groups of note, aligning their Department with the management and development classes of the fast-growing metropolis. The craftsmen (and they almost always were men) of Hollywood – set painters, carpenters and others – conducted the first strikes, mostly unsuccessful, against the studios in the early 1920s. Any evidence (usually supplied by Red Squad police spies friendly to the studios) of their attending union-related meetings usually resulted in firing with no recourse. 'As a result of such suffocating monitoring, the upsurge of labour proceeded fitfully in Hollywood', according to historian Gerald Horne.

The International Alliance of Theatrical Stage Employees (IATSE), created in 1893, proved one of the unions tolerated by Hollywood's major studios. Since the mid-1920s, IATSE had openly desired to unite all the various craftspeople unions in Hollywood under its umbrella. It was encouraged in these efforts by the major studios' signing of the Studio Basic Agreement (SBA) in 1926, which granted motion picture industry unions the ability to negotiate standardised wages and working conditions. The next year, as 'soundies' debuted, sound technicians multiplied, becoming increasingly important in the filmmaking process, but their benefits, wages and conditions were not guaranteed under the 1926 agreement since their services were not yet a factor in that pre-sound era. Between 1927 and 1933, IATSE and the International Brotherhood of Electrical Workers (IBEW) battled for the right to represent these well-paid new workers. The Columbia studio was not a signatory to the initial SBA, and paid its sound technicians two to three times less than union-represented soundmen and mixers. IATSE viewed this as an opportunity to lead a strike against the studios which, when the smoke cleared, it hoped would show IATSE to be a deserving representative of all soundmen under its union umbrella.

The strike added to various tensions between management and workers during the year *Footlight Parade* was produced. It initially stopped all work for two weeks at Columbia Pictures, leaving 800 people idle except for 'writers on unfinished stories and executives'. Two weeks later, on 24 July, the strike expanded to include eleven studios, including all eight majors, putting 5,000 unionised employees (lab workers, film editors, studio projectionists, studio mechanics and of course, sound technicians) and 27,000 employees overall out of work. The local IATSE representative threatened to call out all projectionists and stagehands nationwide if demands were not met soon.

But the studios did not stay idle for long, and in most cases, hardly at all. Several of the studios pulled in other unionised (including from IBEW) or non-unionised workers to replace the strikers, and considerably increased their police forces. With probable lobbying from the brothers Warner, infamous for their resentment of unions, the Burbank city council passed an ordinance forbidding picketing on the Warner lot. The studios worried that acceding to IATSE's demands would encourage IBEW workers to demand similar concessions. The two unions battled for control of the professions they represented, and for the favour of the studios, not an auspicious situation for the workers represented in this industrial action. The striking soundmen wanted to limit their hours to 48 per week and set overtime rates, relatively mild reforms which the studios claimed would cost them at least a million dollars per year. They also demanded the reinstatement of the screen credit they received in the first years of sound films, and insisted that their actions were in line with President Roosevelt's National Recovery Administration (NRA) reforms to raise wages and limit hours in order to increase jobs and thereby the volume of money spent in the economy. But Pat Casey, who handled labour relations for the Motion Picture Producers and Distributors Association (MPPDA, the trade organisation for the major studios), publicly countered that the union's original plan to strike and close down studio production would throw thousands out of work in Hollywood, which would actually counteract the spirit of the NRA reforms.

A week later, on 31 July, IBEW served an ultimatum on the Hollywood IATSE local. If they refused to withdraw support for the sound technicians and their bid to exclusively represent them, IBEW would 'be forced to abrogate all agreements with IATSE and take over all electrical work in the studios', including that of sound technicians. The United Brotherhood of Carpenters and Joiners also signalled their willingness to accept jobs vacated by striking IATSE workers. IATSE's hubristic bid to represent all film craftspeople looked ready to fold; most workers were not supporting their cause or openly defying it. The studios' refusal to meet with the local IATSE leader and their public contention that their production rate was '75% normal' boded ill for IATSE. One of the productions somewhat affected by strike action was *Footlight Parade*, where a recording of one of the songs for the film was delayed by three days. By 5 August, the MPPDA's union negotiator recognised IBEW as the union for all the studios' electrical workers, including soundmen and lighting technicians formerly with IATSE. Two days later, some IATSE soundmen were reported abdicating to IBEW, and the studios vowed to retain any scabs that filled in for the striking workers, and also vowed they would negotiate wage scales and other issues for the 'boothmen' (as *Variety* termed them) when the then-current SBA expired in 1934.

By the time IATSE announced the production of a short film outlining its position and countering IBEW's arguments, the battle was largely over. As the usually anti-union *Hollywood Reporter* surmised, 'the unions were wrong and had the good sense to quickly realize it'. But it was realised too late for many of the striking IATSE workers to keep their jobs in the aftermath of the failed strike. According to *Variety*, IBEW's victory in the 1933 strike meant the 'breaking of the back of IATSE', at least temporarily. They also reported that the studios were awarding three to five year contracts to technicians (including soundmen) who refused to strike or who returned before the strike ended.

With all studios in financial straits except for the barely-in-the-black MGM, unions faced a difficult time amassing power in 1933, but Horne argues that IATSE's leadership learned what it took to succeed over the long run. The leadership that brought IATSE its defeat in 1933 did not last much longer. In the words of scholars Paul Buhle and Dave Wagner, the 'barely disguised Jewish mobsters' William Browne and Willie Bioff took over as IATSE president and international representative respectively in 1934 with the help of Al

Capone and assorted henchmen, taking millions in large yearly payments from major and independent studios, basically in exchange for guaranteeing (often with muscle) labour peace in Hollywood. The IATSE officers were determined not to be outmanoeuvred again, even if it took patronising organised crime to assert their superiority among Hollywood unions. A surprising amount of hob-nobbing between studio moguls (including Harry Cohn at Columbia, Joseph Schenck at Fox, Harry Warner and, later, Lew Wasserman at MCA) and mob men ensued for decades afterwards; evidently, such associations and the back-door payments that followed from them were preferred to awarding their workers fairer pay or conditions. According to Horne, organised crime figures also invested in the major studios before and after World War II, while increasing IATSE's membership by thousands by also including soundmen, gardeners and electricians into their union. Corruption was rife. According to film historian Robert Sklar, under the Brown and Bioff administration 'neither membership meetings nor elections for local officers were permitted'.

Meanwhile, behind the cameras and scrims, working life for Hollywood craftspeople during the 1930s got much worse. As mob influence coalesced in IATSE between 1933 and 1937, conditions and salary predictably worsened for the average studio craftsman, particularly since Browne and Bioff drew huge kickbacks for supposed services to the union (and long federal prison terms when they were finally kicked out in 1939). Meanwhile, for the rank and file, wages for IATSE craftspeople dived by more than a third between 1929 and 1937. Their workers were expected to be on call at all times of the day every day, with little notice of when their services were needed, overtime rules were tightened, and unpunished sexual harassment went on the upswing. In addition, IATSE 'sent [out] numerous messages affirming racialism' and people of colour, particularly African Americans, were almost never seen in studio jobs. Women were relegated to female-associated jobs far from power or the best-paying positions. Hollywood could often be a cruel workplace, whether one was a union or non-union worker.

The eight-week 50 per cent salary cuts instituted during March and April 1933 were not the only salary cuts endured by the players who made extravagant musicals like *Footlight* possible.[2] As the popularity and profitability of the Warner Bros. Great Depression Musicals became clear, wages for chorus girls dropped. Chorus girls employed on *42nd Street* received $66 per week, while those on *Footlight Parade*, produced just a few months later, received only $50 per week (over $900 in today's dollars), nearly a 25 per cent drop, just as *Variety*, in an article entitled 'Hollywood Gals Again Eating', reported that average wages for chorus girls were between $60 and $85. The drop in pay was almost certainly related to the efforts by the major film companies documented in the previous chapter to limit salaries of talent. In both cases, they were paid extra for overtime. One could argue that the work was more taxing on *Footlight* than on *42nd*, particularly in the waterfall sequence. In addition, hours worked were frequently long and punishing. On 9 September 1933, for example, records show that crew and cast worked on the 'Shanghai Lil' number for 14½ hours, then returned the next day and did 13½ hours. In the staged mêlée during that sequence, chorus girl Lorena Layson (later the wife of Louis B. Mayer) accidentally took a punch, knocking her unconscious and necessitating a stopping of filming while she revived. These conditions were onerous, but as a September 1933 government hearing revealed, chorus girls in stage shows often worked just as hard and long for half the money or less.

The marathon pace tired even Busby Berkeley, let alone the actors and dancers. Part of his exhaustion was due to his labouring on two musicals at two studios simultaneously. Goldwyn had not signed Berkeley to a long-term contract since his independent production company made so few films, so he loaned Berkeley to Warners for the Great Depression Musicals, where, unbeknownst to Goldwyn, he signed a long-term contract with Zanuck and Warners, who offered him director credit for his dance sequences. For weeks during the filming of *Footlight Parade*, he worked on Goldwyn's lot by day and secretly in Burbank at Warner's by night, surviving on cat-naps. Goldwyn brought a breach of contract suit against Warners over the incident, which he lost several years later.[3] Recalling the period, Berkeley said that 'there was fun and there was certainly excitement but what I mostly remember is stress and strain and exhaustion'. In a 1966 interview he praised the fortitude of the 'girls' who laboured on *Footlight*:

> I had 16 magnificent girls under contract and I engaged others for each film. My beauties each earned $64 a week, which isn't bad if you consider that we were then in the middle of the depression. But they worked long hours. There was no union to tell us to stop at six o'clock. I remember the shooting of 'By A Waterfall'. I took close-ups of the girls in the water at 3:30 in the morning. And that didn't keep me from calling them back at eleven the same morning to go on! I think the people with whom I worked all liked me in spite of this heavy work, and they were all very nice to me.[4]

Of course they were 'nice' to Berkeley, one of the most famous directors in Hollywood, the man who auditioned and employed them. They knew they were lucky to have jobs at all, let alone prestigious ones that dozens if not hundreds of women would have gladly taken in their stead. But that didn't necessarily mean they were thrilled with their working conditions. Warner Bros. vice-president Edmond DePatie, in a 1965 oral history, confirmed that studio employees were 'exploited en masse' and that they worked 'every Saturday night, fifty two weeks a year'.[5]

Warners was not alone in this practice; other studios kept similar hours. After starring in the successful *Broadway Melody* for MGM, Bessie Love was placed in musical after musical, 26 films in the 1926–30 period, until she felt physically drained and worried about whether such relentless and typecast film appearances represented the best career strategy:

> I got a little fed up . . . [established MGM star] Marie Dressler said she would spank me if I didn't stop [the studio from placing her in so many movies]. I wanted to, but when you sign with a big studio, you must expect to do what you're given, or you don't sign with them! After all, working in any big company like MGM is being part of an assembly line. I was a wheel-horse . . . At the time we had no unions and we were worked all hours. They were really terrible; to get the film out before anybody else could beat them to it, we worked day and night. The film had a 4-week shooting schedule, and we would have to be on the set ready to shoot at 9 am, and we wouldn't finish til 9 or 10 at night. I remember we were often exhausted from working such hard and long hours.[6]

Joan Blondell, speaking about filming the Great Depression Musicals, voiced the same sentiments:

> The hours were awful because we didn't have any unions then and we worked any time they wanted. You could find yourself coming in at six o'clock in the morning and working til midnight and being back at six the next morning. You'd have breakfast at 6:30 and nothing till lunch at 3:00PM. People were about ready to fall over . . . I think Warners specialised in that sort of toughness.

Her *Footlight* co-star James Cagney's autobiography describes their Warner work schedule in almost exactly the same terms and times, adding: 'the studio put [pressure] on us because they wanted to get the thing done as cheaply as possible'.[7] It was a cruel market. According to Bessie Love, the studios 'establish stars, and after that they use them in vehicles to help get young stars established by co-starring [with] them'. Blondell, Cagney and Love possessed the talent and personality to enjoy steady work in movies and TV for about half a century, but most actors did not enjoy such a career. Berkeley and probably all directors also felt this pressure emanating from success in the Hollywood studio system, the fears of being replaced, and the vagaries of trying to please studio executives and audiences while building a long profitable career:

> I worried about being able to come up with new ideas, and then I worried about how they would go over with the public. My musical routines for

> Warners used to . . . [cost] big money in those days. When you're spend-
> ing money like that, you have the executives breathing down your neck.
> It was gruelling and sometimes terrifying, because you couldn't give
> way to despair or lack of confidence . . . As anyone in the entertainment
> business knows, becoming successful is not nearly as hard as staying
> successful.[8]

The film industry labour system leaned in a lopsided manner towards management priorities and profits, even for the stars whose names, faces and performances brought in millions of admissions. Under the restricted and exclusive
multi-year contracts (often for seven years) signed by most actors, they could
not refuse roles assigned by the studio. If they did, they were suspended without
pay until they relented and played the part, or the studio found another role
for them. The time spent on the sidelines by actors because of their refusal
was added to the back end of their contract, making their obligation sometimes longer than seven years. Writers and directors also signed such deals.
Warner director Irving Rapper felt that actors and directors no longer valued
by management were offered projects that studio brass knew they would
not accept so that the studio could avoid paying them. Rapper bragged that
during his career at the studio he had 'more suspensions than the Golden Gate
Bridge'. Eventually, in 1944, in a case brought by Warner Bros. star Olivia
de Havilland, the California Supreme Court ruled that contracts lasting more
than seven years constituted a form of 'peonage' and the practice was discon-
tinued, but in the 1930s such documents proved widespread and powerful. In
addition, while the signee could not break off the contract, the studios inserted
clauses that allowed them an option to cancel the contract with no penalty
every six months. 'You could keep a beginner on the payroll half a year for the
weekly salary of a star, and what better way to charm visiting journalists or
public figures than to provide them with beautiful young women or handsome
young men, designated "stars of the future", as studio guides?', noted film
scholar Robert Sklar. 'Mostly their contracts were allowed to lapse after half a
year; if by chance one broke through to stardom, he or she was sewed up tight
for years to come.' The Warner contracts also featured clauses that allowed
the studio to not pay their contract employees for up to four weeks per year.[9]

The 'loaning-out' of actors represented perhaps the practice that best demonstrated the relative powerlessness of most contracted film stars.[10] When
producers or directors felt that a part could not be filled adequately by their
studio's stable of contract players, they hired talent from rival studios on a
one-time-only basis. The studio that needed the actor paid a sizeable premium
to the studio that held the actor under contract, which did not usually trickle
down to the actor. For example, on *42nd Street*, the leads Warner Baxter and
Una Merkel were both 'loan-outs'. Warner Bros. guaranteed four weeks of

work for Merkel at a rate of $650 per week, and paid MGM a three-week 'carrying charge' of $1,950. The cheque was made out to MGM, not Merkel. In these cases, the loaning of the actor generated considerably more money than their home studio usually paid the actor, not only saving the studio in salary costs, but also representing a money-making opportunity. With Baxter, Warner paid the Fox studio approximately one-fifth of his yearly salary of $156,000 for just six weeks of work. Warners also furnished all travel and hotel expenses for the two stars. For Fox and MGM, substantial profit was made and expenses lessened with no financial risk. And the stars' association with this smash hit enhanced their box-office appeal for their home studios without the studios forwarding anything for publicity or distribution expenses. At the same time, of course, Baxter and Merkel's salaries were stuck at their pre-*42nd Street* rates of pay.

'Loaned out' actors usually saw none of this largesse, and they knew it existed; such deals were often announced in movie periodicals and even the *Los Angeles Times*.[11] As Warners star Edward G. Robinson wrote concerning this topic, 'It was not uncommon for the studios ... to make money on our flesh'. But he also noted that studios were at times loath to engage in the practice because if another studio furnished a hit for their contracted star and made millions in the process, then the home studio proved 'not as bright or clever' as their competition. Yet, he observed, 'each studio wanted the other's contract players. If it sounds contradictory, why are you surprised?' In June 1933, MGM star Myrna Loy went public with accusations that the studio tended to only lend out contracted players when they were exhausted from their regular work schedule, 'unable to give competent performances', and when they 'should be resting'. When loaned to Jesse Lasky's company, she informed the proprietor:

> I think it is only fair that you should know my true condition before putting me into your production. Then, if you still want me, I will play in the picture, I have worked 44 weeks out of the last 52, and am under the care of a physician. In the last production I made at Metro I collapsed and they had to take one scene 10 times before the director gave it his okay.

Lasky cancelled the loan. The article intimated that a recent proposed loan of Clark Gable to Fox folded for similar reasons.

As usually is the case in Hollywood, ego played a significant role on both sides of the 'loan-out' transactions. In an interview decades later, Blondell still sounded annoyed by the extra pay for her services Warners received and kept when they loaned her to Sam Goldwyn for *The Greeks Had a Word for Them* (1932). Such unequal chattel-like arrangements further explain the resentment that led to the establishment of the Screen Actors Guild in 1933. Actors were not the only group who could be loaned out: Goldwyn biographer A. Scott Berg reported that the producer personally made $90,000 (about $1.6 million in today's dollars) loaning out Oscar-winning film composer Alfred Newman to other studios during 1936 and 1937.

However, as scholar Emily Carman pointed out, loan-outs weren't always bad for stars. They also sometimes allowed them to break the monotony of working at the same studio, especially a studio like Warners that tended to tightly typecast actors once they became successful in a certain kind of role. Warner star Bette Davis, for example, used her appearance in RKO's *Of Human Bondage* (1934) to establish herself as a serious actor, beyond the more lightweight roles Warner assigned her previously. Hollywood actors with more savvy agents began placing loan-out restrictions in contracts, especially during the second half of the 1930s, but Irene Dunne's 1931 contract (orchestrated by agent Charles Feldman) awarded her 50 per cent of all loan-out fees, and her 1937 contract with Universal forbade loan-outs altogether (as did Carole Lombard's contracts of the late 1930s, designed by her agent Myron Selznick).[12]

Blondell's anecdotes from her years at Warners during the 1930s portray a studio hell-bent on receiving the maximum from their contracted players to the point of denying them personal lives.[13] *Footlight Parade* represented just one of the eight films she did for the studio in 1933, a slight respite from the ten she appeared in the year before. At one point during 1933, she announced she was 'through with pictures forever', but changed her mind fairly quickly, explaining at the time that her previous statement came from 'a case of nerves but [Warner Bros.] have been very kind and have agreed to let me appear in only six pictures a year'. This episode might have been what she was referring to when she told author John Kobal about the only time she refused to report to a Warners set:

> One year in the Thirties . . . I did eight pictures and I was so exhausted that I got in my car and I drove home and had a bath and got into bed and stayed there for about four days. I mean, I was starting to stutter and my eyes were blinking! I couldn't even look at anyone steadily – that's how tired I was. After four days I went back to the set and of course they docked me for it – took part of my salary away.

The studio's policies during this period mandated that Cagney, as well as other actors and technicians, were, in Cagney's words, 'forced to work almost every Saturday night and often into the early hours of Sunday. Getting off for a national holiday during the week meant they would have to work the following Sunday without pay to make up for that holiday.' Studio moguls even harassed actors away from the studio. Bette Davis, who claimed she was 'never late' when arriving at Warners for work every morning, recalled that 'on the rare occasion when I socialized in Hollywood . . . I'd meet Jack Warner at a party as he was leaving[;] he would wag his finger at me like the father of a delinquent', reminding her to get to sleep early since she had a six a.m. make-up call the next morning. 'I was made to feel like a four-year-old', she complained decades later.[14]

With such harsh work conditions, it came as no surprise that actors skipped town in haste as soon as their films wrapped.[15] Such ruses allowed actors to have time away before their next film was assigned by the studios without running into contract troubles. 'That call of the wild that has players ducking out of town for hideaways in the woods and mountains as soon as a picture is finished gives plenty of headaches to studio heads, especially in view of the 75 per cent of films that need doctoring after previews', wrote *Variety* in 1933. 'Actors have the habit of hitting the quiet places . . . without leaving a forwarding address . . . it generally is some spot away from telephone, telegraph or other normal means of communication.' The article told the recent colourful story of Warners hiring a small airplane equipped with a loudspeaker to track wayward contract player Walter Huston in the San Bernardino mountains for retakes. This represented a situation the studios loathed, which reportedly gave executives 'grey hairs', but which they also contributed to because of the hours they demanded of workers.

In such circumstances, having, let alone maintaining, a family life represented a daunting challenge. The Production Code that studios were asked to promulgate in their films starting in 1930 privileged a traditional morality stressing the championing of marriage and children, but work conditions within the studios did not encourage such a lifestyle for its female stars. As Leo Rosten reported in his study of Hollywood during this decade, stars' personal lives were often turned into 'business institutions' that promoted them and their upcoming films in movie magazines, women's magazines and national newspapers. These periodicals often played up stars' emphasis on a domestic life in their real life, and some even applied pressure on recently married female stars to give up their careers, but the marathon hours that actors worked seemed to preclude a traditional family life. Such pressures, Rosten noted, did not promote 'domestic security' among more famous Hollywood personnel, particularly with the 'unfounded gossip' typically circulating around the movie colony. 'In order to get their faces on the pages of the fan magazines and screens of every small town in America, most of [the actresses] had to put aside home and hearth', observed film historian Jeannine Basinger. Though media depictions of their personal and professional situations could be unrealistic or even hypocritical, the female stars of this era still played an important social role, even if such trailblazing rarely elicited comment at the time: 'These movie stars, particularly the ones who survived to become the screen's exaggerated women, were the nation's first army of prominent career women.'[16] Blondell provides an illustration of the contrast between family and career during this period in Hollywood:

> It was difficult . . . working and having children. I made six pictures carrying my son and eight with my daughter [including the Great Depression Musical *Dames* in 1934]. They'd get me behind desks and tables and things to hide my tummy! I'd have off about two weeks to have the poor child and then get right back to work. The only other vacation I had was in the middle of a picture called *Back In Circulation* with Pat O'Brien [in 1937]. My appendix blew up and they took me to hospital. Well, the shooting was nearly over, and they wanted me to start in another [film], but the doctor said I couldn't leave the hospital. They made a deal with the doctor to take me by stretcher to my house up on Lookout Mountain [in Laurel Canyon], and they had the set designer come and make what looked like the scene we were in when my appendix burst. There was a crew of sixty up there – sound and cameras and everything – and they changed the end of the story so I could be sick in bed! They didn't waste any time at all with me.

In the same interview she recalled that, while filming *Dames*, she had been fitted into tight corsets to hide her pregnancy and 'thought I was going to die. I passed out a couple times.' But Blondell refused to accept the idea that she had been mistreated by Warners: 'I couldn't have worked for all that time feeling mistreated.' In some ways, she seemed to blame herself and her work ethic for what occurred during those years:

> I guess it was the old trouper tradition of the show having to go on. I really didn't fuss about anything, I don't know why. There are times when I think I really should have . . . I never got away from my nothing salary, I didn't fight enough.

Blondell rued her lack of 'fight' decades later, but she did have counsel at the time that advised otherwise. Her co-star and close friend Cagney recommended that a work stoppage between films would produce the salary results she wanted, and encouraged her to go for it, as he had. In the weeks after the *Footlight* premiere, she publicly terminated her relationship with the William Morris Agency when it recommended that same course of action – threatening a walkout in order to win a salary increase. Her letter to her agent stated: 'This advice is so inconsistent with my interest and good business that I am an utter loss to understand how an agent of yours could so seriously advise me [in this manner].' She also claimed that the agency did not act aggressively enough to obtain the highest fees for her services. While it advised her that she could earn only $2,250 per week for a 'personal appearance', she said she was able to earn $3,000.[17]

While Blondell largely acquiesced in her studio treatment, even at the cost of her health, Cagney aggressively fought Warner Bros. numerous times during the decade, particularly when he felt his compensation did not measure up to the proceeds of the films he starred in. Fierce debates over profit sharing and the proper rate of remuneration for stars of hit pictures had percolated at least since the mid-1910s negotiations between Mary Pickford and Famous Players studio founder and mogul Adolph Zukor. Pickford felt frustrated and cheated seeing her internationally successful films (which she often chose herself and commissioned the writers for) subsidising Zukor's poorly performing films, a situation she viewed as reducing her rightful compensation. Zukor listened to the world's most popular woman and, wanting to keep her within his stable, awarded her a cut of her films' proceeds and half the profits, starting in 1915. The next year, Zukor created a production company for her that she owned, basically becoming her business partner.[18] Cagney was neither as popular nor as lucky as Pickford in this regard, and the Warner brothers were loath to grant any raises that would set precedents for other actors on the lot. As his fellow Warner actor Bette Davis remarked decades later:

> Talking pictures had made it necessary to hijack talent from New York but the [film industry] powers ... often don't know what to do with talent. The insecurity of most of these moguls made them wary of a literate group of kids from the theatre [such as Blondell, Cagney, Davis and others]. They wanted younglings they could mold. They wanted to create personalities, not be challenged by them.[19]

In 1930, Cagney signed a five-year contract with Warners paying $400 per week (approximately $5,700 in current dollars). The next year, his indelible performance in *The Public Enemy* propelled him to stardom, inspiring at least one Manhattan theatre to schedule screenings all night to meet customer demand. Immediately thereafter, Warners, as it did for all of its rising stars, placed Cagney in numerous similar typecast roles one after the other, most of which were box-office successes, such as *Taxi!*, *Winner Take All* and *The Crowd Roars*. The studio also demanded promotional appearances, even for films he did not star in. The Warner-sponsored cross-country train to Roosevelt's inauguration that publicised *42nd Street* represented one such excursion for Davis as well as Cagney. According to news reports, neither of them were on the train when it returned for the film's premiere in Hollywood.[20] But with all Cagney's efforts, successes and positive impact on corporate profits for Warner, no raise was forthcoming from his original contract, and no easing of the harsh work conditions, which seemed as important to Cagney as the money. Any and all adjustments would have to be fought for. He felt forced to engage in such behaviour since, as he remarked in one of his autobiographies, 'the actor was not only low man on the totem pole, he was practically buried in the ground'.[21]

Looking around his home studio, Cagney noticed that others were paid far more. Some non-stars at Warners earned up to $1,000 per week. And some actors like Cagney who attracted hordes of paying customers were drawing several times less salary. Cagney's fellow Warner-employed typecast gangster Edward G. Robinson had not signed a long-term contract before *Little Caesar* made him a national figure at roughly the same time Cagney scored with *Public Enemy*. Robinson's independence and sudden notoriety enabled him to sign a two-year, six-picture deal for $40,000 with Warners, ensuring that he would be paid much more and work less than Cagney. Warners star Al Jolson, paid $75,000 for *The Jazz Singer* (1927), signed a three-picture $225,000 deal with the studio in 1928 and felt unhappy about the money since, at roughly the same time, United Artists studio head Joseph Schenck gave Jolson a two-picture deal for a million dollars adorned by a $100,000 signing bonus. In a 1934 letter, R. J. Obringer, head of Warner's legal department, reminded Jack Warner that 'As a result of the Schenck deal and influence, Jolson's attitude toward us became very belligerent and his efforts while making the latter 3 pictures for us were very insincere, with the result that we could not make successful pictures with him . . . we obtained little or nothing of Jolson's real value.' Jolson even asked to be let out of his contract for the third picture. If Jolson felt cheated receiving $75,000 per film, imagine how Cagney felt earning $1,500–$3,000 per picture while Warners cleaned up at the box office. For a comparison with an actor who entered the business at roughly the same time, Marlene Dietrich's first Paramount contract, signed in 1930 before her breakout German film *The Blue Angel* debuted, guaranteed her two pictures at $1,750 per week ($87,000 per year for 50 weeks). Her next contract paid her a quarter of a million for two more films, almost tripling her previous contract. Her first four films were released over a period of about twenty-two months; Cagney's first four were within a period of about six months. 'I kept grinding the pictures out, working at a swift tempo, and seeing everywhere about me the rough-handed treatment of actors by management', recalled Cagney. 'Actors were considered to be expendable material, just like props or makeup. I watched this, and I was to remember.'[22]

Cagney's background made him uniquely suited to take up this struggle. In some ways, he was as much a maverick in real life as he appeared on-screen. He grew up in rough Manhattan neighbourhoods, and as a boy recalled listening to hard-left speechifying in Union Square. As a copyboy on a left-leaning New York newspaper, he heard more such talk. By the time he signed his Warners contract, he probably sympathised with communist views, or at least understood their rationale. Even as his star rose and he became one of Hollywood's most famous leading men, he fearlessly and publicly aligned himself with left-leaning causes: befriending Marxist screenwriters at Warners (including John Bright, who wrote the union-championing *Taxi!* as well as *The Public Enemy* and served as a principal in the formation of the Screen Writers Guild), donating to Kentucky coal miners' efforts to investigate work abuses, and the cause of the nine African American Scottsboro boys implausibly accused of raping two white women, and speaking on behalf of radical labour activist Tom Mooney, who was convicted by faulty evidence of bombing innocent bystanders in the 1910s. Predictably, Jack Warner disapproved of such associations, publicly calling his star a communist dupe and ordering him (in vain) to cease all political activity. According to historian Robert Sklar, Cagney 'became the first major movie industry figure to gain national headlines for a reported involvement in Communist activities'. Such associations were not as incendiary and damaging in the early 1930s as they would become later in the decade for Hollywood personnel, but Jack Warner understandably worried that Cagney's communist sympathies could erode his box-office appeal and profitability for Warner's if his activism went too far.[23]

Unlike most actors fortunate enough to succeed within the Hollywood system, Cagney proved willing to risk his career to secure better pay and conditions, partly out of his refusal to tolerate injustice, and partly because 'he hadn't been all that keen on a movie career in the first place', according to biographer Doug Warren. Cagney's attitude on these issues was 'my way or not at all . . . being a loner made him very difficult to deal with because the usual rules did not apply.' Cagney had succeeded on the legitimate stage and in vaudeville before moving to the movie colony. The thought of returning to that milieu did not trouble him. In fact he felt tempted by it. He also voiced interest in having a career in medicine or farming if his Hollywood career ceased. He saved much from his early career proceeds, and bought a farm in New York, to where he could decamp from Hollywood during salary negotiations and patiently sit out his Warner boycotts while waiting for them to agree to his terms. In 1935, he took on his brother Bill as his manager, ensuring complete loyalty to whatever he wanted to do professionally. As Cagney put it in his autobiography:

> I did an entire series of these walkouts over the years. I walked out because I depended on the studio heads to keep their word on this, that, or other promise, and when the promise was not kept, my only recourse

was to deprive them of my services . . . I'm glad to say I never walked out in the middle of a picture, the usual procedure when an actor wanted a raise.[24]

Cagney's first strike at Warner's occurred during the summer of 1931.[25] Not only was his compensation unsatisfactory, but his original contract promised a twelve-week layoff during his second year, and Warner Bros. reneged on it, forcing him to come to work even though no scripts were ready for him. He initially brought his complaints to Jack Warner, to little or no avail. Cagney reminded him that, during initial negotiations on his first Warner contract, executives promised salary adjustments if his films did well, but such conditions were not written down and would not be honoured. Cagney then disobeyed their order to return, and the studio suspended him, 'officially [holding] back non-existent sums', as Sklar termed it, through the month of August. As was customary, the period of suspension added to the length of his five-year contract. The strike merited a considerable risk by a young star just three months after he achieved stardom; no one else had won against the major studios in such a confrontational showdown. But by September, perhaps realising that Cagney's arguments were not without merit, the studio reinstated him at a rate of $1,400 per week – hardly Jolson numbers, but roughly commensurate with Robinson, and a more than 300 per cent raise. An October 1931 *Variety* article noted how studios were generally 'successful' in their efforts to hold down star salaries, even those guaranteed 'option raises' in their contracts. According to their analysis, Cagney was one of the few in Hollywood during this period of economic dislocation, along with MGM star Constance Bennett, to win such an argument. 'He won, but here was a case of a heavy current b.o. [box office] put against a comparatively low salary figure', *Variety* concluded. 'On the other hand the older line stars, who received ultimatums to forget the option raise or quit, soon came back at the studio's figures.'

Cagney's second strike occurred in April 1932, prompted by the success of *Winner Takes All*, his fifth successful picture in fifteen months. In light of his raise just seven months before, this demand and walk-out could have damaged his image and career if not handled skilfully, particularly since Warners would end the year with a $14 million loss. Cagney knew his current salary was huge, especially compared to most Americans' during the worst year of the Great Depression, but he also felt it unfair that the studio pulled in hundreds of thousands of dollars on the films that he starred in and carried while he made only thousands. To make his request sound more reasonable, he promised publicly to 'accept a proportionately lower salary if and when his pictures decreased in box office returns', according to film writer James Robert Parish. Despite this overture, the brothers Warner again refused to negotiate and Cagney, certain they would never reward his successes for the company with merit pay, abandoned work again.

This strike lasted a lengthy six months, probably in large part due to the intransigence of Cagney and Jack Warner. Neither had much experience or interest in backing down. When the two men verbally jousted on these issues, Cagney the Irish American peppered his statements with Yiddish obscenities picked up from his old New York neighbourhood. Cagney also grew a moustache to show his unwillingness to work on a movie set. For Jack Warner, unsurprisingly, a contract, even if one-sided, needed to be honoured. He threatened Cagney (as well as other future striking Warner players such as Bette Davis and Olivia de Havilland) that he could fix it so that he would never work in Hollywood again, a potent if not entirely realistic threat for a new movie star. According to agent Dick Dorso, intimidation represented one of the main weapons that Hollywood moguls, particularly Jack Warner, brandished in negotiations:

> [The executives] knew nothing about handling people. They ruled by fear. This was characteristic of everyone in their position . . . They had to intimidate you before you intimidated them. Nobody said, 'sit down, tell me what the problem is and let's deal with it.' They wanted to establish the edge right away . . . the big studio execs were all the same – they yelled at you. So much of it was visceral. If you had a good stomach, good seat of the pants, and reacted properly to actors or properties, you'd be successful . . . In person, Jack Warner was overbearing, he was arrogant.[26]

And, it is safe to assume, so was Cagney. Their spats over the years were legendary, lasted over a period of nearly two decades, and earned a place in Jack Warner's autobiography. 'Cagney filed so many suits against us that our lawyers went out of their minds', he wrote in a tone that suggested the mutual respect of long-time warriors. 'We had to settle each suit by giving him a new contract, but I suppose in the long run he was worth it. He was a tough opponent in the legal ring . . . murder on technicalities.' Cagney's tactics apparently got under the executive's skin over time. Edward G. Robinson, the Warners star who boasted in his autobiography that he tended to solve his salary disputes privately, recalled Jack Warner complaining to him 'tearfully' in Europe during the mid-1930s about Cagney and Bette Davis' demands for 'more money and script approval'. He couldn't fathom the 'ingratitude' of the 'nobodies that he'd transformed into stars, arranged for them to have money, deference, houses, international fame. And how was [Jack] being paid back? They were nailing him to the cross.' Robinson reminded him that these stars also did a lot for him over the years: 'I advised Jack L. to share the wealth, that an actor did not necessarily mean money by wealth; he also meant some determination in his own fate.' No reply was recorded. In the same book, Robinson averred that an actor needed to protect himself 'or you would become indentured labor – the Hollywood ideal!'.[27]

The 1932 strike resolution was complicated by another studio offering to purchase the remainder of Cagney's contract for $150,000. *Variety* reported that while Cagney was not working for Warner during his walkout and considered himself a free agent (Warners emphatically disagreed with this interpretation), 'several Broadway legit offers' were made to him, including one from producer Billy Rose. Though all were refused, these overtures demonstrated the power Cagney had amassed within the industry in a short time. Perhaps to infuriate Jack Warner even more, Cagney announced intentions to start his own film production company during this period, and after three months of his strike predicted that the chances of his finding common ground with his studio were 'dim'. He also offered to star in three films without remuneration if Warners agreed to terminate his contract and make him a free agent, also vetoed. In late August, the MPPDA, in a meeting chaired by Jack Warner, adopted a resolution inspired by Cagney's actions, declaring: 'All members at no time in the future shall employ any artist who has refused to comply with his contractual obligations to any producer of motion pictures.' With this ruling, the major Hollywood studios ensured that no studio could employ Cagney or any other actor who, because of disputes, declared his contract invalid. In the end, the Academy of Motion Picture Arts and Sciences (AMPAS) dispatched director Frank Capra to mediate the festering and highly public Warner/Cagney dispute.

Cagney won most of what he wanted in a September 1932 settlement. Warner Bros. bumped his salary up to $3,000 a week, with steady raises to $4,500 by 1935. Furthermore, the actor only had to make four films per year, with top billing in all of them, and it appears that he no longer had to shill on the stump for Warner films he did not star in. But Warners' hardball tactics surfaced in the fine print. The new contract mandated that $1,250 of Cagney's weekly salary 'would be held back – placed in a trust account as a hedge against future walkouts or production disruptions by the actor', according to Sklar. 'In this manner, the studio could announce that Cagney's salary had been raised only $350 a week, rather than $1,600.' Warners also inserted behaviour-related clauses into the agreement. Cagney had to cease giving accounts of private studio business matters to film journalists, and be 'punctual and professional' in all dealings with the studio. Even with such paternalistic edicts inserted into his new contract, Cagney's relationship with the studio apparently survived, as can be surmised from his aforementioned acceptance of an – almost certainly temporary – February 1933 pay cut.

The $3,000 weekly salary applied while Cagney filmed *Footlight Parade* during the summer of 1933, far more than any other actor received for the picture. Warner stalwarts Joan Blondell, Cagney's co-star, and Guy Kibbee made $750 per week, and Ruby Keeler, evidently not on a weekly wage, made $10,000 overall. Cagney earned $27,000 for the film. Enjoying the early stages of becoming one of Hollywood's most accomplished and long-lived stars, Cagney possessed a leverage his fellow cast members did not share, and he pushed it to the maximum, far beyond what others were willing to do; no one in the *Footlight* cast and perhaps no one at the Warner studio in 1933 could have pulled off what he accomplished for himself. Cagney seemed to have more of a grasp of the overall economics of the motion picture industry than his most of his peers. In the mid-1930s, Cagney had an eye-opening experience when a theatre owner informed him that 'I have to take five [Warner] dogs to get one Cagney film'. Block-booking policies of the period forced most theatres to show all of one or two studio's offerings every week of the year, good or bad. If Cagney was worth that much to exhibitors, how much could he be worth to the Warner Bros. studio that paraded his films worldwide? He determined to find out.

Cagney knew his fellow cinema thespians watched his struggles closely. 'Many of Jimmy's fellow contract players were intrigued with the test of strength; it would help determine their own futures', noted Warren in his Cagney biography, co-written by Cagney. 'Others were against the audacity of the upstart actor, who, in their opinion, should have been thankful for what he had.' But as seen with Blondell and others from this chapter, much unhappiness existed about relatively low pay and punishing work conditions, yet few dared to knock the system in a meaningful way, even though Cagney advised others to adopt his approach. 'Cagney was a big fighter and he used to say to me I just should get up and walk out', Blondell observed, looking back at the situation in the 1970s. '"That's all you have to do [he said], and then you'll get what you want and get some decent money."'[28]

But few followed that perilous path, despite Cagney's success. Winning parity under the restrictive Hollywood contract system entailed a decades-long struggle before successful actors, aided by savvy agents, received the kind of compensation they believed they deserved for the money they brought in to studio coffers. Following the consolidation and vertical integration of the major studios in the mid-1920s, Cagney was the first major star under a long-term contract to challenge the apportioning of profits. Even before Leo Rosten posted numbers showing how Hollywood executives took a larger percentage of their company's profits for themselves than almost any other major American industry (see Chapter 3), Cagney scored an important financial precedent, the facts and results of which were published in the trade press for all in the industry to contemplate. 'It wasn't until some of us began to do a little walking out that the studios' total dictatorship over talent began to diminish', he boasted in his autobiography. In the months before he filmed *Footlight Parade*, Cagney had fought hard and risked his career to receive his share of profit for the skilled work he loved to do that proved exceedingly popular, a situation very close to that of Chester Kent, the energetic prologue creator he played in the film. Like Cagney, Kent had to be willing to walk out and give up everything before being offered a deal commensurate with his true worth. It represented yet another parallel between *Footlight* and the political and cultural history of its time.

After 1932, Cagney continued in this iconoclastic vein, becoming one of the first members and officers of the burgeoning Screen Actors Guild in 1933, during the controversial years before the major studios formally recognised the union in 1937. Fellow actors in subsequent years, particularly Warners actors such as Bette Davis, Olivia de Havilland, Kay Francis and Edward G. Robinson, picked up Cagney's cudgel and challenged the terms of their labour as well, on issues of compensation, artistic control and their need to break out of relentless artistically suffocating studio typecasting. Even before those actors rebelled against Warner policies, Danae Clark's research indicated that three of the actors in *42nd Street* clashed with Warner Bros. over labour issues. Guy Kibbee, inspired by the March 1933 salary cuts being extended for a week and being laid off for three weeks without pay, declared his contract void. His frustration must have been exacerbated by *42nd Street* earning record grosses during the same period. It is not clear how this situation resolved, but Kibbee was on board for the next three Great Depression Musicals. Clark also cited *42nd Street* star Bebe Daniels rejecting several scripts from Warner during 1932, which led to fraught contretemps with Darryl Zanuck and an eventual contract renegotiation in Daniels' favour. George Brent refused to report for a Warner film several months after *42nd Street*, 'result[ing] in his suspension' and 'a letter [from Warner Bros.] disclosing his action to nine different studios' to ensure he could not jump ship.[29] Because the Warners seemed particularly strict in upholding their lopsided contracts, this may have marked the reason so many actors rebelled there.

While studio work conditions, even for stars, were often punitive and pay not commensurate with profits generated, recent research indicates that many of these problems were alleviated and sometimes entirely remedied by savvy management.[30] During the 1930s and 1940s, Hollywood agents, led by Charles Feldman and Myron Selznick, designed 'independent' contracts for (often female) film stars that did not tie an actor to a studio for years, and, more importantly, bestowed more and sometimes complete control over film appearances and compensation. Long-term studio contracts provided valuable financial security, but these agents devised a way to enhance artistic freedom and compensation for stars willing to risk leaving the usual studio employment structure.

Feldman and Selznick's experience in the film studios before becoming agents earned them valuable knowledge of studio business practices: knowing how moguls thought, and how much they could actually pay a star who consistently brought in substantial returns. For example, in her 1939 Selznick-designed contract with RKO, Carole Lombard, probably the most popular film actress of the period, won the contractual right to choose her 'director, cinematographer, story, costume designer, make-up artist, hairstylist and even her publicist', drawing $100,000 per film plus a percentage of box-office profits. For her 1940 contract, she received a percentage of box-office grosses from the first ticket sold. Not only did she (and Selznick at a 10% commission) directly participate in the success of her films, but such profits were taxed at 25 per cent capital gains rates instead of 77 per cent charged for salary at personal income rates. 'We'll get ours for what we do now, not for what we may have done seven years ago', Lombard triumphantly informed the press. Similar 'independent' contracts were won by Feldman and Selznick for other female stars such as Clara Bow, Claudette Colbert and Katharine Hepburn, among others. As early as 1930, female stars Constance Bennett, Irene Dunne and Barbara Stanwyck signed 'limited non-option' freelance contracts with studios that increased their independence and earnings, suggesting that the problems that Warner stars such as Blondell, Cagney and Davis, as well as actors at other studios, endured were due not just to exploitive labour practices, but also to a lack of skilled management. No surprise, then, that Cagney in 1932 and Blondell in 1933 fired their William Morris Agency agents.

Similar high-profile industrial struggles erupted elsewhere, as actors during this period began to push back against restraints of the studio system. Marlene Dietrich briefly refused to meet with Paramount in late 1932 when it wanted to discuss her making a film without director Josef von Sternberg, the man designated in Dietrich's contract as her only permitted director, and who had helmed her previous film successes. Her $4,000 weekly salary was temporarily withheld; the studio sued her for over $182,000 in production costs on a non-Sternberg film and unsuccessfully tried to enact an arrest order to ensure that she would not leave for her home country of Germany where studios were bidding for her services before the termination of her Paramount contract in March 1933. In the end, Paramount decided to continue paying its biggest star her weekly retainer and dropped its suit, reasoning correctly that it stood a better chance of enticing her to their side if it quit alienating her. But this conflict, and others Dietrich endured while at the studio, centred more on issues of artistic control; unlike Cagney's situation at Warner, her financial compensation seemed sound to all parties. Elsewhere in Hollywood, actresses Ann Harding and Ruth Chatterton 'jumped studios . . . negotiated or renegotiated contracts to give them more choice over roles between 1931 and 1933', according to scholar Mary Desjardins, while actresses Kay Francis and

Chatterton signed contracts to new studios before their old contracts terminated, a practice that raised the ire of the studio moguls, since it took away the absolute control over actors and their careers that they preferred. Such actions led to bitter accusations of 'star-raiding' between the various studios, one of the major flashpoints of controversy brought up during the bitter negotiations for a National Recovery Administration (NRA) code of film industry practice during the fall of 1933, which will be covered in the next chapter.[31]

The work by employees within the studio system produced magnificent sequences and films at times, but harsh labour conditions ultimately inspired the creation of the Screen Actors Guild and Screen Writers Guild during the decade.[32] The worst years of the Depression seemed to heighten management's desire to film for as few days as possible to cut down costs, extracting as much as possible from workers, and paying them as little as they could. The guilds were spurred on by dissatisfaction and frustration higher up the Hollywood food chain, especially from well-paid actors and writers, but, as is demonstrated in this chapter, lesser-known screen talent also needed and deserved better treatment and union representation.

The studios' March 1933 (supposed) austerity cuts, as well as the demanding schedules they imposed and an unwillingness to allow leading creative personnel to share in the box-office proceeds they generated, revealed the vulnerability of some of the most important yet largely powerless of Hollywood's labour force: the actors and writers. Six actors met that month to inaugurate the Screen Actors Guild. A group of 21 mostly non-star (with the exception of Boris Karloff) actors incorporated the Screen Actors Guild in June 1933 to provide a unified force and voice for actors, vowing to represent neophyte members of their profession as well as the well-heeled. James Cagney was one of the earliest star supporters of SAG, as were his fellow Warner stalwarts Humphrey Bogart, Dick Powell, Edward G. Robinson and Warren William.

Screenwriters also moved to protect themselves during the tense business atmosphere of 1933. Ten writers attended an exploratory meeting a month before the cuts, but the Screen Writers Guild (SWG) was inaugurated a month later on 6 April 1933, promptly withdrawing its writers from the AMPAS company union. With the rise of 'talkies' necessitating full scripts of dialogue, writers assumed a new power and importance in Hollywood, but their treatment did not usually recognise this new status. Although some writers were well-paid (10% in 1934 made more than $10,000 yearly), credit for their work was apportioned by studio producers and executives usually with little if any advising from the writers themselves, with credit sometimes bestowed upon directors, an executive's family members, or others who did little towards the writing of scripts. Since the copyright for scripts rested with the studio and not the writer, and was classified as a 'work for hire', there existed no recourse for an author to insist upon proper credit. And without screen credits, a screenwriter's salary and career stayed stagnant or worse. Studio executives also frequently assigned numerous writers to a film, not informing them about each other. MGM über-producer Irving Thalberg viewed writers 'as interchangeable runners in a relay that he always won', according to Nancy Lynn Schwartz's history of Hollywood writers' struggles. Legendary triple threat writer-director-producer Preston Sturges claimed that his script for his 1933 film *The Power and the Glory* was 'the first story conceived and written directly as a shooting script by its author on his own time and then sold to a motion picture company on a royalty basis, exactly as novels and plays are sold'. Almost every other screenwriter in Hollywood had nowhere near the autonomy and recognised sense of authorship Sturges enjoyed on that film. It represented little wonder that the SWG early on established an official united front with the Dramatists Guild for playwrights in New York, who owned their own copyrights, often earned a percentage of the box-office returns of their plays, and were usually billed on the same level as dramatic actors; their Hollywood brethren yearned for the same kind of respect and compensation.

For both the SAG and the SWG, the significance of the Roosevelt's administration's passing of the National Industrial Recovery Act in June 1933 proved significant and far-reaching. The provision that stamped a government imprimatur of approval on collective bargaining would, eventually, after years of struggle and agitation, bring a new era of autonomy to both these categories of workers.

Though much has been written here and elsewhere concerning the negative aspects of employee relations at the major Hollywood studios, another important side exists to this relationship.[33] It should not be forgotten how much the studios brought to the table. The advantages these companies wielded could not be obtained elsewhere.

A brief examination of Cagney's post-1933 career is instructive in this regard. In 1936, Cagney won a heavily publicised court case freeing him from his Warner contract, mostly on the basis that he and Jack Warner had agreed to have him star in only four pictures per year, yet Cagney had consistently filmed five per year since his renegotiated 1932 contract. The court case was embarrassing for Jack Warner, and Cagney biographer Patrick McGilligan states that Warner blackballed Cagney when he became a free agent, making rival studios hesitant to hire him. Talks with producers Goldwyn, David O. Selznick and even Cagney's old associate Zanuck proved fruitless. Cagney ended up signing a three-picture deal with the fledgling independent Grand National film studio. None of these films was particularly successful, commercially or critically, and the studio ran out of money before Cagney could make the third film. He returned to the Warner fold shortly thereafter as a free agent, finally making the kind of salary he felt he deserved, $150,000 per film with profit participation, right of refusal, twelve consecutive weeks of annual vacation and only two or three pictures per year. The contract, in a first for a Hollywood actor, gave him an option that the studios previously had only reserved for themselves: the right to terminate his contract at the end of every motion picture he starred in or at the end of every year if his relationship with the studio had become 'obnoxious or unsatisfactory to him'. Even with his size-able 1932 raise, Cagney's 1933 compensation of $27,000 for *Footlight Parade* was relatively puny compared to Warner's international profit of at least $1.5 million[34] on the film. Now, thanks in part to his brother William, who had become his agent, he received remuneration and creative authority closer to his true market value. After the Oscar-winning *Yankee Doodle Dandy* (1942), Cagney's greatest commercial success at Warner, he quit the studio again, convinced (probably correctly) that the studio hid revenues for his films (his contract gave him a percentage of box-office gross). The independent film

Figure 4.1   In 1935, after years of restrictive Warner Bros. contracts that paid him less than his box-office value warranted, James Cagney hired his brother William Cagney, a former actor, as his agent and left Warner Bros. The move brought James Cagney a bigger salary with profit participation in his films, but his post-Warners films made with an independent studio and his own production company did less well in the market-place, limiting his compensation. By 1938, James Cagney was back at Warner Bros. (Getty Photos)

studio he then created with his brother William, Cagney Productions, scored no successes either, despite securing solid financing and distribution by United Artists, and paid Cagney much less than he would have received starring in films at his old studio. By the late 1940s, his experiments in establishing independent autonomy essentially finished, he returned yet again to Warner Bros.

With all his talent, moxie and the money he could invest to develop his visions as a successful well-paid movie star, why did Cagney's independent ventures largely fail? There are many reasons, but the most significant are linked with the economies of scale that major studios created and enjoyed at the apex of their power. Because of the efficient and massive industrial assembly line form of production they perfected, they boasted legions of skilled writers, directors, technicians, make-up and costuming experts, and many other personnel employed on economical (if restrictive) contracts, whereas Grand National and Cagney's upstart production company had to hire such personnel from scratch, probably with every new film they produced, a much less efficient model. As Cagney biographer Patrick McGilligan reported, Cagney Productions didn't possess the cash flow to fund the development of numerous scripts for the company to choose from, as the majors did. Directors were difficult for them to procure. The established, vertically integrated studios not only moved much more quickly on the production side than the independents because of these advantages, but also fielded experienced publicity teams and could guarantee national distribution through hundreds of theatres through their block-booked contracts. They owned and maintained the world's best motion picture-making facilities; in 1929 alone, they spent $50 million building new sound stages in the wake of the transition to sound. What start-up could match such resources? Many independent companies, particularly in the 1940s and 1950s, rented the majors' soundstages at a high tariff that necessarily increased their budgets and benefited the majors they were ostensibly competing with. The eight major studios also enjoyed excellent long-term relationships with banks, which provided them with the capital to produce their films – at one point, Jack Warner and Zanuck even served on the board at the California-based Bank of America, which had earned a reputation as the 'movie bank' because of its long history of financing Hollywood product and growth. Through the hard work of establishing connections, the studios also had won access to vast international markets, which added profits that independents either did not have access to or had to spend vast amounts of time cultivating.[35] Producing a film via the independent route during this period would always represent a more expensive, less efficient approach.

It is true that Cagney could have realised a much higher percentage of profit had one of his company's films hit paydirt in the market-place, but the chances of that happening were much less because of his company's less privileged position in the industry, and the added costs incurred by putting together a cast, crew and audience from scratch every time. Cagney Productions' films would always be more expensive to produce and thus return less profit than more efficient streamlined major studio product. With producers with years of hit-making experience residing on every major studio lot, perhaps they enjoyed an artistic edge as well. The long-term fate of Cagney's career tells the tale: his most profitable and best-received films were all made with Warners, from *The Public Enemy* and *Footlight Parade* to *The Roaring Twenties* (1939), *White Heat* (1949) and *Mister Roberts* (1955). As much as he detested certain practices of theirs, he never did nearly as well without them. Nor did actors or directors at other majors until the traditional studio system started to crumble following World War II. As another example, Frank Capra's efforts to exit the major studio system during the 1940s with his independent company Liberty Films yielded similarly frustrating results, with one excellent Oscar-nominated yet commercially under-performing film, *It's a Wonderful Life* (1946).

Because of the necessarily high fixed costs incurred in creating movies efficiently, the studios were often ruthless when it came to enforcing the contracts that ensured their smooth operations and near total control – the film writer David Thomson has termed Hollywood during its supposed Golden Age a 'golden prison' and a 'factory'. But the studios provided hugely valuable services and benefits unobtainable elsewhere. While it is true that these services were largely made possible by the fact that the studios ran oligopolistic operations with such exclusionary practices that no new companies could challenge their hegemony for decades, they still represented the only game in town if one wanted to succeed at the highest international level. Their streamlined system produced numerous masterpieces (amid much vapidity) that still find favour among audiences and critics today. And one could argue that no matter how unfair and inflexible the terms of Cagney's contract, at least he had one – as *Variety* reported in 1932, only 2.6 per cent of motion picture industry workers had 'contracts assuring them of employment for any real period of time'. Actress Bette Davis, who engaged in even more public fights than Cagney did over her Warner contract later in the 1930s, credited the stability that the studios and the moguls who ran them brought to the acting profession. 'It was a handful of suit and clothing merchants [some of the moguls were involved in this industry before they ran the American film industry] who gave the actor the only semblance of continuous financial security he ever had', she stated in her autobiography. 'The destructive aspects of some of these men are properly infamous; but in debt we [actors] are to their gambling instincts.'[36] The tender balance of film artistry and economics has always proven contentious, and still does today. It would be both imprudent and unrealistic to discount either side in this never-ending economic battle.

The year leading up to and including the production of *Footlight Parade* proved a watershed year in the history of Hollywood and its labour force. It saw various wage cuts and work stoppages, the IATSE strike, Cagney's six-month battle against Warners, and more. With all the tension building in the industry from numerous angles, and profits down and losses surging, the major studios might have decided to adopt a less confrontational front. But, in their priorities for writing and implementing the Roosevelt-mandated NRA code for their industry during the fall of 1933, as *Footlight Parade* was being wrapped, their main object would be to make working conditions even tougher and more limiting for their employees. The biggest fight of the year was yet to arrive.

NOTES

1. Sources for this discussion concerning Hollywood unions, craftspeople and the summer 1933 IATSE strike: David Bordwell, Janet Staiger and Kristin Thompson, *The Classical Hollywood Cinema: Film Style & Mode of Production* (Oxon: Routledge, 2002), Chapter 24; Paul Buhle and Dave Wagner, *Radical Hollywood: The Untold Story Behind America's Favorite Movies* (New York: The New Press, 2002): 43–4, 69–71; Gerald Horne, *Class Struggle in Hollywood: Moguls, Mobsters, Stars, Reds and Trade Unionists* (Austin, TX: The University of Texas Press, 2001), Chapter 1; George Murphy, 'A Strike Against Gangsters', in Christopher Silvester, *The Penguin Book of Hollywood* (London: Penguin, 1998): 274–7; Louis B. Perry and Richard S. Perry, *A History of the Los Angeles Labor Movement 1911–1941* (Berkeley: University of California Press, 1963): 327–32; Robert Sklar, *Movie-Made America: A Cultural History of American Movies* (New York: Vintage, 1994), Chapter 5, 171–3; [uncited authors], 'Producers Defy IATSE: Aim to Secure Replacements for Strikers and Keep Plants Open – Men Quit at Midnight', *Hollywood Reporter* (25 July 1933); 'IATSE Strike Folding Up; Green and Casey to Meet in Hope of Settling Differences – Men Claim Promises Broken' and W. R. Wilkerson, 'Tradeviews' [column], *Hollywood Reporter* (27 July 1933).

   Articles from *Variety* by uncited authors: 'Col. Studio Shuttered by Union Walkout over Soundmen's Claims' (11 July 1933); 'Columbia Cancels All Players in 3 Pix Pending Strike Settlement' (18 July 1933); 'Columbia Studio Stopped by Strike; 800 Persons Idle' (25 July 1933); 'Strike Ties Up Hollywood: Put Walkout Up to White House' (25 July 1933); 'Fighting Unions on Coast Take Internal Troubles to Washington but Fail to Find Official Favor' and 'Coast Strike Reports: Studio Prod. Is 75% Normal' (1 August 1933); 'Jurisdiction Clash Between IBEW And IATSE May Give the Electrical Workers Control Over Boatmen', 'Coast Strike Reports' and 'Metro, Warners Lead Studios in Increasing Special Strike Cops' (8 August 1933); 'NRA Moves into Hollywood Studio Strike, Mediator Designated; Men Bolting Union, Back With Prods.' (15 August 1933); 'Outcome of IBEW's Jurisdictional Fight vs. IA May See New Officers' (22 August 1933).
2. Sources for this paragraph: *42nd Street* Contracts For Chorus file (2803 special, 2 of 2), *Footlight Parade* Picture file (2872, 1 of 2), *Footlight Parade* Production – Daily Progress Reports file (1448), all from Warner Bros. Archive, University of Southern California [henceforth: WBA/USC]; Tony Thomas and Jim Terry, with Busby Berkeley, *The Busby Berkeley Book* (New York: New York Graphic Society, 1973): 27, 70; [uncited authors], 'Hollywood Gals Again Eating: Resumption of Musical Pix Puts Chorines Back in Money', *Variety* (20 June 1933); 'Chorus Girls Precipitate Debate: Chorus Girls Toil 86 Hours for $25 Week, Hearing Told', *Motion Picture Herald* (16 September 1933).
3. A. Scott Berg, *Goldwyn* (London: Penguin, 1989): 252–4; Thomas/Terry, 27.

Berkeley's moonlighting and consequent lack of sleep make his achievements in *Footlight Parade* even more impressive.

4. Patrick Brion and Rene Gilson, 'A Style of Spectacle: Interview with Busby Berkeley', *Cahiers du Cinéma in English* 2 (1966): 34.
5. Horne, 45.
6. James Cagney, *Cagney* (Garden City, NY: Doubleday, 1976): 56; John Kobal, *Gotta Dance Gotta Sing: A Pictorial History of Film Musicals* (London: Hamlyn, 1971): 40–1.
7. John Kobal, 'Joan Blondell', *Focus on Film* No. 24 (1 April 1976): 15–16.
8. Kobal, *Gotta*, 40–1; Thomas and Terry, 34.
9. Connie Bruck, *When Hollywood Had a King: The Reign of Lew Wasserman, Who Leveraged Talent into Power and Influence* (New York: Random House, 2003): 113–14; Michael Freedland, *The Warner Brothers* (London: Harrap, 1983): 87; Sklar, 230–2.
10. Sources for this discussion on the 'loaning out' of screen actors: Inter-Office Communication, Mr. Dover to R. J. Obringer, 17 September 1932; L. B. Mayer to WB Pictures Inc. contract, 24 September 1932; Inter-Office Communication, R. J. Obringer to J. L. Warner, 30 September 1932; Inter-Office Communication, R. J. Obringer to J. L. Warner, 1 October 1932. All documents from *42nd Street* Picture file (2872), WBA/USC. Berg, 327; Tom Kemper, *Hidden Talent: The Emergence of Hollywood Agents* (Berkeley: University of California Press, 2010): 41; Kobal, 'Blondell', 15; Edward G. Robinson with Leonard Spigelgass, *All My Yesterdays: An Autobiography* (New York: Hawthorne, 1973): 150–1; [uncited author], 'Too Many Talent "Loans" at Metro', *Variety* (20 June 1933).

    The Warner Bros. Great Depression Musicals after *42nd Street* did not feature 'loan-outs', which probably saved the studio money. For the use of Baxter in *42nd Street*, Fox was paid $31,000, while James Cagney, the top earning actor in *Footlight Parade* and the most popular actor ever to appear in the series, drew $27,000 for his role: *Footlight Parade* 824 Budget, *Footlight Parade* Story – Memos & Correspondence file (2570), WBA/USC.

    Interestingly, Jack Warner refused to ever loan out James Cagney, despite countering many offers; perhaps Cagney was too famous and successful a performer for such treatment to make sense and Warner felt it counterproductive for his studio to compete with his own star.
11. Muriel Babcock, 'Fox Borrowing MGM Star', *Los Angeles Times* (23 Sept. 1932). This story talked about the loaning out of MGM star (and Cagney friend) Robert Montgomery.
12. Emily Carman, *Independent Stardom: Freelance Women in the Hollywood Studio System* (Austin: University of Texas Press, 2016): 26, 49; Kemper, 12, 41.
13. The quotations of Blondell in this section are from Kobal, 'Blondell',; and Pam Munter, 'Joan Blondell: Heart of Gold', *Films of the Golden Age* No. 30 (1 Nov. 2002): 20. Munter offers no citation for the period quotations.

    Blondell's eighteen Warner films in her first two years at the studio seems typical. According to her autobiography (p. 119), Bette Davis appeared in eight films during her first year working at the studio. Cagney appeared in a similar number in his first years, as documented later in this chapter.
14. Cagney, *Cagney*, 63–4; Bette Davis, *The Lonely Life* (New York: G. P. Putnam & Sons, 1962): 141.
15. [Uncited author], 'Coppers and Planes Are Studios' Aspirin for Headaches in Finding Wilderness Hideouts of Actors', *Variety* (11 July 1933).
16. Jeanine Basinger, *A Woman's View: How Hollywood Spoke to Women, 1930–1960* (New York: Knopf, 1993): 186–7; Leo Rosten, *Hollywood: The*

Movie Colony, The Movie Makers (New York: Harcourt, Brace & Co., 1941): 123–4.

17. [Uncited author], 'Film Pay Boost Tip Detailed: Joan Blondell Charges Agency Told Her to Get Rise by Walkout Threat', *Los Angeles Times* (10 November 1933). This theme of Blondell blaming herself for having undergone suffering, instead of blaming the system she worked under, was a common theme in American culture of the period, as discussed in the previous chapter, and in: Lawrence W. Levine, 'American Culture and the Great Depression', *Yale Review* 74: 2 (January 1985).

18. Eileen Whitfield, *Pickford: The Woman Who Made Hollywood* (New York`: Macfarlaine Walter & Ross, 1997): 135–45.

19. Davis, 106.

20. Davis, 124–6; 'Warner Special Train Arrives in Town Today', *Los Angeles Times* (17 March 1933).

21. Cagney, *Cagney*, 46, 63–4; Larry Ceplair and Steven Englund, *The Inquisition in Hollywood: Politics in the Film Community 1930–1960* (Garden City, NY: Doubleday, 1980): 3; Thomas Schatz, *The Genius of the System: Hollywood Filmmaking in the Studio Era* (New York: Henry Holt, 1988): 138–9; Bob Thomas, *Clown Prince of Hollywood: The Antic Life and Times of Jack L. Warner* (New York: McGraw-Hill Ryerson, NYC, 1990): 81; Doug Warren with James Cagney, *Cagney: The Authorized Biography* (London: Robson, 1983): 79–80.

22. Steven Bach, *Marlene Dietrich: Life and Legend* (London: William Morrow, 1992): 114–17, 137–8, 551; Cagney, 46, 51; Schatz, 138–9; Inter-Office Communication, R. J. Obringer to J. Warner, 19 Jan. 1934, from *Big Boy* Artist Contracts file (2869A), WBA/USC.

   In 1936, producer David O. Selznick paid Dietrich $200,000 to appear in *Desire*, making her 'the most highly salaried woman in the world', according to *Time* magazine. Later the same year, producer Alexander Korda paid her $450,000 to appear in *Knight Without Armour* (1937): Bach, 212–13, 220.

23. Buhle and Wagner, 81–2; Cagney, ch. 1; Simon Louvish, 'Top of the World: Portrait of James Cagney' *Sight and Sound* (July 2004): 38–9; Patrick McGilligan, *Cagney: The Actor as Auteur* (San Diego, CA: A. S. Barnes, 1982), Chapter 3; Greg Mitchell, *The Campaign of the Century: Upton Sinclair's Race for Governor of California and the Birth of Media Politics* (New York: Random House, 1992): 58–61, 140–4; Robert Sklar, *City Boys: Cagney, Bogart, Garfield* (Princeton, NJ: Princeton University Press, 1992): 35.

   According to McGilligan and other sources, after *Footlight Parade*, Cagney continued his support of left-wing causes, including aiding Republicans in the Spanish Civil War, supporting socialist Upton Sinclair for Governor of California in 1934 (and rejecting the tax studio heads levied on their employees to support the Republican candidate) and playing a leadership role in the nascent Screen Actors Guild. Cagney became less publicly vocal about such left-leaning topics in the latter half of the 1930s, but was known as someone who did not hesitate to whip out his cheque book to aid people who were suffering. As his brother Bill said: 'When people are hungry and starving, James Cagney doesn't ask them their political beliefs, he helps them.'

24. Cagney, 51; Warren/Cagney, 79–83.

25. This discussion of Cagney's 1931 and 1932 strikes at Warner Bros. is based on the following sources by uncited authors, unless noted otherwise: 'Films' Erratic Salaries: Standardizing All But Checks', *Variety* (6 October 1931); 'Cagney in Town', *Variety* (5 July 1933); 'Cagney Sees Warner Out, May Produce', *Variety* (23 August 1932); 'Cagney–Dvorak's Contract Breach Scored by Coast Producers' Ass'n, Which Votes "Hands Off" Policy', *Variety* (30 August 1932);

'Cagney–Warner Tiff May Go to Academy For Final Arbitration', *Variety* (6 September 1932); 'Academy Insisting on WB–Cagney Mediation as Obligation to Industry', *Variety* (13 September 1932); Cagney, 46–51; Patrick McGilligan, *Cagney: The Actor as Auteur* (San Diego, CA, 1982), Chapter 3; James Robert Parish, *The Tough Guys* (New Rochelle, NY: Arlington House, 1976): 29–32; Robinson, 306; Sklar, *City*, 35–42; Warren/Cagney, 79–90; [uncited author], 'Warner Bros.', *Fortune* (December 1937): 218.

Five hit films starring Cagney from April 1931 to July 1932, in chronological order: *Public Enemy, Blonde Crazy, Taxi!, The Crowd Roars* and *Winner Take All*.

26. Cass Warner Sperling and Cork Millner with Jack Warner Jr, *Hollywood Be Thy Name: The Warner Bros. Story* (Rocklin, CA: Prima, 1994): 226–7.

27. Robinson, 110, 142, 177–80; Jack Warner with Dean Jennings, *My First Hundred Years in Hollywood: An Autobiography* (New York: Random House, 1965): 228.

28. Cagney, 51–2; *Footlight* 824 Budget, ibid.; Kobal, 'Blondell', ibid.; Warren/Cagney, 81–3.

29. Danae Clark, *Negotiating Hollywood: The Cultural Politics of Actors' Labor* (Minneapolis: University of Minnesota Press, 1995): 102–3.

30. This discussion on 'independent' actor contracts of the 1930s and 1940s is based on: Carman, Introduction, 24, 62–78; Tom Kemper, *Hidden Talent: The Emergence of Hollywood Agents* (Berkeley: University of California Press, 2010), Chapter 1, pp. 30, 40, 131, 244.

Such 'independent' deals for actors (particularly female stars, according to Carman) that paid royalties from the box-office gross were much earlier and better than the 1950 deal that agent Lew Wasserman designed for Jimmy Stewart on the film *Winchester 73*, which is often cited as the first time actors received such percentages. The Stewart deal was based on net profits, not the gross, so it wasn't as lucrative or immediate as Lombard's 1940 deal. Such deals, of course, also brought less compensation than a guaranteed salary if the film bombed in theatres. Some men were also involved in deals that featured compensation from box-office net or gross, usually in lieu of a higher set salary, such as director Ernst Lubitsch and actor William Powell in 1938: Carman, 74, Kemper, 48–9.

31. Bach, 162–6. For more on Bette Davis's, Olivia de Havilland's and Edward G. Robinson's fights with their Warner Bros. studio contracts, see Bruck, 113–14; Davis, *Lonely*, Chapter 11; Mary Desjardins, 'Not of Hollywood: Ruth Chatterton, Ann Harding, Constance Bennett, Kay Francis, and Nancy Carroll', in Adrienne L. McLean, ed., *Glamour in a Golden Age: Movie Stars of the 1930s* (New Brunswick, NJ: Rutgers University Press, 2011): 23–5; Michael Freedland, *The Warner Brothers* (London: Harrap. 1983): 55, 78–84, 100; Robinson, 110, 150; [uncited author], 'Warner', *Fortune*, 218.

32. This section on the beginnings of the Screen Actors Guild and the Screen Writers Guild is based on the following sources: Tino Balio, *Grand Design: Hollywood as a Modern Business Enterprise 1930–1939* (New York: Scribner, 1993): 153–5; Larry Ceplair and Steven Englund, *The Inquisition in Hollywood: Politics in the Film Community 1930–1960* (Garden City, NY: Anchor Press/Doubleday, 1980), Chapter 1; Lary May, 'Movie Star Politics: The Screen Actors' Guild, Cultural Conversion, and the Hollywood Red Scare', in Lary May, ed., *Recasting America: Culture and Politics in the Age of Cold War* (Chicago: University of Chicago Press, 1989); Marc Norman, *What Happens Next: A History of American Screenwriting* (London: Aurum, 2008), Chapter 9; Nancy Lynn Schwartz, *The Hollywood Writers' Wars* (New York: Knopf, 1982), Chapter 1; Preston Sturges, 'The Wrong Racket', in Christopher Silvester, ed., *The Penguin Book of Hollywood* (London: Penguin, 1998): 157–63.

33. Sources for this section on the economic advantages of major studios: Rudy Behlmer, *Inside Warner Bros. (1935–1951)* (New York: Viking, 1985): 63; McGilligan, Chapters 5 and 8; Bob Thomas, 105–78; David Thomson, *The Whole Equation: A History of Hollywood* (New York: Vintage, 2004), Chapter 12.

34. As was documented in the previous chapter, *Footlight Parade* made $2.4 million internationally on a production budget of roughly $460,000. With promotion and distribution costs not included in that tally, the total profit to the studio can be estimated at at least $1.5 million and probably $200–300,000 more than that. The details concerning Cagney's 1937 contract with Warner Bros. are taken from: Kemper, 131,200; Thomas, 105–6.

35. Material concerning soundstage construction and banks: Horne, 7–8.

For more on Hollywood's pursuit of international markets, see Ian Jarvie, *Hollywood's Overseas Campaign: The North Atlantic Movie Trade 1920–1950* (Cambridge: Cambridge University Press, 1992).

36. [Uncited author], '25,000 in Films, but only 650 by Contract', *Variety* (2 August 1932); Davis, 93–4.

5. THE NRA CODE

Most histories of the American film industry, if they delve into politics at all, chart the beginning of Hollywood's political consciousness to the contentious 1934 California gubernatorial election. Leo Rosten, in his book on the industry, claimed that this occasion marked 'Hollywood's first entrée into politics'. And indeed all eight major studios became involved in re-electing the rather dull Republican candidate Frank Merriam against author Upton Sinclair, the Socialist candidate on the Democratic ticket, using the kind of strong-arm tactics they usually unleashed against their own employees and competitors. They made short films, insisting that California theatres show them, spreading untrue propaganda about Sinclair without allowing him the opportunity to respond. They forced their employees to contribute to the Merriam campaign, sometimes under threat of firing, and pressured them to vote for him. It was an ugly, divisive campaign, but the studios got their man elected.[1]

But 'Hollywood's entrée into politics' occurred before 1934. We have already seen the involvement of Louis B. Mayer and the Warners in presidential elections, and even before then, Charles Chaplin and Mary Pickford partnered with the government in selling World War I bonds, and Al Jolson stumped and wrote songs for various Republican candidates during the 1920s, among other examples.[2] But the long and antagonistic fashioning of the National Recovery Administration (NRA)'s code of practice for the film industry during 1933 (negotiated as *Footlight Parade* was being written, filmed and released) represented a turbulent political event that pre-dates and informs the 1934 gubernatorial election. The NRA code process exposed deep resentful fissions

within the Hollywood film community that would never fully heal, and ultimately portended doom for the way in which the major studios preferred to
do their business. In addition, this months-long ordeal occurred in full view
of the national press: every twist and turn in the process, and every revelation
concerning the way the moguls and stars earned their money, became common
knowledge. A spotlight flooded onto the soundstages and executive suites of
filmdom, and many, including, apparently, President Franklin Roosevelt, were
not pleased with what they saw.

In the summer of 1933, however, the initial prognosis for the film industry's
co-operation with the NRA looked positively rosy. Roosevelt proclaimed that
the NRA would eventually be viewed as the 'most important and far-reaching
legislation ever enacted by the American Congress'. Senator Robert Wagner,
primary instigator of including the right to collective bargaining for labour
in the legislation, predicted it would 'Bring this country out of depression'.[3]
Within months, both statements proved wildly optimistic and off-base.

The NRA, signed into law for a renewable two-year period on 16 June 1933
by Roosevelt as part of his administration's National Industrial Recovery Act
(NIRA), sought to implement an unprecedented (before or since) reorganisation of the American economy aimed at restoring employment and ridding the
economy of dangerous waste. By setting price controls, production quotas,
maximum working hours and a minimum wage for hundreds of industries
nationwide, the NRA hoped to stop overproduction and cut-throat competition that, according to the administration, hurt companies and put people
out of work. Gen. Hugh S. Johnson, head of the NRA, explained that the
organisation hoped to achieve 'a balanced economy as opposed to the mur-
derous doctrine of savage and wolfish individualism, looking to dog-eat-dog
and devil take the hindmost'.[4] It evinced an ameliorative and humane effect
as well, contributing much to the demise of sweatshop and child labour, and
setting unprecedented standards for minimum wages and maximum hours,
even if some industries did their best to ignore them. But, as Goldman Sachs
film financier Waddell Catchings noted, Hollywood had long operated on a
'rat eat rat' basis;[5] its modus operandi was inimical to many of the notions
promulgated by the NRA, and it would not adjust easily or well to its dictates.

Perhaps most controversially for the union-averse film industry, the NRA
established collective bargaining as a right for workers. It temporarily waived
anti-trust laws so companies within industries could work together to (theoretically) secure the best outcomes for workers, bosses and the American
economy as a whole. The programme had teeth as well – the federal government could revoke the business licences of companies that disobeyed provisions
of their industry's code. The idea was that, with the government watching over
the process and ensuring an equal playing field, management and employees

would both sacrifice some advantages to increase employment and put pay cheques into more people's pockets, improving the national economy during this period of severe economic privation. But much resistance to the NRA developed. It gave the federal government almost unlimited and hotly contested powers over the economy and individual businesses. For laissez-faire business-minded Republicans, it looked like a hubristic act of un-American constitutional heresy, an interference with markets and Adam Smith's 'invisible hand' surely doomed to fail.

During the summer of 1933, however, Hollywood made a point of showing its enthusiasm for the NRA and its goals, with Warner Bros. leading the parade. In the 8 and 12 August 1933 issues of *Variety* and *Motion Picture Herald*, a multi-page ad for Warners' upcoming slate of films was designed to look like a Roosevelt-era government document. A huge replica of the NRA Blue Eagle insignia adorns a page 'announcing' in tall bold letters 'the national recovery ... code for the motion picture industry'. The next two pages are designed to resemble the vow that a government witness takes in court, with an oversized drawing of a hand raised high. 'I solemnly swear', the ad proclaims, making its appeal to theatres to carry the 1933–4 slate of Warner films, to 'wholeheartedly resolve to subscribe to every one of the 60 points of Warner Bros. Recovery Program for 1933–1934.' *Footlight Parade* registered as the first of the 60 points listed. The same issue of the *Herald* featured a two-page preview of the aforementioned multi-page Warner ad, with two large NRA eagles spread over the whole of the space, and large letters proclaiming 'We're On Our Way To The New Era'. Three weeks later, the studio's ad claimed its films would provide exhibitors with 'the short road to recovery'. Such ads, combined with the appearance of the NRA eagle and a portrait of Roosevelt in a patriotic tableau at the end of *Footlight*, marked the high point of Warner's public enthusiasm and identification with Roosevelt and the New Deal.

In the same issues of *Variety* and the *Herald*, MGM and Paramount also featured the NRA Blue Eagle in ads for their forthcoming slates of films, but did not align themselves as closely as Warners. MGM paired the NRA insignia with its trademark lion and proclaimed 'prosperity!'. Paramount featured a smaller reprint of the NRA insignia; its ad pointed out how fewer working hours under the NRA could translate into more leisure hours for the public to see movies in, meaning added profit for theatres and the studios.

Seeing the NRA eagle used by companies in ads was not unusual for the period. For example, in the front section of the *Los Angeles Times* on 21 September 1933, the insignia can be seen in ads placed by a range of products and industries, including Adohr milk, Fuller paint, Knapp-Felt hats, Harris & Frank clothiers, Goodyear tyres, Colgate toothpaste and major department and grocery stores, and in every movie theatre ad, as well as on the masthead of the *Times* itself every day. But none of these companies identified with the

New Deal and its policies in quite so close and enthusiastic a fashion as Warner Bros.

The studios, particularly Warner, publicly gave the impression of being supportive of the NRA, vowing to quickly formulate an NRA code for Hollywood. This did not connote a purely altruistic or patriotic attitude. They hoped that, if they were seen in public doing their part for the New Deal, by changing their business for the good of the country and hiring thousands more workers, and by featuring the NRA Blue Eagle insignia at the start of their films and in all their ads (as the major studios largely did in this period), the public would reward their stance and their sacrifice with good will and additional box-office receipts. After all, as one major Hollywood figure noted in the *Hollywood Reporter* that Depression-saddled summer, the motion-picture industry needed an economic boost: 6,064 of 13,247 theatres nationwide were closed. An NRA Day parade in New York City, with 6,000 motion picture industry employees participating, probably represented the pinnacle of the industry's public embrace of NRA goals. Organised by various top-level executives, including Harry Warner, the marchers included workers from the studios' East Coast headquarters (including 'practically all employees at the Warner home office'), personnel ranging from ushers to owners of 'practically' every cinema in New York, the MGM Leo the Lion mascot, 'theatre bands', radio and 'legitimate theatre' workers, as well as married Warner stars Al Jolson and Ruby Keeler. Chester Hale, the New York musical producer on which *Footlight* lead character Chester Kent was probably partly based, brought a troupe of his 'dancing girls' to the event that released pigeons into the crowd and formed the letters 'NRA' in one of their routines, a scenario resembling the final minutes of *Footlight Parade*'s on-screen celebration of Franklin Roosevelt and the NRA Blue Eagle.[6]

Will Hays, president of the Motion Picture Producers and Distributors of America (MPPDA), began meetings concerning the code in June 1933. Several press accounts from July and August predicted a speedy resolution of the code, with the industry expressing a desire to be the 'first [to complete an NRA code] for Roosevelt'. *Variety* offered readers an optimistic portrait of co-operation between the major segments of motion picture industry – production, distribution and exhibition – and assured readers that 90 per cent of the code was already completed by August, with 'representative indie [independent] distributors, according to their own spokesmen . . . in harmony with major distributors on practically all important points', with the same supposedly also bearing true for the independent theatre owners who avoided block booking their films with the major studios.[7]

Such optimism was misplaced, to say the least. The disagreements unearthed by the shaping of the document were too profound to accommodate quick resolution. Though articles in the press kept appearing throughout the summer and fall predicting a final wrap-up of the film code, the process ground on. The Roosevelt administration ordered all NRA codes finished and submitted by 31 August, but the film industry code would not be finished and approved by Roosevelt until late November, almost five months after initial predictions of completion. No other industry in the United States took so long to accomplish the task; 690 codes were on the books by the end of August, and of the major American industries, only Bituminous Coal's code was approved as late as 18 September.[8] The motion-picture industry represented a special and particularly intractable case.

Even before the code's completion, major studios and exhibitors were following the general reforms proposed by the NRA and supporting the president within their businesses in unprecedented ways.[9] A few days after Roosevelt took office, the independent theatre chain Allied States Association of Motion Picture Exhibitors, which would prove a significant irritant to the major studios during the code negotiations and afterwards, nationally distributed slides, trailers and lobby cards to theatres across the country urging cinema audiences to 'SUPPORT YOUR PRESIDENT'. 'Roosevelt is doing a great job . . . restoring order out of banking chaos . . . paving the way for prosperity', the notices read. 'Our lot may be tough, but his is tougher, so let us all help him as best we can.' In August, 6,000 theatres received a fifteen-second insert to be shown as part of every film programme that featured the NRA Blue Eagle symbol and the words 'This theatre is an NRA member. We do our part.' 'Nearly all' theatres in New York City's Times Square sported homemade NRA flags by August, quite a commitment when one considers that NRA rules forced employees to just eight hours per day, cutting the pay of many existing employees, while forcing theatres to hire more personnel and usually pay more in payroll costs. Executives' hours were not curtailed. The same situation applied at the major studios as well. Such situations caused tensions, since 'white-collared' management employees often ended up putting in far longer hours than lower-ranked employees whose weeks were capped at 35 or 40 hours under NRA regulations. 'Every one, except the bosses, expects raises and weekends', *Variety* trumpeted, assuming that a lowering of hours at the same weekly rate of pay constituted a raise.

As a result of this policy, Paramount reported that its weekly salary expenses jumped to $10,000 (roughly $185,000 in today's dollars), adding around forty employees overall. MGM and Fox posted gains of 60 workers each, with the latter studio cancelling pending vacations for personnel in the wake of NRA reforms. By the end of August, *Variety* claimed that a total of 30,000 additional employees were hired by the film industry (a March 1934 *Variety* article reported that the industry employed 389,000 overall). Union employees were usually allowed to keep the hours and conditions mandated in their contracts, which were often better than those employed under studio contracts experienced. The industry did its part, but worried about financing the government-mandated hiring. The *Hollywood Reporter* predicted that the situation would force the major studios to 'produce a larger number of pictures of a wider general appeal, at costs which can show profits'. Under NRA codes, the industry could also raise admission prices to cover those new costs, which made a difference since the studios earned a percentage of the box-office take and admission prices had previously been dropping steadily to help lure in larger audiences during the Depression.

Warner Bros. took the lead among the major studios in producing film shorts that hailed the NRA and Roosevelt's approach to combating the Great Depression.[10] During the summer of 1933, Harry Warner chaired a committee of studio executives charged with preparing 'propaganda pictures and recruit[ing] theatre screens for showing them'. Each of the eight major studios created an NRA-promoting short film at their own expense. One thousand prints were struck of each film for a total of 64,000 theatre showings.

An eccentric short film entitled *The Road Is Open Again* marked Warners' contribution to this series. *Variety* noted that 'a personal angle between [Harry] Warner and the President, plus the NRA supervision, makes this commercial short a quasi-official venture'. It opens, as most of these shorts did, with a notice superimposed over the Blue Eagle insignia: 'N.R.A. Official Featurette – Patriotically Contributed by Motion Picture Industry'. Dick Powell, the star from all the 1933 Warner Great Depression Musicals, portrays a composer, much as he did in *Gold Diggers of 1933*. This time, he's trying to write a 'patriotic song' about the NRA, as portraits of presidents Washington, Lincoln and Wilson hang behind him. When he takes a nap at his piano, those presidents magically appear, after a brief montage suggesting the crises they faced (the Revolutionary War, the Civil War and World War I). Lincoln reads a newspaper whose front page hails 'one million jobs created by the N.R.A.', and he proclaims that 'things are getting better every day'. Washington concurs: 'Well, Abe, it looks as though we can stop worrying about our country. President Roosevelt has it headed right again.'

This discussion finally awakens Powell, and he admits to confusion about what the NRA does: 'if you'd explain it to me, it might give me an idea for my song'. The presidents describe the organisation's plans and goals in complimentary terms, with Lincoln comparing his freeing of the slaves to the NRA's provisions of 'freeing the slaves of the sweat shops . . . and giving the toilers a chance to enjoy the beauties of life'. Washington concludes that, with the NRA, 'the road to better times will be open again', which causes Powell to snap his fingers in inspiration: he's got his idea for the song. As he plays his piano, the presidents disappear, their job done. With characteristically overdone brio, Powell sings directly to the movie audience: 'there's a new day in view . . . there is hope in the hearts of men, all the world's on a way to a sunnier day for the road is open again.' It sounds like one of the Great Depression Musicals songs with a patriotic march beat added, which makes sense since it was penned by Sammy Fain and Irving Kahal, who wrote 'By a Waterfall' for *Footlight Parade*. At the end of the film, the audience is encouraged to sing along as the song's lyrics are superimposed upon the screen over a montage that includes images of people shopping in a crowded store, speeding railroads, farmers threshing wheat, the Statue of Liberty, the US Capitol, and a clip of Roosevelt smiling and taking off his hat as massed voices and the lyrics on the screen proclaim: 'BROTHER DO YOUR SHARE!' The last image, very similar to the images seen near the end of *Footlight Parade*, is a snapshot of a smiling Roosevelt superimposed over a waving American flag. Though its promotion of the NRA is sincere, *The Road Is Open Again* also serves as excellent marketing for the Warner Bros. Great Depression Musicals.

Even MGM, headed by Mayer, Hollywood's most influential Republican, contributed an NRA short. Comedian Jimmy Durante, billed as 'an eminent authority on the NRA', hosted its clip. He appears on a small stage, with an NRA 'We Do Our Part' flag behind him, singing and gesticulating at the audience with his usual charmingly gruff vaudeville energy: 'you and you and you and you, you've got a president now, he gave the land a new deal . . . put shoulders to the plow, he gave us what we asked for, now pay him back somehow!' With a goofy smile and the cornball gesture of placing his hand to his heart, Durante closes with: 'if the old name of Roosevelt makes the old heart throb, you take this message straight from the president and give a man a job!' Durante stops singing, steps off the stage, and interacts with his audience. He asks a banker if he drives himself to work; the banker says he doesn't and offers Durante a cigar. 'Keep your cigar and hire a chauffeur, keep a man from being a loafer!', Durante shoots back, and proceeds to steal all the cigars from the banker's pocket and place them in his own. Durante also tells an exterminator in the audience (played by Moe Howard, one of the future Three Stooges) to make sure he offers his workers 'a nice weekend vacation', a benefit accruing from the shorter working hours mandated by the NRA. Once again the image of the president appears as Durante raises the NRA flag at the back of the stage to reveal an oil portrait of Roosevelt adorned by an American flag.

Newsreels, usually shown before all feature films, also provided generous publicity for the NRA during the summer of 1933. Pathé's *Roosevelt Asks for Your Cooperation* featured Roosevelt explaining the concept behind the NRA, as various American families representing a diversity of ages and classes (but not races) listen closely and nod their heads. At the end of Roosevelt's speech, one father surrounded by his family remarks: 'well, dear, it looks as if we have the right man in the White House. He sure is leading the country to better times.' His wife agrees. In Pathé's newsreel *Nation Unites to Support Roosevelt*, several leaders of well-known national businesses including IBM endorse the NRA's aims, while *Blue Eagle Wings Way Over Nation* featured Roosevelt administration members, including General Hugh S. Johnson, asking for the nation's co-operation. *NRA Spirit Sweeps Nation!* included numerous shots of the NRA insignia in shop windows around the country, including at theatres. In this clip, Sol Rosenblatt, the man charged with writing the NRA code for the motion picture industry, was allowed more time than anyone else in the preceding films to communicate Hollywood's views on the topic. 'Every group in the motion-picture industry has pledged the president . . . that not only will the motion-picture industry immediately write and enforce its own codes under the [NRA], but will extend every facility from every group and division to enforce all of the codes.' Universal and Hearst Monotone also released highly complimentary newsreels lauding the accomplishments of Roosevelt's famous first 100 days. This spirit of optimistic co-operation and enthusiasm from Hollywood, particularly the major studios, did not last long.

The summer and fall of 1933 saw much additional promotion of the NRA in the media.[11] On the day in September when it was announced that every theatre in the country was prefacing its offerings with an NRA emblem, the Knapinski family of Milwaukee, WI, 'enthusiastic supporters of the President and the NRA', named their child Franklin Delano Blue Eagle Knapinski. Popular bandleader Phil Spitalny wrote a march saluting the NRA. The NRA's publicity committee asked legendary Broadway songwriter George M. Cohan, whom James Cagney would win an Oscar for portraying roughly a decade later, to contribute 'a new patriotic ditty' hailing the NRA for a national radio broadcast. The clamour over the NRA even attracted screenwriter, actress and sex symbol Mae West to weigh in on the situation. For her, the NRA code did 'not go far enough'. She recommended a 'special code for bachelor girls' in light of the fact that they have more time at their disposal since they are working less:

> Men friends: no single woman shall have more than three male admirers – one 'steady', one tall, dark and handsome and one for laughs. This would pass the men around more [just like the NRA passed around jobs more] and give deserving girls a break.

> Gifts from men: A girl shall take no more than she can get. These shall be limited, however, to jewelry, motor cars, flowers, furs and candy.

> Entertainment: She shall do what her escort wants her to do, go where he wants to go, except when she would like to do something different.

This avalanche of free promotion offered to Roosevelt and his NRA programme, which this chapter merely touches on, connotes something unfathomable in the present day. Even in the face of the events such as 9/11 and the 2008 economic crisis, one cannot imagine today's film industry and mass media enabling and voicing such fervent public support for government policies, however well-intentioned. It also gives context to the appearance of Roosevelt and the NRA Blue Eagle near the end of *Footlight Parade*. As scholar Giuliana Muscio found in her examination of Roosevelt's presidential papers, while the administration allowed film clips depicting the president in newsreels (and of course promotional NRA films), it drew the line at his moving image being included in feature films. In such situations, content could not be controlled by the White House, and it worried about potential associations with off-colour or just plain bad films. Roosevelt and his long-time press secretary Stephen Early understood the power of the president's image. They exhibited a mass media savvy no previous administration could come close to matching, but they also realised that such appearances could be overdone or even backfire on them, and closely guarded the president's presence in Hollywood films. Since only a painting of Roosevelt was featured in *Footlight*, it appears that Warner Bros. did not have to approve this through the Roosevelt White House, but as Muscio documents, all the major Hollywood studios, including Warners, wrote long and fawning letters to convince the president's handlers to approve moving images of Roosevelt inserted into their feature films and consistently failed.[12]

But Warners' identification with and enthusiasm for the NRA, the New Deal and even President Roosevelt would not endure. They would not long abide by the ethos of the NRA, even though their marketing and the appearance of Roosevelt and the Blue Eagle in *Footlight* proved their status as the NRA's biggest Hollywood supporters. Throughout 1933–5, they, along with their fellow film moguls, violated the spirit and letter of the NRA code, ensuring as much as possible that the economic pain and sacrifice of the Great Depression in Hollywood was visited upon artists and technicians, not studio heads and executives. They used the making of the code to attempt to cement and further the advantages they enjoyed as a vertically integrated oligopolistic business, preserving their unparalleled advantage in production, distribution and exhibition while offering little to other interests in the motion-picture industry. Such behaviour garnered considerable, mostly negative, notice around the country.

The major three players in the making of the NRA code from the government side became household names in Hollywood circles, their names regularly printed in bold headlines in show business periodicals and national newspapers between 1933 and 1935. First on the list was President Roosevelt, already a familiar figure, of course, but his keen interest in films and filmdom was only becoming known as the NRA motion picture code was being written. Roosevelt did not work directly on policy minutiae concerning Hollywood's code or the other hundreds of codes his government supervised. But he had to sign off on the final product; he had Hollywood friends, did comment on the film code during the process, and seemed particularly concerned about issues of compensation and whether independent interests in the industry were being served in a fair way compared with the major studios which largely dominated the proceedings. Roosevelt, a fan and student of film and Hollywood like no previous president, understood its significance not only in terms of campaigning and governing, but also in terms of the importance in a democracy of securing a diverse national mass media.

In 1923, before he became the governor of New York, he wrote a 29-page movie treatment for a proposed biopic of American Revolutionary War naval hero John Paul Jones.[13] Roosevelt, a former Assistant Secretary of the US Navy under President Wilson, was an avid student of naval history, had done research for a never-realised Jones biography and kept a bust of Jones in his office for years. He sent the treatment to mogul Adolph Zukor at Famous Players, where after a year of making the rounds of the studio, the idea, like most suggested to Hollywood by inexperienced screenwriters, came to nothing.

During his first year in office, according to *Variety*, Roosevelt viewed 1,327 film reels (a reel holds 15–20 minutes of film), '202 reels more than the average stenographer or clerk. It is also four times as many pictures as witnessed by Hoover and almost five times as many as Coolidge viewed when in office.' His film viewing proved so prodigious that the White House had to hire its own film operator from the Navy. Accompanied by his family or advisors, Roosevelt screened 83 features (about a third of those released within the period), 73 short subjects and '500 reels of news'. The two feature films of 1933 that dealt most directly with the subject of the Presidency, *Gabriel Over the White House* and *The Fighting President*, he saw twice. Roosevelt 'saw the most reelage when confronted with the gravest problems of the country' because he believed that viewing such footage 'provides him with a [sic] opportunity of getting closer to the people'. As his wife Eleanor wrote in 1938, Roosevelt's film habit comprised 'the one and only relaxation which my husband has'.

As pointed out previously, dozens of Hollywood stars attended Roosevelt's 1933 inaugural, and this trend continued throughout his four elected terms. He enjoyed hosting film denizens for his White House dinners, such as Melvyn and Helen Gahagan Douglas, Douglas Fairbanks, Jr and early Screen Actors Guild president Eddie Cantor, as well as several studio heads including Harry and Jack Warner and Darryl Zanuck. 'Roosevelt showed no signs of being dazzled by Hollywood glamour', concluded journalist Ronald Brownstein, in his book documenting connections between the White House and Hollywood. 'His attitude toward it was entirely utilitarian. He manipulated the stars and the studio fathers the way he manipulated Congress and his own bureau-cracy.' The denouement of the code-writing process and Roosevelt's post-1933 actions concerning the film industry confirm Brownstein's observation.

In May 1933, soldier, lawyer and manufacturer Gen. Hugh S. Johnson became the man Roosevelt put in charge of the NRA.[14] The native Oklahoman, aged 51 when appointed, was a close friend of Roosevelt intimate and advisor Bernard Baruch, and had previously served in World War I with Baruch on the War Industries Board, which co-ordinated and oversaw the production and purchase of war materiel during World War I. In its marshalling of national economic output, the NRA 'patterned' itself on the War Industries Board to an extent, according to historian Martin Rubin. This probably served as one reason why Johnson was chosen for the job. In newsreels, Johnson appeared dour, heavily scripted and perhaps a little soused. Within the administra-tion he was known for a fondness for drink and for abundant and creative cursing, as well as for memorable if undecipherable aphorisms. At its outset, he perhaps naively predicted that the NRA would 'eliminate eye-gouging and knee-groining and ear-chewing in business'. He understood early on the daunt-ing task of organising the affairs of hundreds of industries under the aegis of the federal government: 'It will be red fire at first and dead cats afterward.' His prognosis proved largely correct over the next two years. As the *Los Angeles Times* remarked, 'Johnson will have the most extensive powers ever wielded by one man over the private business enterprise of the nation'. Its front page above-the-fold bold headline nicknamed him 'Dictator for Industry', probably reflecting the *Times*' right-wing-leaning distaste for the organisation he led.[15] Another important facet of Johnson's job was deciding when it would prove useful to bring Roosevelt into NRA code negotiations (usually only on crucial hard-fought issues where his advocacy could urge executives to compromise for the sake of the country), and when to shield him. With the various very public controversies surrounding the motion-picture code during 1933–4, this proved a particularly important segment of his remit.

Sol A. Rosenblatt, a Harvard Law graduate, former lawyer for the Democratic National Committee and current lawyer for Columbia Pictures, became the NRA Deputy Administrator supervising the fashioning of Hollywood's code and its administration.[16] He also handled the writing of several codes for other amusement industries. Relatively young (32 in 1933) and armed with an ability to represent himself and his cause well on film, Rosenblatt possessed enough inside experience to play a sharp psychological game in his quest to investigate and regulate Hollywood's business practices. Well before the code became law, he became known in the trades as 'Rosy'. A *Variety* feature enti-tled 'Rosy Knows Too Much' painted a picture of Rosenblatt and his assistant holding court in a five-room suite at the luxurious Beverly Wilshire hotel as he grilled various film industry representatives (including studio moguls), his interrogation style supposedly taking on an effective amalgamation of 'Father Confessor' and 'Big Bad Wolf'. The act evidently worked, with many executives 'crying copper' and 'spilling everything' concerning their Hollywood brethren.

Variety also reported that Rosenblatt was aided in his film industry research by NRA 'undercover investigators' compiling reports on Hollywood practices in the preceding months, which enabled him to 'surprise the picture magnates with his intricate knowledge of the industry'. Whether such NRA skulduggery really existed or just represented mogul paranoia was never substantiated. With hundreds of industries to administer, it stretches credulity to imagine the NRA sending spies in the opening months of the organisation's existence to one of the hundreds of industries they would have to supervise. Rosenblatt smartly never denied such rumours. He also seemed to possess a realistic understanding of Hollywood's political dynamics and how they would fit into the construction of the NRA code. In August, when show business periodicals and Hollywood execs unanimously insisted a final code agreement was imminent, Rosenblatt alone told *Variety* that he believed 'the industry is in a muddle and has not even gotten into preliminary work on a code formula', an astute and largely confirmed prediction.

The writing of the NRA motion-picture code provoked a fierce power struggle within the industry, the most contentious since independent filmmakers fled west in the 1910s to evade the fees and lawsuits of Edison's Trust. Such rancour was not surprising, as the scope of the job was daunting – according to Rosenblatt, it took '276 classes of labor and employers to make a single motion picture'.[17] The inner workings of Hollywood had never been codified in such a precise fashion. Every segment of the industry, from the moguls and the creative workers in Hollywood to the nationwide distributors and theatre owners realised they needed to manoeuvre quickly to seal the best deal for themselves in the code as early as possible. In addition, each group aggressively made the case for its interests in the public arena, trying to sway general opinion to its side. Industry rivalries and resentments brewing for decades rose to the surface and became public knowledge.

From the start, the major film companies dominated the proceedings, with Harry especially, as well as Jack Warner, intimately involved.[18] Will Hays and his MPPDA attorney initiated the code-writing process during June 1933, taking recommendations in private from 'producing heads' (heads of production at the major studios), drawing up a preliminary version of the code that Rosenblatt would later refine. This so-called 'Hays group' set the precedent for the big eight studios being in charge, with all other groups coming to them and making requests for what they wanted to see enacted. This situation could not conceivably have gone another way. With their strong vertically integrated structures in place, the major studios enjoyed an oligopolistic control of the American film market, and would be picking up the majority of the tab for NRA code reforms. To a large extent, they *were* the industry, and they naturally would not countenance any reforms that challenged their hegemony.

Independent exhibitors and distributors, as well as actors and other creative and contracted studio personnel, soon realised that the major studios would not be looking out for their best interests and would in fact attempt to drive their salary and benefits downwards. Consequently, they did their best to lobby for their own provisions into the code, with varying degrees of success. For example, representatives from the Academy of Motion Picture Arts and Sciences (AMPAS), the Hollywood company union (supposedly) representing actors, meeting with the 'Hays group' in July, asked for a cessation of the practice of loaning out actors, an action rumoured to be also favoured by the Roosevelt administration. AMPAS further asked for a lowering of production work to 48 hours per week, a significant drop but still above NRA mandates for a working week. Producers refused both requests immediately, proving once again the Academy's general impotence. The *Hollywood Reporter*, which generally took the viewpoint of the major studios, reported that Academy representatives hoped NRA provisions would 'prevent unscrupulous fly-by-night' independent film producers 'from producing "quickie" pictures for ridiculously low costs by taking advantage of the employees on both salaries and long hours of work'. The 'Hays group' didn't mind if such policies eliminated some of their competition, especially competition that didn't have to pay for the expenses of running a major film studio, in the name of producing economic fairness under the insignia of the NRA. The major studios took care to ensure that the code-writing process retained a veneer of fairness for all film interests involved, but made sure that major decisions went the way that they desired.

Production costs represented one early concern that lasted throughout the code-writing process.[19] With salary costs increasing due to NRA regulations, the salaries of Hollywood's best paid workers, particularly actors, were singled out for contributing to rising production expenses even though early NRA regulations left such higher salaries unaltered. Between 1929 and 1933, according to the NRA's research, production costs decreased by 35 per cent, but salaries only went down 16 per cent, and overall, salaried employees (usually the most famous and valuable employees) took up three times more in production costs than hourly studio workers. Some outside observers felt that the film industry's supposedly bloated salaries had contributed to the run of receiverships and bankruptcies suffered by major studios during the Great Depression. NRA rules held forth on minimum salaries, but said nothing concerning maximum salaries. Creating a day of reckoning for movie stars by reining in their remuneration seemed to constitute a major goal for the studios during the construction of the code, something the studios had wanted to do for years. And if this were to be executed correctly under the guise of the NRA, the moguls could cast such a move as a patriotic act.

What's more, 'picture scouts' visiting Washington to discuss the NRA code during the summer of 1933 reported back that government figures seemed interested in maximum salaries and were considering looking into the matter, especially after reports cited that over 350 Hollywood figures earned yearly incomes over $100,000 (about $1.85 million in today's money). *Variety* predicted in July that 'the [decadent] Roman salary day won't last long'. 'We have got to reduce the present high top level and increase the ridiculously low levels now existing in this industry, in salaries as in everything else', insisted Harry Warner. 'I believe you can increase the number of people to be employed by 20 to 30 per cent and not use any more money than is being used now.' And who in the studio's present employ would take the salary cuts to increase employment without raising overall payroll costs? Certainly not extravagantly paid executives like Harry and Jack Warner, as was proven when they unilaterally excused themselves from the industry-wide salary cuts instituted during March and April 1933. The other highest paid employees were movie stars.

But not everyone bought the premise that actors were mostly responsible for out-of-control Hollywood budgets. In one meeting between Rosenblatt and many of the studio moguls, Paramount head Adolph Zukor accused Mayer and MGM of being the principal cause of rising budgets, with their policy of 'pay[ing] any price without regard' for talent, and raising production standards with luxurious and elaborate set designs for films like *Grand Hotel* (1932). Mayer countered that MGM only desired 'to acquire personalities and material that would assure box office success'. Rosenblatt himself blamed the talent raiding between studios (particularly by Darryl Zanuck at Twentieth Century) for contributing to soaring industry expenses, and hoped to secure provisions against it within the NRA code. The general public did not have the facility to judge such industry-centric talent issues, but they could easily understand the enormity of the salaries of movie stars such as James Cagney and his studio bosses Harry and Jack Warner when they totalled several times what President Roosevelt made per year during a time of economic dislocation. The salary issue continued boiling throughout 1933 and 1934.

In the early going of fights over the code, Warner Bros. showed conflicting if not hypocritical behaviour by simultaneously being out front in their support of the NRA, yet questioning whether their company would take part in the code.[20] In July, they threatened to leave not just the code-writing process, but the MPPDA, if Will Hays used the auspices of the NRA to dictate too many of the terms of the industry. No other studio made such public threats against the NRA. The brothers Warner chaffed at accusations made against them of 'star-raiding', and Hays' initial draft of the code included a provision outlawing such behaviour. The year before, in a widely publicised case, Warners scooped up the contracts of stars Ruth Chatterton, Kay Francis and William Powell before their previous studios had a chance to make an offer and before their contracts had formally expired, a protocol usually followed in Hollywood. In addition, as mentioned in Chapter 3, Warners secretly employed Busby Berkeley during the evenings for *Footlight Parade* and offered him a long-term contract while he concurrently worked during daytime hours on a musical for Samuel Goldwyn. This situation created an intriguing conundrum: Warners insisted on the right to not follow industry protocol when hiring stars away from other studios, undermining other studios' contracts, yet vehemently attacked those actors in their own studio who dared to question the terms of their original contracts once they became successful stars who helped the studio earn hundreds of thousands if not millions of dollars. Apparently, the sanctity of contract did not go both ways in Burbank.

Later in 1933, Goldwyn brought Jack Warner before an MPPDA meeting, hoping to sanction and punish his studio's behaviour in the matter of (as Goldwyn put it) 'pirating' Berkeley. The MPPDA refused to act, and Goldwyn's reaction made the front page of the *Los Angeles Times*. 'When Jack Warner was brought before the producers association to explain his bootlegging, his answer was "What can I do about it?"', Goldwyn complained. 'Mr. Warner could do nothing about it and the [MPPDA] can do nothing about Mr. Warner. So I resigned [from the MPPDA].' He said he refused 'to be a member of any organization that harbors and protects the Warner brothers'. Their studio peers were clearly not enamoured with the Warners. In July, *Variety* described them in a headline as 'pretty grouchy', and reported that 'in big membership circles', probably meaning in the eyes of their fellow MPPDA members, 'the brothers from time to time have been regarded as greedy children who have tried to grab all of the popsicles'. As cantankerous underdogs who worked for decades before becoming the last company to vertically integrate and join the ranks of the other major studios, and who worked on lower film budgets than most of their competitors, the Warners were much more comfortable going along with their own policy, and not aligning with others. Harry Warner, who represented his company at the NRA code-writing negotiations during 1933, was 'vehement' that Warner Bros. would only be represented by itself, and 'declared' his company 'off codes until the right one came along and there was a cessation of selfish motives'. The sometimes vague and confusing dual nature of his message to fellow studio heads is evident in this statement made at an industry meeting about the NRA code in August 1933:

> We are not seeking anything more than anybody else's [*sic*]. We are willing to cooperate to see everyone get hearings in Washington. If that

fair deal is not provided I am going to fight. We are not against anything.
We are in favor of everything.

Such contradictory sentences pressed together in close proximity might have
been plucked directly from the absurd proclamations of the politicians portrayed and mocked by the Marx Brothers in *Duck Soup*, a hit Paramount
film released during code negotiations in the fall of 1933. In the end, Warners
joined with its MPPDA brethren in writing the code, especially when it became
clear that the major studios would evince dominance over its results, allowing
them to enjoy new controls over talent and agents that they had longed to have
for years. And even after the Warners signed on to the final code, they would
continue to insist on maintaining a level of independence in their actions; such
behaviour, while irritating to others, was firmly ensconced within the long-
term personality of the company.

In an 8 August 1933 speech at the New York Bar Association that marked
the first official industry meeting concerning the NRA code, Rosenblatt set
his goals for the enterprise. He said he favoured a single code, not separate
ones for production, distribution and exhibition since those interests were
intricately linked. The major studios also owned major interests in all three
segments. Rosenblatt stressed a single code because in the previous few weeks,
at least seven industry leaders had written their own draft of the NRA code,
including Hays, Mayer, AMPAS' president, and Abram Myers, head of Allied.
Every one of the seven spoke briefly at the event. Rosenblatt emphasised that
he wanted the industry to write its own code, so that the government did not
have to step in as it had threatened to do if the process were not completed by
the end of the month. As the *Hollywood Reporter* put it a few days later, 'it is
best for the industry to give itself a little spanking, rather than have the government administer the whipping'. Rosenblatt also recommended that the issue of
film censorship, which was in the press frequently because of groups pointing
out recent violations of the 1930 Hays Code, be considered separately from the
NRA code process, a position the major studios supported.

Rosenblatt further 'mentioned that while he had not invited labor representatives to the meeting he was negotiating with such leaders separately and
their aims would be considered in the code'.[21] Not an auspicious situation for
labour: the major business interests of the film industry were already presenting their plans in a public context with labour pointedly left out of the proceedings. It represented another sign that, in the writing of the code, the major
studios' interests would reign paramount.

At Rosenblatt's New York meeting, he assembled three committees comprising
at least a dozen well-known industry figures each, in the fields of production,
distribution and exhibition, charging them with drawing up proposals for

code provisions dealing with their segment of the industry and asking them to identify any lingering controversies that could not be resolved within their committee.[22] These sessions were private, apparently not minuted or reported upon, and little is known about them other than that committee members and the witnesses they called worked day and night on their portion of the code for close to a month. All parties came together to share their progress and air differences with as many as 600 spectators from 12 to 15 September 1933 at the US Commerce Building in Washington, DC. Most code matters were ironed out by the committees, but several issues took months to resolve (and some would not be resolved even when the code became law in December). Rosenblatt broke the industry groups into smaller sessions, hoping to find compromises by grouping different personalities and segments, to no avail. On 25 September, after what the *Los Angeles Times* termed 'another weekend of factional bickering', Rosenblatt told the conferees that he would write the contested parts of the code himself, trying to work out fair compromises between positions. The day before, the *Times* proclaimed that the code would be sent to Roosevelt for approval in less than a week. Two days later, it reported that motion picture industry insiders conceded 'the end . . . is nowhere in sight'. On 30 September, registering the brewing resentment in Hollywood, MGM placed a striking two-page ad in *Motion Picture Herald* featuring its Leo the Lion mascot standing with his fist in the air next to a message in tall bold lettering: 'Gentlemen! Quality cannot be coded!'. On 2 October in Washington, Rosenblatt announced his interpretation of how the controversial issues in the code should be resolved, and, as reported by *Film Daily*, 'the independent delegates, representing [independent] producers, distributors and exhibitors, broke out in open revolt. They waxed emphatic . . . that [Rosenblatt's] provisions were unfair and workable.' Actors, writers and agents soon declared similar sentiments.

The issues that held up industry approval of the NRA code were numerous.[23] Most centred on the balance of power and profit between major studios and independent forces, as well as highly paid creative workers. A few days following their walkout on Rosenblatt, the independents wrote him a group-signed letter arguing that 'the proposed code fails to deal with many major abuses that affect the industry', fails to prevent 'oppression of small enterprises', and 'tends to promote and perpetuate unfair and monopolistic practices'. Unsurprisingly, block booking emerged as a major issue. Many theatres, especially those represented by Abram Myers' Allied association, wanted to purchase films in open competition, to screen quality major studio films without being forced to show their less desirable product, and to enjoy the right to buy films from independent producers as well. Rosenblatt countered by noting that his plan allowed theatres to 'reject 15% of the feature films assigned [by the major studios] and [that they were] required to pay for only half of those eliminated'. But what he refused to recognise was that such an arrangement meant that major studios continued dominating and dictating what each block-booked theatre screened over the course of the year, and forced them to pay for pictures they did not want.

In addition, the major studios wanted to outlaw double features, bingo games held before screenings known as 'Screeno', and 'the giving away of premiums' such as dishes and other prizes to increase attendance.[24] The majors apparently felt that such activities detracted from the value and class of their output. Also, double features brought in less money per film, since they took up twice the theatre time of a solo attraction, slicing in half repeat performances of the day's programme and depressing box-office returns. The studios also seemed worried that a blanket exhibitor policy of double features would necessitate an impossibly expensive doubling of production costs to meet the demand, although the NRA, focused on creating more jobs, seemed to relish that prospect. Such major studio policies were in some ways counterproductive – local theatres resorted to tactics such as double features and Screeno to bring in more audiences to see the studio's films, from which, of course, the studio retained a percentage of the proceeds. Eventually, in August 1934, in a move for which the NRA took partial (and perhaps undeserved) credit, the major studios capitulated on this issue when a majority of them voted to allow double features, but not the other promotional gimmicks previously mentioned. *Variety* claimed the majors mostly united on this to 'keep the [blue] eagle's talons off . . . any other regulations of trade customs'. Giuliana Muscio surmised that this deal represented a quid pro quo, allowing independent exhibitors their double features if they stayed silent on the issue of block booking, which a perusal of *Variety* during the fall of 1934 and all of 1935 indicates that they largely did.

In this environment, independent exhibitors walked a fine and difficult line. There weren't enough independent features for them to show 52 weeks per year, and the independent studios did not possess the resources to promote a film as effectively as the majors did, which usually meant they made less money than major studio films. At some point, then, the independent exhibitors were forced by the structure of the market to deal with the majors, often on a regular basis on disadvantageous terms. And if they weren't affiliated year-round in a relationship with a major studio, they usually received a film on its third, fourth or even fifth run, months after their local block-booked theatres showed the film, if the major studios' distributors even allowed an indie exhibitor to show a particular studio's films (and sometimes they didn't). No wonder such theatres employed giveaways and games to lure customers to their theatres showing a months-old film. Sometimes, as detailed in a government hearing in the spring of 1934, independent exhibitors were only allowed to show major studio films if they purchased large numbers of shorts along with the features.

The owner of the independent Eagle theatre in New York complained that Columbia Pictures made him buy 976 shorts in order to have the privilege of screening some of their features – he claimed it would take two and half years to use all those shorts in his programmes. But he did it because he felt he had little choice. Independent exhibitors from around the country at the hearing testified that 'unfair practices used in metropolitan areas . . . are prevalent even in the sticks'.[25] Rosenblatt's code reforms helped a little around the edges for this demographic, but largely preserved the heavily slanted status quo.

Rosenblatt inserted safeguards into the code that he insisted would provide 'ample protection' for independents. NRA grievance boards would be created to arbitrate disputes between indies and the majors. 'The code is intended to aid and assist small enterprises and give them a forum for the first time in the history of the industry to which they can come for aid and assistance.' But signs were not auspicious for those independents. The code would largely keep block booking as the industry standard, enshrined by government decree. Rosenblatt was asking the independents to trust him, but if the code-writing process was major studio-dominated, it did not bode well for what would transpire for independents when they complained to the code-mandated grievance boards, and they knew it.

News reports about the code negotiations tended to view the objecting independent cohort as 'insurgents' (a loaded word), selfishly keeping the industry from agreement, when they were actually fighting to have control over their own livelihoods. As the *Los Angeles Times* reported: 'Contrasted with the position of the insurgents, major [studios] and [their] affiliated exhibitors indicated more or less complete satisfaction with Rosenblatt's efforts.' Well of course they did. Their way of doing business was preserved, while independents would be forced to fight on for their issues after the lopsided code was passed. 'Neutral observers inclined all along to give the insurgents a break, feel they are entitled to more consideration than they are receiving', surmised *Variety* in an article entitled 'Indies Booted Their Chances at Code Hearings'. 'The indies, to date, have not only allowed themselves to be out-generaled, over-pressured and what-not by the majors, but have deliberately blundered and muffed tactical points.'

The drive by studio moguls to pin the blame for rising production costs on actors, and the attempt to reduce actors' pay cheques via the NRA code, spurred the thespians into even more action.[26] Already in 1933, they had set up the rudiments of the Screen Actors Guild (SAG), but the lack of respect shown actors during the code debacle helped bring many more of them into the fold. If actors were going to be blamed by the moguls for the economic troubles within the industry they ostensibly controlled, the actors were going to fight back by renouncing their AMPAS representatives and signing on for SAG en masse. Hollywood thespians mounted a spirited publicity campaign, pelting Washington and local NRA representatives with telegrams, scheduling mass meetings and insisting that salaries should be limited only by the free market.

Another factor in the mounting SAG rebellion was the majors' lack of interest and initiative in creating a system of impartial arbitration and mediation between actors and the studios. Rumours in the press signalled possibilities of this happening, but nothing transpired. Instead, as film historian Danae Clark found, 'the result was a conflationary discourse' carried on within the industry and trade magazine journalism 'whereby an actor's degree of cooperation with the studios got translated into his or her degree of patriotism and support for Roosevelt's policies' and the film industry in general. Such tactics worked earlier in 1933 when most contract employees approved their own temporary salary cuts, but such arguments proved far less convincing months later during the final weeks of NRA code negotiations.

When the preliminary version of the code came out without provisions for arbitration or mediation, this provided another reason for actors to seek protection by forming their own union. On 4 October, shortly after the indies walked out on Rosenblatt, almost every major Hollywood star gathered for a meeting at a private home, and among those switching from AMPAS to SAG representation were Warner stars Cagney, Paul Muni and Ann Harding, joined by such luminaries as Gary Cooper, Groucho Marx, Robert Montgomery and many more. Four days later, 1,200 actors and writers gathered at the El Capitan, one of Hollywood's premiere first-run theatres, for a joint meeting between SAG and the Screen Writers Guild (SWG), to unite and bring even more publicity to their mutual cause. Stars were significant to the nascent SAG in terms of gaining publicity and power, but president Eddie Cantor stressed that their organisation needed to focus on the more quotidian members of their profession: 49 per cent of Hollywood actors made less than $2,000 per year, many had to purchase their own wardrobe and nearly all kicked back 10 per cent of their pay to an agent. Screenwriters were in much the same position as actors, as salaried studio employees threatened by initial NRA code provisions. Six weeks before the meeting, the SWG's executive board issued a statement proclaiming that the code 'declares war on the industrial workers' and will bring 'industrial peonage' to screenwriters. Many rejected AMPAS, signing on with the SWG, which grew to 750 members during its first year.

The El Capitan meeting successfully publicised actors and writers' problems with the code and the major studios in general. They were particularly alarmed by clauses 4 and 5 of the code, which meant to drive down their earning capabilities and contractual freedoms. The myriad provisions in these clauses promised to enhance the studios' long-held desires for more control over their workforce and the elimination of competition, firmly cementing into place the plantation aura that the major studios preferred in their hiring practices. For example, if the Agency Committee of the NRA code wished (five of the committee were major studio representatives, joined by an agent, actor, writer, director and technician), it could require all agents in Hollywood to register with it, and even permanently bar certain agents from the industry. Agents drove up employee salaries, particularly the most successful ones, and studios had wanted to place them under their thumbs for some time.[27] This represented a particularly bold power grab. It gave the major studios the opportunity for control over a class of motion-picture employees they did not hire or pay, since agents are compensated on the basis of a percentage of their client's earnings. This provision ostensibly sought to intimidate and even restrict agents, reducing potential competition and costs for the major studios.

An anti-talent-raiding clause in the NRA code, probably partly inspired by Warner Bros.' actions in this realm, further tipped the balance in the direction of the largest Hollywood studios. It mandated that no studio could make an offer to a salaried employee until the last 30 days of his contract, and allowed the home studio to always have a chance to match any offer. It also forbade any studio fomenting 'dissension, discord or strife' between another studio and its contracted employees in order to inspire an employee to be 'dissatisfied with his subsisting contract' (little recognition of the existence of women was present in code language). It forbade any 'large financial inducements' to sign contracts, sparing the major studios another expense. Also, as Laurence W. Beilenson, the legal counsel for the SWG and SAG during their early days, has written, 'for three to six months after the expiration of the employee's contract – the number of months depended on the size of the salary – the code, through a system of notification, gave the studio . . . what in effect amounted to a right of first refusal on the services of the actor, writer or director.' The major studios were particularly sensitive about 'star raiding' not only because it represented the loss of a star to competition (stars raised audience levels, increasing studios' exhibition profits), but also because such moves wasted months of expenses spent planning the pirated star's next films.

Another code provision attempted to assuage the fragile egos of studio chiefs and keep them and their services free from criticism. The code barred the 'defamation of competitors by falsely imputing to them dishonourable conduct, inability to perform contracts, questionable credit standing . . . or by the false disparagement of the grade and quality of their motion pictures or theatres'. Who knew that the tough Jewish immigrants and sons of immigrants who founded modern Hollywood were so sensitive at their core? In order to stem future Cagney-style contract rebellions, the code allowed the blackballing of any employee who 'has refused without just cause to render services under any contract of employment' if such action was approved by the Code Authority, another committee with a majority of its membership representing the eight major studios. Such laws and provisions did not prevent a contract employee from moving to another studio, but they did attempt to intimidate and pressure employees to stay with their current employer, no matter how unpleasant or unfair their working situation. They tilted the board even further against employees in the direction of Hollywood moguls and executives. Actors, as well as cameramen during this period, also protested that the NRA-mandated 48-hour week would not be applied to them; the studios obviously did not want to give up the crushing six- or seven-day weeks described by Cagney and Joan Blondell in the previous chapter.

Perhaps most odious of all to those gathered at the El Capitan, the so-called salary clause of the NRA code sought to place an industry-wide $100,000 yearly limit on all contract salaries, with $10,000 penalties assessed to violators. At the theatre and in a message sent to Roosevelt about the 'sinister provisions' of the proposed code, 'all the important stars' threatened to walk out of the industry for a year if the provision were made law. Screenwriter Oliver H. P. Garrett reminded the audience that the major studios 'had sold them a bill of goods during the 50 per cent emergency [cuts] period' in March 1933 and were attempting to sell them 'another bill of goods now'. Film star Frederic March used statistics to argue that the money paid to talent only comprised 40–50 per cent of production budgets. Unfortunately, he did not possess author Leo Rosten's statistics released later in the decade that demonstrated how major studio executives paid themselves at a rate higher than all other American executives except for one industry, when comparing their salaries to company profits. John Howard Lawson, avowed communist and first president of the Screen Writers Guild, shouted to the assembled crowd:

> The producers are not going to get away with it. We're going to fight. We won't allow them to place the burden for all their waste and inefficiency on to the creative talent which is responsible for every dollar brought into the box office. We must stop racketeering that is existing in this industry.[28]

The term 'racketeering' at the time was usually reserved by the press and federal law enforcement officials to describe the crimes of legendary gangsters such as Bonnie and Clyde and John Dillinger, who roamed, robbed and killed across middle America, particularly during 1933. The subtle reference and comparison made by Lawson almost certainly must have been purposeful.

In any case, the El Capitan event was successful, in terms of generating publicity about the creatives' worries about the impending NRA code, and in terms of membership recruitment. At the close of the evening, 183 new SAG members signed up, including three featured in the Warner Bros. Great Depression Musicals: Guy Kibbee, Ned Sparks and Warren William. The outcry by actors and writers against the code proposals, particularly its salary provision, seemed to succeed on at least one count; as a result of the protests and publicity, Rosenblatt was summoned to the White House in October to talk to officials there (but not to Roosevelt) about the 'legal aspects' of penalising excessive salaries. At the time, the outcry also seemed to succeed on another count: the uproar caused by SAG and SWG impelled the securing of last-minute code provisions for actor-producer and writer-producer committees that promised more significant representation in the creation of 'fair practices'. 'They were included in the final code in an effort to quiet the artists', reported labour historian Murray Ross, and the ruse worked. But after enactment of the code, the committees never met or accomplished anything, because the major studio executives refused to name their members of the committees for seven months. After they finally did so, the studio representatives declined to put across proposals or participate in meetings, despite the actors and writers sending protest telegrams concerning the situation to President Roosevelt. In the end, the actor and writer code committees amounted to just more cynicism and effrontery from major Hollywood film producers.[29]

Each side continued to militate against the other in the press concerning the salary debate during October, trying to win public opinion and the favour of the Roosevelt administration.[30] Gen. Johnson, while supposedly taking 'no formal stand' on the issue, said that he had been told that compensation for Hollywood actors was 'grotesque' and that 'financial differences in the industry can be traced in large measure to the payroll burdens'. Rosenblatt argued that huge studio salaries 'result in unfair and destructive competition'. Johnson also added, without naming a source, that 'less than 500 persons had been drawing 51 per cent of the total salaries paid by studios'. Ironically, Johnson seemed to favour the salary clause in numerous press interviews, while also questioning the legality of the NRA ruling on maximum salaries. Eddie Cantor, the new president of the Screen Actors Guild, responded: 'Studio statistics will disclose that only 10 per cent of the cost of every picture goes to salaries. We, the actors, would like to know where the other 90 per cent goes.' Lester Cowan, president of AMPAS (and Rosenblatt's brother-in-law), in a too-little-too-late attempt to remain relevant to the creatives his organisation claimed to represent, called the proposed salary provision 'outrageous'. He would resign his position before approval of the NRA code; the events of 1933 so rattled AMPAS that it briefly considered eliminating the Academy Awards presentation for 1934. On 15 October, in what looked like an orchestrated attempt to make the actors' side of the argument look bad, the *Los Angeles Times* published the weekly salaries of dozens of top Hollywood stars from Greta Garbo ($9,000) to James Cagney (wrongly pegged at $2,800 – it should have been $4,000), with no notice made of high executive and management salaries. Later that month, in another seeming attempt to dispel sympathy for the stars' position in code disputes, the *Times* published a front-page story in its entertainment section with little attribution or specific names concerning film stars fighting 'for each other's servants' because 'faithful retainers' were supposedly 'scarce in Hollywood'.

Rosenblatt reminded the press and actors protesting the code that the salary provision would apply to 'executives as well as employees'. While this was ostensibly true in the provision's wording, it represented a stretch to believe that this would prove true in reality. Under the code, the decision on whether a salary was excessive would be made by the Code Authority, a committee of ten high-ranking industry members. Five of those ten would always be affiliated with the major studios, whether in the production, distribution or exhibition fields (for example, when the code was approved in November, Harry Warner served in this capacity). The other five were 'unaffiliated producers, distributors and exhibitors', one of which, starting in November, would be a representative from Universal Pictures. It meant that at least six of the ten Code Authority members were part of the big eight studios that ruled the roost in Hollywood, and a spring 1934 report by a government review board argued that, when taking into account the distributors and exhibitors serving on the authority who did most or all of their business with the major studios through block-booking arrangements, the number of members of the authority affiliated with the major studios was actually eight. Would major studio executives (or those whose livelihoods depended on the major studios) vote against the salaries of fellow studio executives, no matter how disproportionate those salaries were compared to those of executives in other industries, or even within their own? Would even an independent exhibitor wishing to have favourable terms on the most profitable major studio films bite the hand that feeds? It seems doubtful.[31]

In a story usually pitched in the press as related to the investigation of motion-picture salaries, the Federal Trade Commission announced in November that it was 'asking 2000 companies to furnish data on the salaries of their execs and directors'.[32] The point that such coverage seemed to make was that it wasn't just Hollywood denizens being picked on concerning high salaries. But there seems to be no evidence from the *Times* or other newspapers that executives or high-paid employees from other industries had their salaries dragged before the public as film stars did in what looked to be a deliberate attempt to undermine and intimidate them. Also, none of this publicity noted that, as this book has demonstrated in its analysis of Cagney's salary negotiations, big pay cheques earned by stars (and probably executives as well) usually reflected their market value – how their skills, image and personality brought more customers to the box office. While studio executives brooked no compunction about rewarding themselves on the basis of criteria such as profits accruing to their companies, they strongly resisted paying the market value of the creatives in their employ for the same reasons.

Further curtailing of creatives' rights were announced. In early November, *Variety* reported:

> The committees designated by the code authority will be instructed to disencourage . . . the retaining by film interests of high pressure lawyers to rep[resent] them at [Code Authority] hearings. The schedule calls for shutting off such lawyers; in this way it is expected the actor or exhibitor will be forced to realize that he could have done a better job before the Code Authority or grievance board than the barrister whom he retained.

No creatives (actors, writers, directors, cinematographers, etc.) or other non-executives were represented on the Code Authority, as originally laid out in the code, unless a 5–5 deadlock existed on a certain issue, in which case 'one representative' of that 'class' of employees could temporarily serve on the Authority to break the tie.[33] Imagine the situation if you were an actor taking a grievance to this board, filled with representatives of your bosses, with no peer of yours in attendance. What would be the chances of getting a fair hearing in this system, especially when lawyers were not supposed to be brought to such hearings? The system appeared designed to intimidate resistors or 'insurgents' from bringing their issues for consideration. Once again, in numerous ways, the deck was stacked in favour of the majors and their preferred ways of doing business from the beginning. In this instance and others, the idea that management and employees both needed to sacrifice under the NRA had never been taken seriously by the executives.

Meanwhile, as the major studios were violating the spirit if not the letter of the NRA provisions they vowed to uphold in their code dealings, Jack Warner served as chairman of the NRA State Recovery Board, issuing numerous appeals on behalf of the organisation.[34] The appeal garnering the most coverage was his 'concerted drive against . . . rackets and profiteering under the guise of the Blue Eagle insignia' that pretended to serve NRA dictates only to 'coerce [illegal] membership fees from employers and employees alike'. A fine of $500 and six months' imprisonment could follow for 'any person falsely representing himself to be operating under the agreement'. Some of these 'racketeering groups' and 'protective associations', Jack claimed, falsely used the NRA imprimatur to justify illegal price increases. The groups also promised employers 'protection' from 'labor troubles of any kind', a similar situation to that of the Hollywood major studios, which paid millions in bribes to mobsters William Browne and Willie Bioff – thugs who disguised themselves as IATSE union's top officers and enacted a forced labour peace through intimidation. Ironically, at roughly the same time, IATSE and the Motion Picture Machine Operators union sent telegrams to Roosevelt and Johnson protesting the major studios' use of NRA Blue Eagle imagery in their marketing since they were simultaneously 'conducting a campaign to destroy the principle of collective bargaining' in their NRA code machinations. By October 1933, the *Motion Picture Herald* reported that Jack had 'settled eight incipient strikes and taken action on a mere 3,914 complaints of NRA violation as part of his chairman role'. Jack also urged California 'housewives and consumers' to 'save a job' by purchasing as many consumer goods as possible. The idea, further spread 'coast to coast' by Mary Pickford via NBC radio, the top network in the country, was that since industrial plants were making moves to hire idle workers to resuscitate the economy, consumers needed to 'do their part' to help the economy at local cash registers.

In the last month before Roosevelt signed the motion-picture code, tensions mounted. The major studios tried to beat back any last-minute challenges to the code they largely fashioned and dominated, while dissatisfied creatives and independent studios, distributors and exhibitors vowed to 'fight on and on' for what they felt to be fair treatment. At the same time, optimistic signs were sprouting in the economy at large after six months of the NRA's existence. Gen. Johnson announced in November that the NRA had put somewhere between 3 and 4 million Americans back to work, and statistics indicated that both industrial production and factory employment had climbed 25 per cent between March and December 1933, although inflation grew as well, with the cost of living rising 8 per cent in that same period. Statistics like these inspired *Time* to name Johnson as its man of the year and feature his portrait on the magazine's cover, a prestigious honour. However, subsequent historians have argued that much of the 1933 economic gains represented a temporary boomlet as companies bought materials and manufactured quickly before the NRA's wage and price controls kicked in. Historians also generally agree that the NRA did evince at least an initial positive effect, and kept the economy from atrophying further. In the film industry, for example, theatre attendance improved, and the *Motion Picture Herald* reported that, between April and September 1933, 598 theatres across the country had opened their doors for business, 'mostly reopenings of previously darkened houses', and 185 theatres were engaging in 'either new building or extensive reconditioning'. Cautious optimism was expressed in numerous movie trade magazines.[35]

Yet, fights and issues perpetrated by the code continued and increased.[36] On 27 October, the motion-picture code was sent to Johnson, appended with the signatures of 'virtually all the major producers and distributors' and the theatres affiliated with them. The salary clause was included, as was block booking. On the other side of the docket, according to the *Los Angeles Times*, the 'insurgent faction' of indies and creatives were 'uncompromisingly opposed' to the pact, making 'angry complaints' that 'Rosenblatt has yielded in every dispute to the majors'. Johnson, who also referred to the non-major studio participants in the code as 'insurgents', called the Hollywood code 'the most complex I've got' and expressed his full confidence in Rosenblatt, declaring that 'complaints of unfairness on Rosenblatt's part [are] entirely baseless and criticism of the code unjustified'. The *Times* predicted Roosevelt would sign the code 'within a few hours of it being received', but it took almost a month. On the day *Footlight Parade* premiered in Los Angeles, the *Times* wrote: 'The NRA tonight appeared headed for a blowoff over the motion-picture code with prospects for early promulgation of the agreement growing slimmer.' No other NRA code in the country experienced such delay between submission and approval. The reasons cited in the press included: further study of the legality and practicality of the salary clause, discussions concerning different wage scales for non-contract workers, and the President and his staff wishing to investigate whether the major studios had run roughshod over the concerns of the independents in fashioning the code, as the latter group protested.

The delay proved so vexing to the major studios that they threatened to back out of the entire deal if the code did not gain complete and immediate approval.[37] *Variety* reported in mid-November that high-ranking Hollywood executives wanted to 'demand . . . that the code be immediately submitted to President Roosevelt for signature, or that it be officially torn up'. 'In the event of any radical changes' that the President might insist upon before signing the document, the executives also insisted that they should 'be allowed to return to Washington in full force and state [their] own versions' of the code. Hearing reports that the major studios hoped the code would be 'tabled', government sources warned the industry that they 'had better dissipate all ideas of treating the code lightly and try and make it work or else the government is likely to hand [Hollywood] something far tougher than the [current] formula. This, it is concluded, might very likely be out and out federal regulation.' The producers had the code pretty much the way they wanted it, and did not want to countenance any backtalk, from independents or from Washington, DC. More than four months of meetings and negotiation had brought much impatience and frustration, but the major studios' behaviour in the final stretches did resemble that of spoilt children who want it their way or not at all. In late October, the *Times* reported that 'undue political influence has been charged against one or two picture companies in the framing of the code'. Could this new strategy of pressuring the Roosevelt administration to approve the film code by threatening to walk out have been promulgated by the brothers Warner, who not only were known in the industry for wanting 'all of the popsicles' for themselves, but had pulled a similar tactic and threatened to walk out on code negotiations during the summer? It seems possible that the *Variety* article had the politically-connected brothers in mind.

The major studios further argued in the press that the delay was costing the industry millions, and driving morale down.[38] 'Hundreds of deals' were supposedly suspended in distribution and exhibition, and a 'general uncertainty in production' reigned because of 'Washington's tardiness'. Some legitimacy clung to this argument: it was somewhat difficult to close deals when no one knew exactly how business would be conducted after the code was signed into law. But the changes were not going to be extreme – unless Roosevelt radically rewrote the code, which he had not done for the more than 700 codes already approved, the major studios would still be running the show both in Hollywood and along the vertically integrated pipeline to theatres. Also, the NRA had already set policy on maximum wages and hours, so anyone trying to surmise the expenses for a new theatre or film-related company would have a good idea what to expect. It was noted ruefully in the press that Roosevelt had recently signed a dozen NRA industry codes into law on the same day, while the film code lay dormant on his desk for two weeks. Sources, probably from the major studios, complained that double features and giveaways at theatres had risen 25 per cent since the code had been sent to Washington, and that box-office returns faded 5 per cent in the same period. But with reports of the time also indicating an increase in ticket sales not seen since before the Great Depression, it was difficult to sympathise with such contradictory figures. Roosevelt was being blamed by Hollywood for the code delay, but the real problem was that the code-writing process had exposed an unusually combative and divided industry. Perhaps Washington was not so tardy as the moguls were intransigent. Roosevelt and Johnson obviously felt they needed to take extra time with the film code to ensure they were not caught approving a lopsided document that codified bad business policies, sowed further distress and unfairness, and made the government complicit in the bargain.

A final attempt by the creatives to alter the emphasis of the still-unapproved film code occurred over the Thanksgiving holiday during the last days of November.[39] Popular screen comedian, Roosevelt acquaintance and SAG president Eddie Cantor visited the President at his Warm Springs, GA retreat, along with writers Fannie Hurst and Robert Sherwood, the latter of whom had served as a presidential speech writer for Roosevelt. Some in Hollywood groused about this; the *Motion Picture Herald* argued that a more experienced film executive should have had the President's ear at this late junction in code negotiations, instead of a 'merry, whimsical song-and-dance man'. Naturally, the salary clause issue came up. Cantor made some personal and unrealistic speculation about the possibility of spreading out the overall economic effect of actors' high salaries by paying them smaller weekly amounts over the course of a decade, a notion that when reported in *Variety* was virulently opposed by Cantor's own union. This concept did not fly, but another point Cantor made seemed to resonate with the president. Roosevelt wanted to know why an actor should make more than $100,000 per year, more than the President earned. Cantor pointed out that whatever amount of money Roosevelt was not paid for his work 'stayed in the pockets of the American people', according to labor historian Nancy Lynn Schwartz, 'but if actors and writers made less, it just stayed in the pockets of the [studio] producers', executives and moguls. The argument may have influenced Roosevelt's future actions.

On 27 November, Roosevelt approved and signed the film code, adding altera- tions of his own.[40] Cantor and fellow star Marie Dressler were appointed to serve as non-voting Code Authority members so that 'squawking actors', as *Variety* termed them, could have a (relatively powerless) voice in film industry matters. (A few days later, Dressler resigned from the post, claiming it too demanding; no replacement was announced) In a positive outcome for the cre- atives, the salary and anti-raiding clauses were suspended for 90 days pending further study by Johnson and the White House. Roosevelt also reserved for himself and Johnson the power to override any Code Authority decisions or changes in its membership. According to a front-page article in the *Los Angeles Times*, these actions 'aroused outspoken antagonism of industry leaders'. In a decision that went against the creatives, particularly actors and cinematog- raphers, the code allowed certain contract studio employees to work beyond NRA dictates on maximum hours if 'intimately involved with production'. It was difficult to discern whether this rule represented a backtracking of NRA policy, or a recognition of the special nature and reality of making feature films. Nowhere in the debate over salaries was it mentioned that perhaps another reason why salaries were so high for star talent was because of the marathon hours usually demanded of such employees.

Distrust between the government and the major studios was palpable, both in alterations to the code and in exchanges about the code in the press follow- ing the president's action. Reports swirled of a pending Congressional inves- tigation of the film business. Johnson remarked that no NRA-coded industry would receive more careful scrutiny, because of the breaches in the film world that the code-writing process revealed, and the general sniping at the code in Hollywood – probably also because of the outsized amount of time and effort it took to assemble the code compared to the case for other industries. For example, in addition to the code prepared by Rosenblatt, '47 antagonistic groups' offered their own versions of the code to the federal government. It represented a lot for the NRA to wade through, encompassing as much or more hassle than they experienced supervising any other major American industry.

For the independent forces in filmdom, without movie stars or literary per- sonalities at their disposal to make personal cases for them at the White House, the results of the final code were not as positive. Perhaps no other outcome was possible under the circumstances, but the fact that many independents, including Allied, dropped out of the codewriting process early on when they realised their interests would probably never get a fair hearing didn't help their cause. Giveaways, raffles and other promotional devices were forbidden by the code, with the potential penalty of a boycott by distributors for theatres found indulging in the practice. The indie exhibitors, according to *Variety*, predictably 'scored the compact as monopolistic and trespassing on their rights'. As they had promised for months, the independents, led by Allied, kept the pressure on against what they viewed as the unfair oligopoly-rewarding aspects of the code for as long as the NRA existed, which led to accusations in the press of them being 'antagonistic' towards the organisation. But their beef was more against the major studios than the government body.[41]

The signed pact made the major studio-dominated composition of the Code Authority public for the first time,[42] making it obvious that the majors controlled the majority needed to pass or defeat any provision if they united. But such an outsized advantage was not sufficient for the major studios. Seemingly incensed that some key matters would be left hanging for 90 days and that Roosevelt and Johnson could veto Code Authority decisions, they assembled another rebellion in order to pressure the administration for more concessions, threatening to become the first industry to challenge the NRA's constitutional legitimacy all the way to the Supreme Court.[43] 'The NRA and major filmdom are reported to be at the crossroads', *Variety* reported a week after Roosevelt approved the code. In the same article, anonymously quoted film executives claimed they couldn't manage to effect $10 million in employee raises under NRA rules without cutting production costs somewhere – they were probably especially thinking about cutting star actors' salaries, which Roosevelt's suspension of the salary clause had rendered impossible for the time being. As scholars Larry Ceplair and Stephen Englund put it: 'Now that it was clear that real labor-management bargaining, and not salary fixing, would have to occur, studio management opted out.' Or at least they tried to do so. There was scuttlebutt intimating that industry leaders might withdraw their signatures and refuse to abide by the code, and worries that this would bring further federal involvement in their business and alienate millions of their customers who patriotically supported the NRA. During the first week of December, representatives from all the major studios 'pleaded' that Roosevelt rescind his modifications of the code. Some called his emendations 'Federal dictatorship'. Brief messages featured in the 1934 *Film Daily Yearbook* from famous Hollywood executives such as B. P. Schulberg (MGM), Adolph Zukor (Paramount) and Albert Warner praised the NRA, yet behind closed doors these executives did all they could to defy and destroy the film code.

The provision that allowed Roosevelt or Johnson to reverse any Code Authority decision apparently made the studio moguls particularly nervous. A committee of film executives headed by MPPDA head Will Hays headed to Washington asking for 'greater self-regulation' under the NRA pact. Perhaps not wanting to risk the industry testing the constitutionality of the NRA, Roosevelt awarded them half a loaf; Johnson could not overrule the Code Authority, but Roosevelt still reserved that right. In exchange, the studios were asked to create policies of arbitration and mediation, which did not occur until long after the NRA's demise in 1935. Hays described the administration's actions as 'very satisfactory'. He and his studio employers were also undoubtedly pleased by a ruling the same week which proclaimed that no Code Authority member could be added or removed 'without sanction of majority of the industry members of the code authority'. This amendment made major studio dominance under the NRA iron-clad, and probably ensured that film industry lawyers would not draw up legal challenges to the NRA.

In addition to their concerns over the cost of actor salaries, the major studios also publicly complained about the potential economic impact of administering the NRA code itself.[44] The industry claimed it spent over $1 million in expenses to write the code, and predicted that the Code Authority meetings would cost at least $500 per hour. 'In other words', *Variety* portended, 'those Authority sessions are going to be more costly than telephone calls to Europe.' But their worries were unfounded. After six months of operation, the Code Authority's costs amounted to just $71,046, less than half of the estimates published months previously – quite a bargain when compared with the $1 million major studios spent per year to keep Hays' MPPDA organisation running.

Another surprise unleashed by Roosevelt within the fine print of his code approval centred on the issue of film censorship, a hot topic in Hollywood at the end of 1933, as various groups, particularly Catholics, agitated for stricter adherence to the 1930 Production Code.[45] During the code-writing process, various sources either predicted that film censorship would form part of the code or thought it needed to happen. Most in the industry were against conjoining the two issues, but Rosenblatt argued that including the Production Code represented 'the best insurance against outside censorship' of the industry. The NRA code as submitted to Roosevelt vaguely required the industry to 'pledge its combined strength to maintain right moral standards', with no description of what that might entail. Roosevelt felt more was needed, and confided later that deciding on the best way to deal with the contentious issue constituted another reason for his delay in signing the code. He appointed Dr A. Lawrence Lowell, president emeritus at Harvard, to a non-voting seat on the film industry's Code Authority. The news of this appointment brought 'unconcealed resentment' and protest among film executives, according to the *Los Angeles Times*. Lowell had earned infamy as a vocal exponent of enhanced film censorship, as well as an opponent of block booking who recently admitted having seen only three films in the preceding two years. Johnson admitted that the move signalled Roosevelt's intention to influence the industry to use the Hays Code to regulate itself more strictly.

It may have represented no accident that in the same week the code was approved, the film *Elysia*, a quasi-documentary depicting life in a nudist colony with cartoons of nude nymph-like females in its ads, was showing in theatres. Such features were a perennial if not common attraction for urban theatres wishing to draw Depression audiences. In the Los Angeles area, *Elysia* ran for more than a month. No major studio contributed to the film, but the industry's critics associated such releases with the industry at large, not the small-time producers who brought it to the screen.[46] Millions during this period were not only angry but felt betrayed by major and minor studio fare that abandoned the precepts of the Production Code. Much more so than today, movie-going in the 1930s was viewed and enacted as a family activity, with cartoons and serials for the kids, and newsreels and trailers for the adults before the main feature. Family admissions also brought increased revenues. The existence in the market-place of films like *Elysia* eroded the industry's family-friendly atmosphere and threatened audience support, one of the reasons the industry finally capitulated to the July 1934 strengthening of the Production Code. Lowell's appointment was so disastrously received that he resigned it in less than a month; Roosevelt and the NRA couldn't force the industry's hand regarding the censorship issue, but the industry ended up administering its own medicine, admittedly under pressure.

Other industries also experienced problems in forming and adapting the NRA codes.[47] While cotton manufacturers initially appeared to improve the horrible work conditions and pay of their employees and deal with previous long-term overproduction liabilities, many individual companies found ways around such reforms in the long term, and most of the other largest American industries also refused to reform so easily. Early in his tenure, Johnson's staff informed him that the NRA's enforcement powers to punish offenders under the system would not pass constitutional muster if tested, which is why propaganda and patriotism were brandished by the organisation more than penalties. Perhaps the film moguls had realised this, or had been informed of it by their legal staffs. Their boldness in threatening to abandon the film code in order to obtain more of what they wanted (or keep smaller interests in the industry from getting more of what they wanted) makes more sense in this light. Auto magnate Henry Ford did the same thing and, unlike the film moguls, followed through with his threat because he refused to abide any agreement allowing collective bargaining. As historians Bernard Bellush and Ellis Hawley documented, numerous examples existed of Johnson and other senior NRA staff making concessions to the needs and desires of industry and big business in the formulation and execution of NRA codes, often at the expense of the interests of labour and consumers.[48]

In most ways, the film industry's NRA code followed the pattern of other large industries. Historian David Kennedy's conclusions concerning the NRA's significance demonstrate that the MPPDA served a similar role in the film industry to other dominating producers in different industries:

> Various trade associations, like the Iron and Steel Institute or the National Automobile Chamber of Commerce, cloaked now with the vague mantle of governmental authority, effectively became the code authorities for their respective industries. They ignored the anti-trust laws with impunity and enforced production quotas and price policies on their members. Typically, the largest producers dominated the codemaking bodies, producing squeals of complaint from smaller operators, labor and consumers. Though the NRA contained both a Labor Board and a Consumer Advisory Board, and though in theory both those interests were supposed to be represented in codemaking and code administration, in fact fewer than 10 percent of the code authorities had labor representation and only 1 percent had consumer members.

The motion-picture code followed suit in this realm, with its policy of no workers or creatives serving on its Code Authority as fully voting members. In the end, the high fixed costs which kept competition from developing against the big eight studios since their vertical integration during the mid-1920s lay behind their oligopolistic practices. They basically ruled their industry, which meant that they could get away with such behaviour, and nothing the NRA or independent film industry forces could do would change that power equation. Similar situations, and similar impotence resulting from the NRA's reforms, also existed in the steel and automobile industries. The NRA's mandate of collective bargaining, though successful during 1933 in the case of mine workers, generally brought results not unlike those found in the film industry: a company union slanted towards management was proffered instead of authentic representation. The workers were almost always on their own in their struggle for a true union, especially since the government could not yet enforce its own provision: hence the redoubling of efforts in Hollywood for the SAG and SWG. The government offered a legal opportunity to capitalise upon, but left labourers alone to take it on for themselves. Still, 1.17 million American workers were in involved in strikes during 1933. Famous actors and well-paid writers in Hollywood possessed leverage to create powerful unions for themselves relatively quickly, but most American workers were not so fortunate and grew disappointed with the Roosevelt administration's unfulfilled promises in this area. Eventually, after World War II, section 7a, the collective bargaining clause, would engender a revolution in the economic and personal well-being of the American worker.

Rampant mind-boggling bureaucracy represented another inherent problem with the NRA, limiting its effectiveness.[49] 'There are boards and committees for any and all occasions', observed *Variety*. 'So many of them, Washington contacts of filmdom reveal, that they seem to overlap in various instances or to nullify the work of each other.' For example, when seeking redress on issues of fair trade practice, a complaint could travel from a local industry griev-ance board, to the Code Authority, then on to the Divisional Administrator (Rosenblatt, in the case of the film industry), then on to the National Compliance Board and the National Compliance Director. If the complain-ant still felt dissatisfied, he or she could submit the issue to Johnson, and from there go on to the US Attorney General and the Federal Trade Commission, with the US District Court serving as a last resort until reaching President Roosevelt, where the chain finally stopped. In April 1934, it was announced that ten boards would be established around the country to watch for viola-tors of the NRA film code, adding 70 workers to an already sprawling NRA bureaucracy. Such myriad and intersecting pathways could not have helped the NRA's popularity or utility.

In addition, the organisation probably tried to codify too many industries. Historian William Leuchtenberg pointed out the multitude of NRA codes: 'Code 450 regulated the Dog Food Industry, Code 427 the Curled Hair Manufacturing Industry and Horse Hair Dressing Industry, and Code 262 the Shoulder Pad Manufacturing Industry. In New York, I. "Izzy" Herk, execu-tive secretary of Code 348, brought order to the Burlesque Theatrical Industry by insisting that no production could feature more than four [strippers].' It sounds humorous until one calculates the time and money used to formulate and police each code. Historian Amity Schlaes found that in the NRA's first year, '10,000 pages of law had been created, a figure that one had to compare with the mere 2,735 pages that constituted federal statute law . . . the NRA had generated more paper than the entire legislative output of the federal government since 1789.' Narrowing NRA focus to the largest most important industries and regulations in the country, where it would have done the most good, would have saved time and effort and probably would have produced a better overall economic impact.

Though the major studios eventually mostly won their arguments, the NRA code-making process exposed their modus operandi to the public and the government like never before. Overall, it represented a short-term loss for the crowd not affiliated with the majors, but it created the stirrings for a long-term win. The worst nightmares of the independent and artistic forces in the film industry mostly came true: the federal government's intervention justified and strengthened the major studios' position and business model, making it even more difficult if not impossible for any true competition to emerge against them in the short run. The absence of anti-trust worries instigated unprecedented collusion at the top of the film industry, and the result decidedly did not produce the balance of interests between workers and management that the NRA hoped to effect.[50] Yet, along with the contract rebellions of Cagney and other actors documented in the previous chapter, the code experience also represented a significant first step towards breaking the stranglehold the majors enjoyed over the careers of the various creatives they employed, as well as theatres and distributors around the country. Like most efforts to bring more equality and balance to American society, righting the balance in Hollywood would take a long time. Too long. The NRA, particularly in Hollywood but also around the nation, did not live up to its initial promise among workers, but it allowed them a glimpse of the possibilities, commencing a difficult and sometimes violent path towards strong independent unions and industrial reform.

Warner Bros., the studio that on-screen represented the struggle of everyday people like no other, took the lead in using the occasion of the NRA code to resist the struggle of its own workers, attempting to strip away as many advantages from them as possible (and mostly succeeding). Other major studios followed suit. By the end of 1933, none of the major studios sported the NRA Blue Eagle logo in its advertisements. Just three months earlier, all the studios, particularly Warner Bros., were doing so avidly. Warners and MGM took the lead in stripping the logo from their marketing even before the code was approved, RKO and Paramount were the last to drop it from their advertising.

The NRA experience during 1933 and afterwards demonstrated that the Warners were not the loyal supporters of Roosevelt and the New Deal that they claimed themselves to be in the media. The underdogs championed by the Warners in films such as *I Am a Fugitive from a Chain Gang* and dance routines like 'Remember My Forgotten Man' and 'Shanghai Lil' from the Great Depression Musicals were not championed by them in real life. Quite the contrary. The Chester Kents of 1933 Hollywood did not win their battles and achieve autonomy or fair compensation. No immediate comeuppance against the powers that be surfaced in real life; the studios ingeniously and successfully engineered NRA negotiations to preserve their overwhelming advantages. If anything, the Warners during 1933 code negotiations (and afterwards) seemed more aligned with MGM head Louis B. Mayer's rock-ribbed big-business-friendly Republican party ethos than their publicised reputation for streetwise and hardscrabble production, and support of FDR and his New Deal agenda.

But interesting parallels exist between these NRA struggles and *Footlight Parade* in 1933. Like Kent, actors, writers and other creatives end up returning and working within the system for their old bosses even after various abuses have been revealed. The artists' love and passion concerning what they do, and the difficulty of finding employment at a high level of their professions that allows them a mass audience, are factors used against them by management.

Figure 5.1   After Chester Kent (played by James Cagney) has learned that his
partners have hidden profits from him, they are embarrassed, and scared
he'll walk out on them, so they offer him a 'new deal'. He fires back:
'Yeah, and I'm the dealer!' But similar victories for Hollywood creative
labour during 1933 were rare in real life, as the making of the 1933 NRA
motion-picture code demonstrated. From *Footlight Parade* (Warner Bros.,
1933).

Where else could 1930s film actors, or a musical prologue creator like Kent,
go to? The major studios and the fictional Frazer and Gould agency are pretty
much the only game in town. In real life, Cagney possessed the star power and
the moxie to dramatically increase his salary, but most of his compatriots either
didn't have the leverage to employ it or felt afraid or disloyal about doing so,
even when they were clearly being taken advantage of by management. Just as
in *Footlight*, creative theft served as a key theme in NRA negotiations, perhaps
not via outright stealing as done by Frazer and Gould's executives and the
Gladstone company's spies, but by the major film companies and their representatives not properly remunerating talent on the basis of the rewards their
contributions made possible. Chester Kent eventually won a 'new deal', rede-
fining himself as 'the dealer', but labour progress in non-fiction Hollywood
proved much slower. We know now that Kent's cherished musical prologues
vanished from the show business landscape by the mid-1930s, while major film
studio hegemony in production, distribution and exhibition would subsist for
nearly another decade and a half. In both the NRA negotiations and *Footlight*

Parade, the struggle for respect for one's talents and contributions, perhaps even more than money, was paramount, and difficult to come by. Were the chorus girls in the Great Depression Musicals (whose salaries dropped during the course of 1933) artists moving in impressively choreographed lock-step fashion or just examples of glamorous corporate subordination?

The obstinacy and narrow-mindedness exhibited by the major studios helped break their back in the long term, ending their supposed 'Golden Age' after World War II. The various cinematic, governmental, political and economic reverberations of 1933 were essential in uncovering and encouraging a gradually building sense of rebellion and unfairness within the motion picture industry labour market.

NOTES

1. Leo Rosten, *Hollywood: The Movie Colony, The Movie Makers* (New York: Harcourt, Brace & Co., 1941): 134–5. A more complete description of the 1934 California gubernatorial campaign with full sources appears in Chapter 6.
2. Ronald Brownstein, *The Power and the Glitter: The Hollywood–Washington Connection* (New York: Pantheon, 1990), Chapter 1; John Morello, 'Selling the "Available Man": Albert D. Lasker, Advertising and the Election of Warren G. Harding', paper given at the Historians of Twentieth Century United States (HOTCUS) Conference, Middelberg, the Netherlands, June 2012.
3. Ellis W. Hawley, *The New Deal and the Problem of Monopoly: A Study in Economic Ambivalence* (New York: Fordham University Press, 1995): 19–20.
4. Arthur M. Schlesinger, Jr, *The Age of Roosevelt: The Coming of the New Deal* (Boston: Houghton-Mifflin, 1960): 84.
5. [Uncited author], 'Warner Bros.', *Fortune* (December 1937): 110–11.
6. [Uncited authors] 'Teeth and Penalties in Code, Says Rosenblatt: Theatres Must Get Away from the Red', *Hollywood Reporter* (9 August 1933); '6,000 March for Film Industry in New York NRA Tribute', *Motion Picture Herald* (16 September 1933). For more on Chester Hale, consult Chapter 3.
7. [Uncited authors], 'Must Jell 50 Codes into 1; Films' Formula Ready by Aug.', *Variety* (4 July 1933); 'Working Faster on Codes; Want to Be The First for Roosevelt' and 'Studios' Code Maybe Ready by July 31', *Variety* (25 July 1933); 'Must Have a Uniform Code; All Branches Concur, Edict', *Variety* (1 August 1933); 'Permanent Code This Week?; But Meetings Are Scheduled', *Variety* (8 August 1933); Tom Waller, 'That Film Code – Wot Grief; They're Working on It, and How', *Variety* (15 August 1933).
8. Schlesinger, Jr, 110–12.
9. Thomas Doherty, *Pre-Code Hollywood: Sex, Immorality, and Insurrection in American Cinema 1930–1934* (New York: Columbia University Press, 1999): 82–5; [uncited authors], 'Allied Suggests Trailers Urging Faith in Roosevelt', *Film Daily* (11 March 1933); 'Academy Code Seeks to Protect The Individual: Would Eliminate Unfair Practices', *Hollywood Reporter* (20 July 1933); '30,000 Ushers Averaging $6 Wkly [*sic*] And Other Minor Trade Employes [*sic*] Now Figured for Minimum Wage', and 'Upping Scales Allowable Is Claim', *Variety* (25 July 1933); 'NRA Is in Action Today: All Studios with Exception of Fox and Paramount Put Office Workers on Forty-Hour Plan', *Hollywood Reporter* (31 July 1933); 'More Employes [*sic*] with NRA Deal', *Variety* (1 August 1933); 'NRA Confuses

Studios, But 400 Added 1st Week', *Variety* (8 August 1933); 'NRA Effect in Far West; Theatres Operate Under Eagle, Except Union Men with Contract', *Variety* (8 August 1933); 'NRA Flags Waving: Nearly All Theatres on B'way in Times Sq. Show Emblem', *Variety* (8 August 1933); 'NRA Trailers Ready for 6000 Houses August 20', *Hollywood Reporter* (9 August 1933); 'Some of the Better Paid Employes [*sic*] Feel That Blue Bird Is Agin 'Em', *Variety* (15 August 1933); 'Manager's Round Table' [column], *Motion Picture Herald* (26 August 1933); '30,000 More Now in Picture Industry', *Variety* (29 Aug. 1933); 'Flinn Submits His C.A. Report; 389,000 Wage Earners in Pictures', *Variety* (6 March 1934).

10. Sources for this discussion on NRA propaganda films: Doherty, ibid.; [uncited authors], 'Warner's Semi-official "New Deal" NRA Short', and 'Harry Warner as NIRA Propagandist', *Variety* (1 August 1933); '64,000 Showings per NRA Short Scheduled', *Variety* (29 August 1933); 'Film Shorts for NRA Shown: Few Previewed on Coast; 1,000 Prints for Each', *Variety* (5 September 1933); 'Eight NRA Films Made; One Release a Week', *Motion Picture Herald* (16 September 1933). The last-named article announces that, in addition to the eight NRA shorts produced by the eight studios, Warner Bros. 'intends to produce an extra short subject entitled "The New Deal"', but no other references or evidence of this film could be found.

The eight major Hollywood studios in 1933 (in alphabetical order): Columbia, Fox, MGM, Paramount, RKO, United Artists, Universal, Warner Bros. *The Road Is Open Again, Give a Man a Job, Roosevelt Asks for Your Cooperation, Nation Unites to Support Roosevelt, Big Companies Endorse, Blue Eagle Wings Way Over Nation* and *NRA Spirit Sweeps Nation!* are all available on YouTube.

Warner Bros. revisited the idea of patriotic shorts, featuring American history figures such as Patrick Henry, in their determined anti-Nazi campaign during 1936–9, years before other major studios dared to alienate Germany, which represented a major film export market for Hollywood: Thomas Doherty, *Hollywood and Hitler, 1933–1939* (New York, 2013): 310–29.

11. [Uncited authors], 'Song of NIRA', *Variety* (1 August 1933); 'Cohan Writing Official NRA Song', *Variety* (15 August 1933); 'Baby Has NRA Link in Name', *Los Angeles Times* (22 September 1933); Grace Kingsley, 'Hobnobbing in Hollywood' [column], *Los Angeles Times* (22 September 1933).

12. Giuliana Muscio, *Hollywood's New Deal* (Philadelphia: Temple University Press, 1997): 92–6; Brownstein, 75–7.

13. This section on Roosevelt and the film industry is based on the following sources: [uncited author], 'Why F.D.R. Is a Film Fan: Sees More Pix Than Any President', *Variety* (21 April 1934); Brownstein, ibid.; Paul Buhle and Dave Wagner, *Radical Hollywood: The Untold Story Behind America's Favorite Movies* (New York: The New Press, 2002): 60.

14. Bernard Bellush, *The Failure of the NRA* (New York: Norton, 1975): 9–10, 30, 122; William E. Leuchtenburg, *Franklin Roosevelt and the New Deal, 1932–1940* (New York: Harper & Row, 1963): 64–70; Martin Rubin, 'The Crowd, the Collective, and the Chorus: Busby Berkeley and the New Deal', in John Belton, ed., *Movies and Mass Culture* (London: Bloomsbury, 1996): 71–2; Schlesinger, Jr, 145.

15. [Uncited author], 'Dictator for Industry Selected by Roosevelt: H. S. Johnson, ex-General, Honored; Budget Chief Lists Tax Plans to Finance Public Works', *Los Angeles Times* (19 May 33).

16. [Uncited authors], 'Rosy Knows Too Much: His Inside Stuff Kayos Hollywood', *Variety* (30 January 1934); 'Permanent'; 'Teeth'.

17. [Uncited author], 'Teeth'.

18. [Uncited authors], 'Academy Code'; 'All Branches of Industry Will Get Chance at Code Framing', *Variety* (25 July 1933); 'Code to Bring Changes: NRA Document Provides for Central Booking Office and Rehashed Old Arbitration Pact', *Hollywood Reporter* (14 August 1933).

19. Robert Sklar, *Movie-Made America: A Cultural History of American Movies* (New York: Vintage, 1994): 170–2; [uncited authors], 'Washington Scans High Salaries: Maximum Money as well as Min.', *Variety* (1 August 1933); '30,000 Ushers'; 'Rosy Knows'.

20. This section on the Warners' NRA resistance and Goldwyn's charges against them is based on the following sources: [uncited authors], 'Warners Pretty Grouchy Nowadays; May Prefer It Altogether Alone Unless Merger with WE Eventuates', *Variety* (4 July 1933); 'Goldwyn Scores Warner: "Reckless Star Raiding" Charged in Statement as to Why He Quits Hays Org', *Los Angeles Times* [front page story] (31 Oct. 1933); Waller, 'That Film Code'; 'Permanent'; 'Teeth'.

21. [Uncited authors], 'Code to Bring'; 'Teeth'.

22. Sources for this paragraph: Arthur W. Eddy, 'A Summary of Events Leading Up To the Motion Picture Code', from the *Film Daily Year Book 1934* (no publishing data, c. early 1934): 596–7; [uncited author], 'Studios Divide on Code: September 12th Hearing Will Bring Widely Differing Views; Acad. – Writers – Agents Active', *Hollywood Reporter* (24 August 1933); W.B. Francis, 'Finale Nears on Film Code', *Los Angeles Times* (24 September 1933); [uncited author], 'Hopes for Film Pact Set Back', *Los Angeles Times* (26 September 1933); W. B. Francis, 'Film Industry Splits on Code', *Los Angeles Times* (6 October 1933).

23. This section on the independents' complaints concerning the NRA code is based on the following sources: Francis, 'Finale'; Francis, 'Film'; [uncited author], 'Indies Booted Their Chances at Code Hearings; Told All', *Variety* (17 October 1933).

24. Sources for this paragraph on double features: J. Douglas Gomery, 'Hollywood, The National recovery Administration, and the Question of Monopoly Power', in Schatz, ed., *Hollywood: Critical Concepts in Media and Cultural Studies, Vol. 3* (London: Routledge, 2004): 246; Muscio, 124; [uncited authors], 'NRA's Doubles Troubles: 2 Majors Would Turn in Eagle', *Variety* (7 August 1934); 'Need Twice as Many Pix: Duals' Decision Seen as a Boon', and 'NRA Legalizes Dual-Billing; U-Col.-Indies Were for 'Em; MG and Fox Joined and Swung It', *Variety* (14 August 1934).

    By early 1935, in a ruling largely redundant by this time, the US District Court in Philadelphia ruled that the major studios could not legally prevent double bills: [uncited author], 'U.S. Court Holds Double Bill Restriction in Contract Illegal', *Motion Picture Herald* (9 February 1935). According to Gomery, after the NRA was declared unconstitutional and disbanded in May 1935, independent theatres resumed promotional giveaways and games until World War II. Eventually, filling in the second-billed movies in double features became an entrepreneurial opportunity for smaller Hollywood 'B' studios such as Republic.

25. Examples of the independent exhibitors' problems in dealing with the major studios are detailed in these accounts of the spring 1934 NRA Review Board investigations: [uncited authors], 'Clarence Darrow's NRA Review Bd.'s Power Has Film Codism Nettled', and 'Darrow Assails Pic Code: Rosy in Battle with Review Bd.', *Variety* (27 March 1934); 'Calls Coders in Quiz to Answer Charges or Face Roosevelt', *Daily Variety* (27 March 1934); 'Indie Exhibs Charge Rosenblatt Ignored Them, Code Gives "Big 8" Stronger-than-ever Dominance', *Variety* (3 April 1934).

    Independent film producers also had the disadvantage of paying large licence payments for sound recording and reproducing devices that the majors and their affiliated corporations had control over. What *Variety* called the 'sound monopoly' 'has killed indie producers ... 10 years ago there were 18 to 20 and now there are only three or four'. See: [uncited author], 'Code Splits Review Bd.; Darrow's Comm. in Two Factions', *Variety* (10 April 1934).

26. This section on the NRA film code's provisions, especially their significance to actors and screenwriters, is based on the following sources: Tino Balio, *Grand Design: Hollywood as a Modern Business Enterprise 1930–1939* (New York: Scribner, 1993): 153–5; Laurence W. Beilenson, 'NRA: Blue Eagles, Sick Chickens', *Variety* (25 Oct. 1983); Buhle and Wagner, 44–5; Danae Clark, *Negotiating Hollywood: The Cultural Politics of Actors' Labor* (Minneapolis: University of Minnesota Press, 1995): 80–1; Tom Kemper, *Hidden Talent: The Emergence of Hollywood Agents* (Berkeley: University of California Press, 2010): 10–11; Murray Ross, *Stars and Strikes: Unionization of Hollywood* (New York: Columbia University Press, 1941): 106–8, 113–15; Nancy Lynn Schwartz, *The Hollywood Writers' Wars* (New York: Knopf, 1982): 28–31; *Code of Fair Competition for the Motion Picture Industry* (Washington, DC: US Printing Office, 1933): 236–42; [uncited authors], 'Talk Hollywood Walkout: But Stars Won't Ignore Contract', and 'Studio Players Plenty Het Up over the Code – Make Sweeping Changes Vs. Producers' Methods', *Variety* (17 October 1933); 'Film Code Problems Aired at White House', *Los Angeles Times* (24 October 1933); 'Code to Bring Changes'; 'Studios Divide'.

  For a useful chart and other statistics and factors demonstrating the small amount of money made by most film actors in 1933, consult: Ross, 107–8.

  Earlier drafts of the NRA code were even more restrictive to agents. In August 1933, the *Hollywood Reporter* wrote about a plan considered for the code that would establish 'a central booking office [for all the major studios] with the salary of every individual in the business ticketed and with all buying of talent done from that office', an excellent way for the major studios to keep an eye on and (probably) intimidate all their creatives' agents. Also, if all studios negotiated contracts for contracted employees in the same building, it would make collusion between them much easier: [uncited author] 'Code to Bring Changes'.

27. For more on the studio moguls' previous attempts to rein in the power of agents, consult: Kemper, 13–15.

28. [Uncited author], 'Studio Players Plenty'.

29. For further details on the ultimate outcome of the NRA actor-producer and writer-producer committees, see the aforementioned Murray Ross book, and: [uncited authors], 'Film Actors Ask Government for Better Work Conditions', *Motion Picture Herald* (12 January 1935); '13 Planks in Producers' Platform to Improve Actors' Conditions', *Motion Picture Herald* (9 February 1935).

30. W. B. Francis, 'Film Salaries Cub Plan Under NRA Disclosed; Code Authority Would Hold Reins; With a $10,000 Penalty Provided for Excessive Payments', *Los Angeles Times* (14 October 1933); Edwin Schallert, 'Filmdom in Revolt against Proposed NRA Code; Regulation of Stars' Salaries Denounced' *Los Angeles Times* (15 October 1933); John Scott, 'Film Stars Fight for Each Other's Servants: "Faithful Retainers" Scarce in Hollywood', *Los Angeles Times* (29 October 1933); [uncited authors], 'Stars' Huge Salaries Explained, Defended: Actor's Day Is Short and Money Soon Spent; Players Popular a Few Years Ago Now Living on Charity', *Los Angeles Times* (22 October 1933); 'Cinema Code Draft Ready', *Los Angeles Times* (22 October 1933); 'No Acad Awa This Year: But Substitute Proposition Formulated by Howard Eastbrook', *Variety* (17 December 1933); 'Groups Asked to Name Academy Awards Committee', *Motion Picture Herald* (23 December 1933).

31. As further evidence of the lopsided nature of the process, film historian Tino Balio noted that only three out of the hundreds of NRA codes enacted nationwide

specifically spelled out the names of those who would be part of the initial Code Authority, and one of those was the motion picture industry, which demonstrates the moguls' anxiety in making sure that they controlled all NRA Code Authority machinations: Tino Balio, *United Artists: The Company Built by the Stars* (Madison, WI: University of Wisconsin Press, 1976): 99–102.

32. [Uncited author], 'High Salary Curb Seen; Fed Inquiry Hints Move', *Los Angeles Times* (19 October 1933).

33. [Uncited author], 'Path Cleared for Code: Code Still Unsigned Formally but Industry Can't Treat It Lightly', *Variety* (7 November 1933); *Code of Fair Competition*, 221–2.

34. [Uncited authors], 'Strike Unions Squawk to President', *Variety* (1 August 1933); 'This Week' [column], *Motion Picture Herald* (7 October 1933); 'Warner Issues "Buy Now" Plea', and 'Mary Pickford Aids Drive: America's Sweetheart Broadcasts Plea for "Buy Now" Campaign', *Los Angeles Times* (15 October 1933); 'Roosevelt Orders NRA "Chiselers" Punishment; Fine and Jail Provided for False Pretenses in Showing Eagle; Specific Rules Issued', *Los Angeles Times* (18 October 1933); 'NRA Racket Drive Begun: Warner Authorizes Action to Curb "Protective Associations" That Gouge Members', *Los Angeles Times* (20 October 1933); 'NRA Enforcement as Seen' *Variety* (21 November 1933).
For the history of Browne and Bioff at IATSE, consult Chapter 4.

35. Arthur Robert Burns, 'The First Phase of the National Recovery Act, 1933', *Political Science Quarterly* 49:2 (June 1934): 161–4; David Kennedy, *Freedom from Fear: The American People in Depression and War, 1929–1945* (Oxford: Oxford University Press, 1999): 177–89; [uncited author], 'Upturn Tidings', *Motion Picture Herald* (7 October 1933); Edwin Schallert, 'Hundred Sixty Millions Films' Bill This Year; Salaries Total More Than Half of Hollywood's Expenditures; Fantastic Spending Explained', *Los Angeles Times* (26 October 1933); [uncited authors], 'Johnson Raps Foes of NRA', *Los Angeles Times* (8 November 1933); 'Indies Booted'.

36. W. B. Francis, 'Johnson Given Code on Films', *Los Angeles Times* (28 October 1933); [uncited authors], 'Work Finished on Film Code', *Los Angeles Times* (5 November 1933); 'Film Code Splits N.R.A. Officials', *Los Angeles Times* (8 November 1933); 'Pay Scale Snag for Film Code', *Los Angeles Times* (11 November 1933).

37. Edwin Schallert, 'New Control May Come from Films' Civil War: Hollywood Split by Factionalism; Hays Group vs. Academy; What Future Holds for Pictures', *Los Angeles Times* (27 October 1933); [uncited authors], 'Path Cleared for Code: Code Still Unsigned Formally but Industry Can't Treat It Lightly', *Variety* (7 November 1933); 'Code Delay Is Costly: Wait Wasting Millions for Pix', *Variety* (14 November 1933).

38. [Uncited authors], 'Code Delay Is Costly'; [probably the work of editor Martin Quigby] 'Calling Mr. Cantor', *Motion Picture Herald* (18 November 1933); 'Code Wait Jumps', *Variety* (21 November 1933); 'Johnson Turns Sphinx on Code Delay; Squawks, Pleas Ignored; Hint Action Within Week; Rosenblatt Chafing', *Variety* (21 November 1933); 'NRA Enforcement'.

39. Beilenson; Schwartz, 28–31; [uncited author], 'Schenck-Cantor See F.D.R.: Visit Warm Springs, Ga., to Present Hollywood's Side', *Variety* (21 November 1933).
According to *Variety* above, humourist and film star Will Rogers was also scheduled to visit the president and discuss similar issues.

40. [Uncited authors], 'Film Code Approved: Surprise Sprung by Roosevelt', *Los Angeles Times* (28 November 1933); '"Pix" [sic] Legislation Worry: NRA Can't Halt Congress' O.O.', 'No Biz Will Receive Such Careful Scrutiny on NRA Code

Enforcement As Will Pictures – Gen. Johnson', and 'Rosy Lauds NRA to Wisc. MPTOA', *Variety* (28 November 1933); 'Analysis of the Picture Code Discloses That the Govt. Hasn't Missed a Thing to Insure Effect', and 'Setting the Machinery of the Picture Code; Alternates OK Industry's Pro and Con on Lowell', *Variety* (5 December 1933).

41. Muscio, 118; [uncited authors], 'Indies March', *Variety* (16 January 1934); 'MPTO Blast Allied as Film Code Obstructor; Flay Group in Letter Broadcast to Exhibs', *Daily Variety* (12 March 1934).

42. The members of the initial Code Authority for the NRA film code: Merlin H. Aylesworth, MGM; Harry Warner and Sidney R. Kent, Fox; Geo. M. Schafer, Paramount; Nick Schenck, MGM/Loew's, representing major producers and chain exhibitors; Charles L. O'Reilly, Nathan Yamins and Ed Kuykendall, representing exhibitors; and W. Ray Johnson of Monogram Pictures and R. E. Cochrane of Universal Pictures, representing indie producers. In this period, Universal was seen as one of the big eight Hollywood studios, though not as powerful as MGM, Paramount and Warners.

43. Larry Ceplair and Steven Englund, *The Inquisition in Hollywood: Politics in the Film Community 1930–1960* (Garden City, NY: Doubleday, 1980): 30; W. B. Francis, 'Film Magnates Lose Code Plea', *Los Angeles Times* (9 December 1933); [uncited authors], 'Film Legal NRA Test? May Yet Be the First to Do So', *Variety* (5 December 1933); 'Johnson's Film Powers Curbed', *Los Angeles Times* (10 December 1933); 'Pix Wins Points from U.S.; Gov't Gives In a Bit Over Code', *Variety* (12 December 1933); 'Forecast for 1934 – by Industry Leaders', from *1934 Film Daily Year Book* [no publisher or date specified, probably early 1934]: 87–111.

44. [Uncited authors], 'Code Authority Costs', *Variety* (12 December 1933); '$500 an Hour for Every Hour the Code Authority Convenes Is Theoretical NRA Overhead', *Variety* (26 December 1933); 'First Acctg of NRA Costs Reveals Under 100G Needed First 6 Mos., or 50% of Orig. Estimates', *Variety* (31 July 1934).

45. Edwin Schallert, 'Hollywood Growls at NRA "Censorship": Appt of Dr Lowell as Code "Czar" Regarded as Unwarranted Attempt to "Clean Up the Movies"', *Los Angeles Times* (3 December 1933); *Code of Fair Competition*, 255; [uncited authors], 'Pictures Deems Itself the Winnah in Film-Crime Commission's Probe', *Variety* (28 November 1933); 'Film Code Approved', ibid.; 'Analysis', ibid. For more on the history of the Production Code, see Chapters 2, 3 and 6.

46. Bryan Foy, the producer of *Elysia*, came to Warner Bros. in the mid-1930s to supervise and produce their output of 'B' movies, none of which had a nudist exploitation element: [uncited author], 'Warner Bros.', *Fortune* (December 1937): 218.

47. Clark, 80; Kennedy, ibid. (the quotation is from pp. 184–5); Leuchtenburg, ibid.; Schlesinger, Jr, ibid.

48. Bellush, 36–46, 107–15, 121, 131–3; Ellis W. Hawley, *The New Deal and the Problem of Monopoly: A Study in Economic Ambivalence* (New York: Fordham University Press, 1995): 56–65, 104–5; Robert F. Himmelberg, *The Origins of the NRA: Business, Government and the Trade Association Issue* (New York: Fordham University Press, 1976): 181, 197, 205–12. Republican Progressives such as Senators William E. Borah (ID) and the mercurial Sen Huey Long (LA) accurately predicted the NRA's potentially damaging bias in favour of large companies at the expense of smaller independent businesses, insisting in particular that the two-year moratorium on anti-trust laws 'would facilitate the blossoming of trusts and combines . . . the result would be increased concentration, rather than more equitable distribution of wealth' (Bellush, 19–20; Hawley, 20).

49. This section on NRA bureaucracy is based on the following sources: Leuchtenburg, 68; Amity Schlaes, *The Forgotten Man: A New History of the Great Depression* (New York: HarperCollins, 2007): 202; [uncited author], 'Picture Codists Return from Capital Further Puzzled by Board – Committee Additions', *Variety* (13 March 1934); 'Blue Eagle Readying for Active Motion Picture Code Enforcement', *Variety* (10 April 1934).

50. One source, out of many consulted, places a more positive spin on the actions of the big eight studios concerning the NRA code: Louis Nizer, *New Courts of Industry: Self Regulation Under the Motion Picture Code* (New York: The Longacre Press, Inc., 1935). While the book features much valuable research into precise details concerning the motion picture code, and access to many who administered it (Rosenblatt is thanked first in the acknowledgements), it is overly sympathetic to the major studios, and often not knowledgeable about what was transpiring outside NRA officialdom and the Code Authority. For example, Nizer puts a lot of stock in the threats of the president and administration to step in if a major industry did not create a code (xv–xvi), but, as has been discussed previously, all parties concerned, including *Variety*, knew that such penalties would not survive a constitutional test – this is why such penalties never happened, not because everyone concerned was so well-behaved, or because the administration used its power so judiciously. On the same page, Nizer incorrectly states: 'Unlike other Industries, the Motion Picture Industry did not present labor difficulties.' For Nizer, the major labour problem was 'overpayment', presumably of movie stars, but he doesn't make this clear on pages xvi–xvii – a point of view that appears to put him on the side of the major studios, without acknowledging the huge uproar of labour interests accompanying the rise of the NRA during 1933 in Hollywood. There are many other examples that could be mentioned about the slant of Nizer's book.

6. POST-1933: A CONCLUSION

The idealism fuelling the participatory New Deal spirit of 1933 dissipated in the years to come. Forces once united came undone. The Warners increasingly separated themselves and their studio from New Deal policies, in trade journals and in their personal lives. As will be shown in this chapter, their move away from Roosevelt can also be glimpsed in their post-1933 musicals. The Roosevelt administration, as the 1930s progressed, adopted a more aggressive approach against the film industry and the Warners, especially after having seen their business tactics up close during the code-writing process and afterwards. During 1935, Harry Warner was once again, as in 1930, in hot water with the government. He could not convince his old ally Roosevelt to ask the Justice Department to dismiss a suit accusing him and the studio of participating in a restraint of trade concerning their theatres under the Sherman Anti-Trust Act. Harry bitterly complained that 'the New Deal pays off its friends with the Sherman Act and causes them to lose theatres'. Certainly, the Warners had been Roosevelt's friends, or at least supporters, in the efforts they made to help elect him in 1932, but had they been his friends since then, in particular during the period when they played a key role in the final significance and overall tone of NRA code negotiations? That is debatable. Warners star Edward G. Robinson recalled Jack Warner dissuading him from 'championing Roosevelt so visibly' in his 1936 election.[1] Just three years previously, of course, Jack was Roosevelt's top man in Hollywood, a ranking official in the California NRA. But Harry and Jack had returned to their Republican Party roots, where Hollywood moguls usually resided.

Part of the Warners' post-1933 political shift was also linked to the 1934 California gubernatorial election, an event that defined Hollywood's political consciousness as much as or more than the NRA code experience.[2] Roosevelt's surprising 1932 California victory initiated a sea-change in the normally reliably Republican state. In 1930, Republicans outnumbered Democrats in the state by a four-to-one margin; in 1934, the parties found themselves in a dead heat, with Roosevelt's popularity ascendant, as seen in the Congressional majorities he eventually picked up in the 1934 mid-term election. Frank Merriam, the 1934 Republican incumbent nominee for governor, had served as the lieutenant governor until his predecessor died five months before the election. Merriam, 68, an Iowa native who had successfully guided both Coolidge and Hoover to the White House as a campaign manager, was, according to author Greg Mitchell, 'an old war-horse as out of step with trend-happy California as a silent movie'. In the August primary election choosing the final party nominees for the office, the Democrat beat him by 90,000 votes out of nearly 800,000 votes cast, with 10,000 Republicans abandoning Merriam to write in the name of the Democratic nominee.

But this wasn't just any Democratic candidate. Upton Sinclair, a famous author and muck-raking journalist for more than three decades, won the Democratic nomination on a socialist platform, promising to end poverty in California (shortened to the epigram 'EPIC'). One of the main ways he planned on achieving this goal was by increasing taxes on businesses, particularly the film business, one of the top three industries in the state. They were ripe for the picking – the top ten studios paid just $3,142 in state taxes during 1932 (less than James Cagney made per week!) and $13,618 the year after. 'We are going to tax the great corporations of this state to make up the present deficit', Sinclair promised on the stump, adding that such a strategy would create a system whereby 'democracy could be made to work'. While Sinclair was not calling for the dissolution of the government, he was calling for something more radical than Roosevelt's NRA: to reconfigure California industry, including Hollywood, into a 'for use' system whose priority would be to give all workers jobs and the wherewithal to live, not a 'for profit' capitalist system. Although Sinclair referred to himself as a New Dealer and a supporter of democracy, and while Roosevelt would have greatly benefited politically from the first Democratic governor in populous California for more than thirty years (especially with his re-election campaign on the horizon), Roosevelt could not bring himself to support Sinclair. Though his legions of critics often argued otherwise, Roosevelt denied that his New Deal reforms were socialistic in nature and insisted they would only apply during the unprecedented economic crisis. He couldn't afford to be associated with Sinclair's rhetoric, even if he was a fellow Democrat.

The Hollywood studios, frightened of being finally taxed at realistic rates for the state resources they used, started an all-out war against Sinclair's candidacy, using for the first time all the power they possessed in the service of a political cause. Sinclair was already *persona non grata* in Hollywood, having failed at writing scenarios for MGM in 1932, and having written a biography of film executive William Fox that blamed his fellow moguls for conspiring to plan his downfall and exposed their questionable financial practices. Not only were those in charge of the major studios virulently opposed to Sinclair's tax plans and ideology, but their livelihoods were threatened by his half-baked and probably unrealistic announced plan to put the state of California into the movie business, showing its own films in its own theatres, helping the thousands of unemployed workers in the film business and, not incidentally, supplanting the work of the major studios whose usual products displayed 'bad taste'. It represented a shot across Hollywood's bow, and they responded in kind. In order to amass funds for their election efforts, the major studio moguls pressured their contract employees to contribute one day's salary to the Merriam campaign. Cagney and Jean Harlow led a rebellion against the 'Merriam tax', with Cagney promising to donate a week of his salary to Sinclair if the Warners made him donate a day's salary to Merriam, but most complied, as they had for the previous year's 50 per cent salary cuts. Half a million dollars raised (nearly $9 million in today's dollars) underwrote Hollywood's activism for Merriam, even though polls showed the great majority of studio employees supported Sinclair.

These funds supported rallies, speakers, radio shows, press releases, photographs, flyers and, most significantly, film production. The studios that had united a year previously to produce patriotic NRA shorts now banded together to release shady, factually dubious anti-Sinclair short newsreels, provided free to theatres across the state. The films showed groups of dirty-looking, menacing Hollywood extras dressed as vagrants massing at the California border, waiting for Sinclair's election to invade the state and take advantage of California taxpayer largesse. The theme continued in newspapers, with pictures published depicting hobos in dilapidated vehicles heading for the Golden State. Most of these pictures were probably staged; twelve days before the election, William Randolph Hearst's *Los Angeles Examiner* and the Republican-leaning *Los Angeles Times* both featured photos of dishevelled teenage stowaways arriving in California railyards from other states. These pictures were actually stills from the Warner Bros. film *Wild Boys of the Road* (1933), as observant film patrons and the young actors featured in the photos realised quickly. In other major studio-distributed newsreels, Merriam supporters were portrayed as upstanding well-dressed citizens (housewives, grandmothers, business executives), while Sinclair supporters appeared threatening, such as the be-whiskered Bolshevik-looking man in one newsreel who remarked: 'Vell, [Sinclair's] system worked vell in Russia, vy can't it work here?' Scholar Mark Wheeler stated that the 1934 California election 'pioneered use of opinion polls, political advertising and public relations strategy . . . commonplace in subsequent American elections'.[3] The studios also tried to reduce support for Sinclair by threatening to move their facilities out of the state, preferably to Florida, whose legislature promptly passed legislation that would exclude the film industry from taxation if it moved there. New Jersey proposed similar legislation.

The studios' misinformation campaign worked. Almost seven weeks before the election, Sinclair led in one poll by a two-to-one margin, and 800 local EPIC Clubs had sprung up around California. On election night, Sinclair gained over a million votes, but lost by 35,000, amid some disturbing evidence (never conclusively proven) of voting fraud favouring the Republicans. But the studios' hard-won victory elicited only temporary relief for them when Merriam hit them with a plan for their vastly increased taxation shortly after his election. Talk of moving their film facilities surfaced again in the press, but the studios stayed put, faced the music, and became even more profitable over the course of the remainder of the decade.

Instead of focusing on the quite legitimate arguments for not electing Sinclair, the studios resorted to dubious images. Perhaps these proved more effective than drawn-out arguments, but their essential falseness showed the Hollywood studios in just as cynical and dishonest a light as any crooked politician. While it is difficult to gauge how the public at large felt about such chicanery, the image of studio management in the eyes of their own workers greatly deteriorated. As in the debacle over the NRA code, it proved yet again that they were out for their own interests and no one else's, and that they would stop at nothing to ensure that their business plan remained exactly as they wished. The creatives and technicians learned their lesson and turned the tables on their bosses. Four years later, Hollywood's best-paid non-management denizens organised a 'Studio Committee for Democratic Political Action', an unprecedented effort from this demographic that assembled the same kind of media campaign as the moguls organised for Merriam in 1934, but without the doctored propaganda. They even requested Governor Merriam relinquish one day of his salary to the Democratic candidate, who ended up winning the election, ending four decades of Republican representation in the California governor's seat. The sour after-taste from the Merriam campaign transformed Hollywood into a Democratic stronghold, which holds to the present day. Hollywood chronicler Leo Rosten quoted one studio management source ruefully remarking that 'I guess we started something in 1934'.

The early months of NRA administration also probably further distanced the Warners from Roosevelt and New Deal policies. Despite the concessions they and the other major studios secured during the NRA code-making process, the bold headline over the *Daily Variety* masthead on 15 February 1934 seemed to express what many in studio management felt in Hollywood: 'NRA FIST HOVERS OVER STUDIOS.' At the beginning of 1934, rumours swirled through Hollywood circles that the US Congress was 'launching a well-mapped campaign for . . . scrutiny of every phase of the film business'. The rumours proved largely correct. The first phase of heightened government scrutiny came with the Roosevelt administration requiring under NRA auspices that all contract and management workers earning over $150 per week (roughly $2,700 in today's dollars) fill out a detailed questionnaire concerning their compensation over the previous three years. Moguls and executives as well as actors and technicians had to fill out the form, the details of which, somewhat ominously, would be shared with the Internal Revenue Service. Questions about stock ownership and supposedly widespread Hollywood nepotism were also included. 'While NRA is close-mouthed about what it will do with the reports, inside tip is that the Government is intensely interested in the balance between total payroll costs and net profit and loss figures', surmised *Variety*. 'If the payroll burden seems disproportionate to enlightened brain trusters [the nickname often given to Roosevelt's cabinet], direct steps will be taken to read-just the ratio under the code.'[4] The question of salary abuses now seemed more focused on executives and moguls than upon the actors on whom the MPPDA had tried to shine the spotlight during NRA code negotiations the previous fall.

The second phase of government scrutiny began in March, when Roosevelt created the National Recovery Review Board in response to growing criticisms of the NRA.[5] Some prominent Republicans and even some fellow Democrats were taking the administration to task about how the NRA tended to support monopoly at the cost of small businesses. Inflated consumer prices and the inability of collective bargaining to take root in the economy were also issues raised by other constituencies. If the Board found monopolistic or discrimina-tory practices being practised by NRA Code Authorities, it could recommend changes. In a moment of what he later termed 'total aberration', Roosevelt chose Clarence Darrow, the legendary but unpredictable lawyer, to head it. It marked Darrow's last turn on the national stage, and not one of his shining moments. Although the Board did publicly highlight important NRA deficien-cies, Gen. Hugh Johnson resented Darrow and the Board's presence, insisting that small businessmen who refused to pay 'code wages for code hours' and took advantage of women, children and people of colour in sweatshop situa-tions were one of the main problems in administering the NRA, and thus did not deserve special investigations on their behalf. He asked Darrow to use NRA personnel in his board's work, and report any irregularities he found to Johnson first before making them public because 'I am the big cheese here'. Darrow ignored those instructions, tended to confer when he could with Roosevelt, which he found easier than most to do, being the most famous attorney in America. As law historian Michael Hannon has documented, over nearly four months the Board 'held 57 public hearings, reviewed 3,375 complaints, and investigated 34 codes', which constituted over half of the total employed labour working in industries operating under NRA codes.

One of the main NRA codes investigated, especially since it drew twice as many complaints to the Justice Department than any other, was the motion-picture code.[6] Darrow summoned all Code Authority members, as well as NRA Division Administrator Sol A. Rosenblatt, to a meeting in Washington on 26 March 1934, asking them to 'answer charges of discrimination and anti-trust provisions' – although, since the NRA waived anti-trust provisions, it is not clear what such violations meant, or even if they were violations. He also told them point blank he would urge the president 'to order a complete rehauling of the [motion-picture] pact'. None of the authority members, or Rosenblatt, would answer the charges, and the Board possessed no subpoena power, so the rest of the meeting consisted mainly of a reiteration of charges by independent film industry interests, led by the inequity of block booking, and how the code heavily leaned towards the major studios. But now, the MPPDA was not shepherding the show; Darrow was, and independent interests got much more of a public hearing than the first time around.

Amid the various charges, a few new angles surfaced. One concerned an indirect accusation of collusion by Rosenblatt, since his former boss at Columbia Pictures, Nathan Burkan, served as one of the main authors of the code on behalf of the major studios, while he also attended exhibitor conferences on the code called by Rosenblatt. Abram Myers, head of the Allied States Association of Motion Picture Exhibitors, one of Darrow's key sources for his accusations and the most vocal of the independents protesting the NRA code, pointed out several other examples of NRA staff with past business connections with the major studios. He also recalled that Rosenblatt had handed him and the other independent exhibitors their final version for the code in October with a 'take it or leave it' attitude while the studio moguls sat in a motel room away from the action waiting for news of the reaction. Harry Brandt, president of New York Independent Theater Organization, told the Board that no independent groups had so far been invited to participate in the writing or administration of the motion-picture code, and that their suggestions were scrapped by Rosenblatt, who also asked independent film leaders attending code conferences to refrain from writing notes on the proceedings. When the White House refused to react to such tales of lopsided dealings, Myers paraded the information to various media sources in the spring of 1934, trying to underline the biased nature of the NRA code.

It was also revealed at this time that Code Authority members no longer attended their own meetings, sending lawyers or sales managers in their stead. Special Assistant Attorney General Russell Hardy made an appearance at the

meeting, confirming that the Justice Department viewed the film code as coun-
tenancing monopoly practices, and that it had recently filed three anti-trust
suits concerning theatre ownership, winning two of them. He also noted that
the Department had taken notice of a significant increase in theatre ownership by the major studios recent years. Overall, Hardy seemed to be using the
occasion to serve notice on the moguls – though it moved extremely slowly in
doing so, the Roosevelt administration eventually acted on those accusations
of restraint of trade against the motion-picture industry.

On 9 April, the Darrow board split in its recommendations to Roosevelt on
the motion-picture code, diluting their ultimate effect.[7] Three of five committee
members, including Darrow and his former law partner William O. Thompson,
sided with independent interests and recommended a 'complete overhauling of
the pact'. The others felt the code should stand. Governor Floyd B. Olsen from
Minnesota, friend of Myers and present at the Board's last meeting concerning
the code, made the sensible suggestion that Code Authority members should
be paid federal salaries, so they weren't beholden to the major studios in their
decision-making, alleging that otherwise decisions upon independents in the
film business were being made by their competitors – a conflict of interest. He
also assailed Rosenblatt for his multiple connections with the major studios,
intimating that Rosenblatt may have not been the best person to shepherd the
code process.

The next week, and for weeks afterwards, the major studios struck back
in force, defending their code and the process that created it.[8] In a long
brief, they attacked the Darrow board's conclusions and witnesses with mostly
dubious counter-arguments. They noted that the independents championed
by Darrow spotlighted only eight of 270 provisions and that most of the
code went unquestioned, which was roughly true, but only because the Board
didn't focus on the complaints concerning the code from studio creatives and
their agents. The majors also claimed that the code required 'great sacrifices'
on their part, and that '89.5% of the clauses were drafted for indies ...
while 99% give them rights they never enjoyed previously' – claims that were
obviously hogwash. They implausibly denied that they controlled the Code
Authority, instead accusing their detractors of using 'mathematical trickery' to
bolster their claims. Some of the review board witnesses, according to major
studio sources, had increased their theatre holdings since the Great Depression
started, while the majors were experiencing troubles with bankruptcy and
receivership, which suggested that independent exhibitors were not doing as
badly as they claimed.

In the end, the major studios explained their position with more honesty,
admitting they controlled the most influence on the Code Authority, which
was 'entirely justified because of the amount of money [they had] at stake'.
They also justified their historic use of block booking. 'The fact that block

booking is and always has been a universal custom of the business leads to the presumption that it is a fair method of doing business', the brief read (somewhat illogically), followed, according to *Variety*, by completely untrue suppositions: 'block-booking does not result in discriminatory leasing, does not "pre-empt" exhibition time and does not require exhibs [*sic*] to "take bad pictures in order to get good ones"'. In their overall thrust, the major studios had a point. The arguments being bandied about by Darrow's board were old, and it did not fall to the government to improve the situation. But couldn't the score have been evened up at least a little bit?

Rosenblatt personally attacked Darrow and his Board, accusing them of 'gross negligence, prejudice, bias, malice, slander, blindness . . . unsupported by a scintilla of evidence'. He complained that Darrow's report, if enacted fully, would place independents 'in the driver's seat', and that while his code entailed 1,200 hours of work, and 206 witnesses in its compilation over more than three months, the NRA Recovery Review board only spoke to 21 of 7,500 theatre operators and took fourteen hours of committee time.

While that comparison may be accurate, it did not take into account the larger context. Darrow's Board subsisted on a budget of only $50,000, could not leave Washington, DC, and did not have subpoena or any other substantive legal power. During a period of close to four months, it investigated 34 codes and reviewed 3,375 complaints. The Roosevelt administration never meant the Board to function as an authoritative last word on the NRA codes; it was looking for abuses in the general programme, and found them, and not only within the film industry. Furthermore, Darrow invited Code Authority members to all hearings (not just those concerning the motion-picture code) and gave them the opportunity to cross-examine any witness on the stand. The members of the motion-picture Code Authority, mostly controlled by the major studios, either refused to participate or refused to attend all of Darrow's board meetings. For them to accuse Darrow of negligence and bias when they never bothered to make their case while the Board met, and then issue a hatchet job of a brief concerning the Board's findings afterwards, was obviously self-serving. Then again, as a strategy, it made sense for them to stonewall for fear of adding legitimacy to a process they strongly opposed – they probably realised that, if they attended, they would only get slapped around in a public forum. They knew their existing system would prevail, because of their general power in the industry and because they knew Darrow couldn't dig up much more than the main NRA figures didn't already know. The major studios obviously held themselves unaccountable; in April, at two hearings chaired by the NRA Labor Compliance Director, no representatives of the major studios attended to hear 1,500 code complaints concerning studio labour conditions, though 'all had been cited to appear as respondents to one or more complaints'.

But the denouement of Darrow's board demonstrated that he wasn't doing his cause any favours either.[9] His final May 1934 report split the Board again, negating its impact. One of its members, banker John Sinclair, resigned before the report's release and gave the president his own minority report, noting that the nature of the Board ensured that it only received one side of the story, usually from those whose views were not represented in NRA codes, such as the independent film interests. To journalists, he accused his fellow board members (almost certainly meaning Darrow and Thompson) of 'utter disregard for fair play'. Such press coverage and the Roosevelt administration's delay in releasing the report (mostly due to Johnson's wish to respond to it) made it a topic of wide public interest. While a preliminary Board report recommended a return to non-NRA-supervised competition, the final report depicted competition as a destructive force that needed to be abandoned. According to historian David Kennedy, Darrow's 'slapdash report . . . suggested both antitrust prosecutions and socialized ownership as remedies'. Such confusing and contradictory conclusions ensured that no reforms commenced. The advocacy of socialism alone probably kept Roosevelt from acting any further on the Board's observations. With Darrow's board finally having no effect in changing NRA structure or emphasis, the Roosevelt administration supposedly assigned 63 'neutral observers' in the field to report on the film code nationwide in another attempt to ascertain how well or badly the code worked and to investigate potential abuses. This action demonstrated that the administration felt uncomfortable with the situation that the motion-picture code presided over, but it evidently could marshal no additional evidence to change it. Nothing was ever heard again concerning those supposed 63 observers, and one wonders if they were ever even deployed.

In September 1934, the salary clause and anti-raiding provisions of the motion-picture NRA code were scrapped, which benefited film stars.[10] Roosevelt had originally ordered a 90-day review of the salary clause when he had approved the code in late November 1933, but the review lasted more than three times as long. Nor was any notice ever made of findings from the financial disclosures required of high-paid film industry employees at the beginning of 1934. Rosenblatt did write a report (released in July 1934) based on the survey findings that provided average incomes of various classes of film workers, but not individual salaries. His report mostly followed the lines laid out in the code at the behest of studio moguls, blaming agents and the 'star system' for inflated actor salaries, and refraining from highlighting the fact that average executive salaries always exceeded average actor salaries by a factor of more than ten.[11] Either way, the report had little new to add, and the Roosevelt administration must have realised that any government attempt to regulate maximum salaries and justify standards of remuneration for private sector employees would have been struck down in the courts. Rosenblatt strongly felt the Code Authority could not legally levy the fines it had called for, and none was ever charged or paid. Also, it is difficult to imagine how one could construct a system that could make such decisions fairly and equitably concerning actor salaries, particularly when the two sides in the negotiations, the studios and the actors/ agents, represented such different and opposed interests. And as Screen Actors Guild president Eddie Cantor told Roosevelt in November 1933, any decrease in actor's pay went into the pockets of the studio moguls and executives – why underpay actors when the extra money just overpaid their bosses? It was better for the government to keep out of such struggles. Cantor and Rosenblatt both supported placing actors on a royalty basis deriving from box-office receipts from their films, but the government, probably again smartly, refused to take charge of such a reform, and the studios, which at this point rarely offered percentage deals to actors, did not even countenance such a move.

Throughout 1934, many, especially New Deal partisans, argued that the NRA had improved the economic situation as a whole in the film industry.[12] Box-office figures rose that year, according to *Variety*. Fox, Paramount and Warner Bros., all of whom suffered losses in 1933, were back in multi-million dollar profit in 1934. The *Motion Picture Herald* reported that 'motion picture stocks and bonds made the best showing of any individual group of issues on the New York Stock Exchange during 1934, appreciating in value some $106,614,125' for a total market value of $457,773,125 (over $8 billion in today's money). Most theatres were pulling in an even more disproportionate amount of cash since they had increased their admission prices that year as part of NRA reforms, partly to pay for the additional labour the administration mandated.

The Production Code Administration (PCA) also took credit for the jump in revenues, arguing that its actions had inspired more people, particularly families, to return to a habit of patronising movie theatres.[13] Starting on 31 July 1934, the PCA replaced the moribund Studio Relations Committee, mandating stricter guidelines and penalties for the censorship of motion pictures, and making sure the major studios adhered to the 1930 Production Code. The nationwide furore concerning Hollywood mores during the spring and summer of 1934 left movie executives with little choice but to acquiesce. Catholics led the way, especially Cardinal Denis Dougherty of Philadelphia, who advised all good Catholics to avoid Hollywood product. 'A shared hatred of Hollywood seemed to imbue Christians of all denominations with a spirit of brotherly love', observed film historian Thomas Doherty, who documented nationwide protests from various Protestants, and the Central Conference of American Rabbis, as well as sociologists researching the harm rendered by movie-going, the results of which research are mostly now dismissed as balderdash. Congressmen of both parties, realising that any association with Hollywood provided invaluable publicity, found it irresistible to be viewed as improving public morality during an election year. Several pieces of legislation (never passed) sought to penalise filmmakers who issued 'suggestive, unwholesome or morally objectionable' product. In order to head off this massed resistance and put their businesses on a financially dependable family-friendly footing, Hollywood cleaned up its own house by allowing the PCA to wield considerable power over its product.

One can gain some insight into the change for films in the post-July 1934 era by examining excerpts from the first report on new films made by PCA head Joseph Breen:

> I am happy to state that perhaps the best commentary on the definite improvement in the quality of our pictures, from the [Production] Code standpoint, is the fact that an overwhelming majority of both pictures reviewed and scripts submitted during the past thirty days, fell into the innocuous *Miscellaneous* category ... never during the two and a half years that we have been writing these reports has the preponderance of scripts of the right kind over questionable ones been so noticeable. This, of course, speaks for itself.
>
> Equally important with the improvements in the moral tone of our product is the fact that ... [w]e have reviewed recently a surprising number of excellent pictures ... gratifyingly free from objectionable elements, and yet seem to have lost no whit of their entertainment qualities. This is the most encouraging of all.

A whiff of self-congratulation wafts through the report, but logical reasons underlay the change of tone evident in Hollywood product. Severe penalties, including five-figure fines and outright banning of a film, awaited those studios whose films did not pass muster with the PCA. With Breen and the PCA involved early in the process of every major studio film, approving scripts as well as song lyrics, there was now less to censor. Elsewhere in the document and throughout Breen's PCA reports of this period he issues critical judgements as well as clearing film content, calling Cecil B. DeMille's upcoming *Cleopatra* film 'magnificent', and the 1934 Warner Great Depression Musical *Dames* 'excellent', though he notes that he and his organisation had to force the studio to tone down the costuming during one Busby Berkeley-designed dance sequence. Berkeley, as usual, stretched censorship rules as far as he could manage.[14] Though the strengthened PCA regime brought benefits as well, it was clear that the more adult, saltier and less censored heyday of so-called Pre-Code Hollywood, which brought to the fore films such as *Baby Face*, *I Am a Fugitive from a Chain Gang*, *I'm No Angel*, *Duck Soup*, *Shanghai Express* and *Footlight Parade*, was consigned to the past, at least for the next quarter-century.

Despite the significant uptick in their business, the major studios still grumbled and expressed paranoia.[15] *Daily Variety* argued in October 1934 that, so far, only labour interests and extras had benefited from NRA code decisions, noting that 75 per cent of labour judgments found in favour of the workers and 'not the producing elements', and 90 per cent of judgments concerning extras favoured the extras. The cost of film production increased 16 per cent during 1933–4 as the code's provisions were enacted, another potential irritant for the studios until one considers the vastly enhanced revenues and profits during the same period.

Nevertheless, even with efforts by the government to strengthen or expand the NRA stalled or dead in the water, the studios feared potential repercussions when Congressional Democrats scored a landslide victory in the 1934 election. *Variety*'s bold front-page headline following the election screamed: 'New Dealers' Film Threat'. They prophesied a 'sweeping Congressional probe' of Hollywood, along with more 'government participation' in business. In January 1935, similar unfounded rumours were published, including that the Roosevelt administration would insist on a Democrat to head the MPPDA. Part of these fears emanated from Hollywood's unsavoury boosting of Republican Governor Merriam. 'The California situation undoubtedly will contribute to movements to put the screws on the [film] industry', predicted *Variety*. 'The charge that Hollywood studios coerced actors, writers and other employees into providing financial aid for the Merriam campaign and ordered persons on their payroll to vote for the Republican ticket is certain to be taken up in the House [of Representatives] and may be the lever with which film enemies will force an investigation.' The one speculation in these press pieces that became reality in the short term was that the Wagner Act, originally introduced through the NRA legislation, passed Congress and became law in 1935. It enshrined collective bargaining as a guaranteed right for workers, something the studios and other large American industries had feared for decades, and would fight hard before accepting.

While the Hollywood community originally viewed Roosevelt as a fan of their industry and a potential ally, by early 1935, and probably much earlier, this relationship was being reassessed on both sides. In January, with the order to proceed provided by Roosevelt, Attorney General Homer Cummings indicted ten companies and six 'first-rank [local film] executives' in St. Louis on anti-trust violations. *Variety* viewed this action as 'the first step in an audacious campaign to pester and goad the industry into launching a new and far more dramatic housecleaning' of their practices. A federal grand jury was also impanelled to investigate similar charges concerning Fox's theatres on the West Coast. Such prosecutions could challenge the practice of block booking without embarking on a direct and constitutionally challengeable attack on the practice. Some of the information reportedly used in these investigations came from Abram Myers of Allied, whose wife reportedly worked in the US Justice Department's anti-trust division. The persistent efforts of independents like Myers to expose the details of block booking and push for reform and action proved an important goad in inspiring the government to keep pursuing the issue. According to scholar Giuliana Muscio, the administration also became alienated from the industry when it produced documentaries promoting the New Deal and its accomplishments during the mid-1930s, and found its access to American movie theatres 'stubbornly hindered by the [film] industry' and its block-booking policies.[16]

Roosevelt obviously had harboured reservations about the motion-picture industry's business model. As his interactions with film industry between 1933 and 1935 demonstrated, its main structure was oligopolistic if not monopolistic, aggressively restraining competition. The policy and the power consolidated by these practices also probably affected the artistic content and quality of American film; as Frank Capra testified at the government's block-booking hearings in the late 1930s, 'About six producers today pass upon 90 per cent of the scripts' made into films. If the NRA could not secure general industry reform and more open competition in Hollywood, Roosevelt and his administration would look elsewhere in an attempt to right the balance.

Starting in 1937, Roosevelt's Justice Department began assembling a case to declare block booking an illegal restraint of trade. Attacking the industry from this angle demonstrated the Roosevelt administration's change of strategy concerning the most effective way to create a fairer economy. Its effort did not represent the government's first attempt in this regard. Between 1921 and 1932, the Federal Trade Commission (FTC) collected '17,000 pages of sworn testimony and 15,000 pages of evidence' about block booking, and even issued a cease and desist order against the practice in 1927, later overturned by the courts (Myers worked with the FTC during this period). With this history in mind, as well as Hollywood's return to and expansion of block booking since 1927, the Roosevelt administration knew it had to proceed carefully in order to win the ruling it wanted. The Justice Department began prosecuting its *U.S. vs Paramount Pictures* case in 1938, testing the constitutionality of block booking and attempting to sever the profitable connection between the studios and their theatres, but it would not be decided in the government's favour until after World War II, nearly a decade later. Warner Bros., and the rest of the big eight studios, were named in the case.[17] The action further separated the interests and affections of Roosevelt and the Warners.

On 27 May 1935, just seven weeks after being extended for another two-year period, the US Supreme Court declared the NRA unconstitutional in a unanimous decision.[18] For the Roosevelt administration, the edict did not surprise, coming amid a volley of Supreme Court-engineered reversals of New

Deal legislation. 'By the end of May the NRA was showing the effects of accumulated buffetings and setbacks', reported historian Ellis Hawley. 'The whole organization seemed demoralized, on the verge of breaking down from overextension, sheer complexity, and internal conflict.' The Court ruled that the administration and Congress overstepped their bounds by regulating firms in matters of interstate commerce, particularly the matter of hours and wages, even if those firms approved and aided the enterprise. The decision was also expected since Roosevelt and his team felt over time that the programme did not work as well as originally envisioned; companies in Hollywood and industries around the country were evading NRA dictates, and the argument that the organisation favoured larger companies had become accepted in Republican as well as in some Democratic circles by 1935.

Roosevelt did not feel 'heartbroken' over the rejection of the NRA. In fact, he told his Secretary of Labour that 'the whole thing has been a mess' and 'an awful headache'. Yet, it temporarily halted the cycle of economic disaster by creating millions of new jobs. It brought a spirit of action from the federal government that, at least in its first year of operation, inspired hope. It explored the idea of what American capitalism could be, and perhaps should be, about: a broader sharing of the fruits of free enterprise. Americans today still fiercely debate the proper role of government in returning prosperity during a period of economic calamity and righting abuses in industry. Although many Americans today would not approve of the principles that animated the NRA, at least it represented a bold (if sometimes misguided) experiment to ease the burdens of those in need. In 1960, historian Arthur Schlesinger, Jr summarised the NRA's ultimate significance:

> The more enduring achievements of N.R.A. lay not in the economic, but in the social field . . . It established the principle of maximum hours and minimum wages on a national basis. It abolished child labor. It dealt a fatal blow to sweatshops. It made collective bargaining a national policy and thereby transformed the position of organized labor . . . It set new standards of economic decency in American life – standards which could not be rolled back, whatever happened to N.R.A. In doing these things, it accomplished in a few months what reformers had dreamed about for half a century.

Many, including some latter-day historians, believed that if Harold Ickes, who headed the Public Works Association (another organisation created by the National Industrial Recovery Act), had steered more money towards the NRA, the programme would have been more successful in meeting its goals. Without extra funding to bolster the programme, the NRA in many ways just spread scarcity further. When the smoke cleared from the NRA's destruction,

Roosevelt, perennially optimistic and forward-looking, shifted his priorities swiftly, ready to implement new ideas to reanimate the American economy when other schemes faded or failed.

In Hollywood, news of the NRA's dissolution evinced little effect.[19] After all, aside from rules concerning pay and hours for workers, the studios were forced to change little of their long-standing business plan by the Roosevelt administration. *Variety*, with typically witty repartee, announced that 'the Blue Eagle is a dodo'. It also advised Hollywood's management denizens to avoid cutting wages and increasing hours to save money, claiming that such measures would represent a false short-term economy. In the immediate aftermath of the decision, most major studio stocks took a dive, with Columbia, Fox, MGM and Warners in particular losing money. While some in the industry wished to live under the code even without the government imprimatur, such talk vanished from the industry trades in less than a month. In June, *Variety* declared that the industry would design 'a code of fair trade policies and a system of arbitration' to ease future squabbles, particularly between the major studios' interests and indie exhibitors, but nothing came of it. The big players in Hollywood quickly abandoned the NRA's examples, for which they had little use in the first place, while some independents hoped in vain to hang on to the original spirit of NRA reforms and some of the provisions that benefited them.

The combined effect of the Supreme Court's rejection of the NRA and the passing of the Wagner Act made Hollywood labour relations, especially between creatives and the moguls, even more hostile. Now that the NRA no longer supervised the use of collective bargaining, all parties in Hollywood existed on their own, and struggles became even more tense, particularly concerning union participation.[20] Wherever possible, the major studios stymied efforts by the Screen Actors Guild and Screen Writers Guild to establish themselves as exclusive representatives of their occupation, acting as if the Wagner Act did not exist. The writers and actors (and later the directors) purposely used the term 'Guild' to avoid the left-wing proletarian associations of the word 'union', but it didn't matter to the big eight, which were adamantly opposed, no matter what the groups decided to name themselves, and had no compunction in employing heavy-handed tactics to head off legitimate employee representation. A common tactic they employed was peeling off the most successful and well-off writers into a competing studio-friendly organisation, as happened with the short-lived Screen Playwrights in 1936. Efforts to renew the AMPAS company union as a viable substitute for the nascent Guild were also tried. The Screen Actors Guild, in which James Cagney served as one of the vice-presidents starting in the spring of 1934, won their battle first, becoming the sole bargaining agent for actors starting in 1937. 'The victories have been victories for the rank and file [actors]', pronounced the *Nation* about the result. 'For themselves the stars have asked and won next to nothing.' Some of these benefits included minimum wages, mandated rest periods between screen calls, established procedures for arbitration and guarantees of continuous employment.

While the Screen Writers Guild was recognised by the National Labor Relations Board as a legitimate union by 1938, its efforts towards recognition took longer than for the actors, since writers experienced more difficulty than actors in withholding their services to force a deal and were not as well-known to the public. Many screenwriters who doubled as Guild leaders were fired in this period, including Dalton Trumbo at Warners and Lester Cole at MGM. Finally in 1941, after nearly a decade of struggle and after threatening an industry-wide strike and amassing a strike fund to show it meant business, the SWG signed its first contract with the major studios recognising their authority in representing Hollywood screenwriters. At the meeting where the deal was finalised, Harry Warner released an outburst laced with a 'string of obscenities' aimed at the union's leaders. It demonstrated how personal and bitter the struggle had become: 'Those dirty communist sons of bitches . . . they want to take my goddamn studio, my brothers built this studio. I came from Europe . . . my father was a butcher', and so on. He was led out of the room with an executive on each arm dragging him away while he continued his rant. Soon after this deal, the SWG also won the right to have screenwriter credit judged by merit and evidence, instead of studio dictates, another important victory.

The Warners' move away from Roosevelt could also be espied in their films of 1934 and afterwards, particularly the Great Depression Musicals. The culture of the Warner Bros. musicals changed. The films referenced the New Deal, openly or subtly, far less than during 1933. The unity and idealism forwarded in films like *Footlight Parade* dissipated. In *Dames* (1934), emphasis is not placed on a strong leader (such as the directors played by Cagney in *Footlight* or Warner Baxter in *42nd Street*) uniting a stage company behind a cause for their greater good against tall odds: instead, the film concentrates on an eccentric tightwad millionaire's relatives trying to weasel him out of his money. In the 1933 Warner Bros. musicals, the prim and proper in society, be they well-off socialites or censors, are in the end unable to resist the romance of a good musical and the lures of pretty 'dames'; they are hypocrites who cannot countenance or fulfil their own desires. This theme continues in *Dames*, but not in the films that follow.

Despite the presence of a couple of cute and spectacular Berkeley routines (the 'I Only Have Eyes for You' sequence is one of his best and most romantic moments), the post-1933 Warner Great Depression Musicals become increasingly formulaic and cliché-ridden, starting with *Dames*. Dull love story contrivances are substituted for the originality displayed in previous films, as seen when the Ruby Keeler/Dick Powell romance in *Dames* is threatened by the hoary device of an innocent kiss being misinterpreted. Rather than featuring a plot that allows women a wider emotional and intellectual range than usual as seen in *Footlight*, *Dames* reverts to type. In *Gold* and *Footlight*, feisty Joan Blondell plays characters that refuse to cash in on a deluded rich male suitor, and demonstrate enough smarts to uncover a larcenous plot. In *Dames*, Blondell's character uses her sex appeal to manipulate and blackmail one of the millionaire's relatives to back the musical she wants to star in, while invading his private space twice wearing a revealing negligée, threatening his marriage.

The Great Depression and the people suffering under it on Broadway and elsewhere are ignored in these later films. Even when Powell's character tells the unwilling manipulated relative that 'you're a great credit to this country for allowing people to work', he's making fun of him – the drama of putting a hundred stage workers out of work and on the street is not present in *Dames* as it had been in previous outings. Whereas the 1933 Great Depression Musicals featured plots often matching the immediacy of Berkeley's sequences, this is much less the case after 1933. One wonders if some of the zest of the previous

Figure 6.1   The post-1933 Warner Bros. Great Depression Musicals changed in tone and theme. *Gold Diggers of 1935* features a cast of characters fixated on acquiring or keeping money, and the material pleasures it brings – quite a change from the camaraderie and hard work ethos usually depicted in Warner's 1933 Great Depression musicals. Here, characters portrayed by Dick Powell and Gloria Stuart celebrate going out shopping with her mother's money. (Warner Bros., 1934)

films, as well as their willingness to include material suggestive of current events, evaporated with the tightening of the Production Code rules, which limited the controversial and adult themes featured in Hollywood films. In any case, the later films did not connect as strongly with the zeitgeist of the period, or with audiences.

The trend continued throughout 1934 and 1935. *Gold Diggers of 1935* (1934), the first film entirely directed by Berkeley, begins with a hobo on a park bench, but he's a theatrical-looking hobo, nothing like the sincerely pained and dirtied souls seen in the 1933 'Forgotten Man' sequence. No images of that sort ever intrude upon the film again. The musical takes place exclusively amid the trappings of the most prestigious vacation resort in the country, a setting so glamorous that it seems as though Warners are competing with MGM for glitzy *mise-en-scène*. Audiences are repeatedly shown the eccentric and emotionally dysfunctional qualities of the rich, who are made to appear completely lost without the ministrations of their maids, chauffeurs and other helpers. At the same time, the workers portrayed in the film are not sympathetic either, as each rung of the service hierarchy in the resort extorts a large percentage of tip money from the rung beneath them. Powell, this time working without Keeler, falls for a well-off daughter, abandoning his long-time fiancée, and sings a surprisingly boring Harry Warren/Al Dubin song to woo his new love. Material pleasures are even more paramount in this film than in previous outings: the rich daughter's goal for the summer is to spend 'mama's dough'; Powell's jilted fiancée no longer searches for the 'finest man in the world', but for a 'rich one'; and when a rich man's stenographer tries to seduce him, she sings 'I'm in the Money' to him, in the hopes that she soon will be. The tired themes of gold diggers and inept millionaires are pursued at the cost of nearly everything else in *Gold Diggers of 1935*, even above the joy of singing and dancing. The 1933 *Gold Diggers* women worked together and suffered together for their mutual benefit – in 1935, everyone is out for what they can get for themselves.

Although Berkeley captured some good performances from his Warner contractee cast, and devises a striking four-minute non-verbal sequence to open the film, he proves in the end unable to enliven a painfully hackneyed script. Perhaps no one could do otherwise. The franchise appears tired, nowhere near the heights of 1933. The marketing was tired, too: the Warner publicity files for *Dames* and *20 Million Sweethearts* (1934) feature the same marketing approach perfected in 1933 with little alteration, including radio and newspaper serials, product tie-ins, manufactured feature articles, advertising matrixes featuring glamorous women, and so forth. *Wonderbar* (1934), starring Al Jolson, featured a minstrel routine so stereotyped and offensive that it not only seemed like an artefact from a previous era, but was also banned when shown on television in future decades. Its plot and setting resembled MGM's *Grand Hotel*, with a dash of robbery and murder added to the clichéd mix. Following

Warren and Dubin's Oscar-winning 'Lullaby of Broadway' from *Gold Diggers of 1935*, the hits began to fade for the songwriting team. Nothing new in these post-1933 musicals or their marketing spoke to audiences, other than viewing Berkeley's latest kaleidoscopic creations. And even those sequences were being limited: a memo from Wallis to Berkeley during the filming of *Dames* castigates Berkeley for planning sequences with too many chorus girls and expensive set construction.[21] The free hand Berkeley enjoyed in 1933 was retracted.

With the post-1933 Warner musicals' lack of connection to the zeitgeist (political and otherwise) of their era, their enhanced tameness from the new adherence to PCA rules and the toning down of Berkeley's creative freedom, it is no wonder that the Warner musicals' quality and appeal kept declining during this period. The pronounced emphasis on glamour in films like *Fashions of 1934* and *Gold Diggers of 1935* might have also worked against the time-tested Warner Bros. studio aesthetic of hard realities and underdog grittiness. Perhaps the studio veered too far away from what it was historically best at. And perhaps it was spreading itself too thin – in 1933, it concentrated on three quality musicals; the next year it issued seven. At the height of the success of *42nd Street* in the spring of 1933, a Harrisburg, IL theatre owner writing in *Motion Picture Herald* raved about the film and its draw among audiences: 'At last we have a picture that gives them real entertainment, and how they go for it.' But, aware of the Hollywood studios' penchant (then and now) for milking successes dry with subsequent spin-offs of successful prototypes bringing diminishing artistic and financial returns, he also voiced his hope 'that we don't have fifty of the same pattern in the next six months'.[22] Warners, and other studios following their lead, failed to heed this warning in the post-1933 period, repeating their fading formula ad nauseam until they had ground the life and soul from it.

Not until Stephen Sondheim's works of the 1960s and beyond would musicals with a strong social foundation and adult content gain a large audience once more. The MGM and Astaire musicals that dominated the genre for decades after the Warner Great Depression Musicals had faded transported audiences to milieux of fantasy or ideal families, without the doses of black-and-white reality the 1933 Warner musicals contained.

The studios, particularly Warner Bros., were not living up to their own soaring and patriotic media rhetoric concerning the New Deal. For a brief time in 1933, the Roosevelt administration and the Warner Bros. aesthetic mirrored each other with their concern over the 'forgotten', down-and-out and struggling denizens of America. The brothers Warner mostly moved away from Roosevelt in the years following the dissolution of the NRA code, seemingly frustrated and disillusioned. If they could not fully control the game, they would walk away from the table and insist upon operating by their own rules for as long as they could. Perhaps there was a price to pay for such intransigence for Warner Bros. (and for other major studios as well). The Warner Bros. musical production unit lost its lustre, became conservative – perhaps a bit like the studio itself and its leaders. Or more accurately, they returned to the conservative political roots they and other moguls had embraced before the coming of Roosevelt. Nonetheless, Jack Warner claimed in his autobiography that he remained friends with Roosevelt 'to the day he died', one of many dubious statements made in that book.[23]

The camaraderie between workers that makes *Footlight Parade* so charming probably never existed in the real life soundstages of Hollywood, particularly on the Warner lot. The Warner brothers, particularly Harry and Jack, had proved themselves as venal and selfish as the management of Chester Kent's prologue company. Through its long-time workplace policies, the studio undermined, underpaid and overworked the talents that made their films – in many ways, the setting, plot and characters of *Footlight Parade* reflected the real conflicts at every level of the studio workforce.

It probably represented no accident that Warner Bros. would not enjoy another massive hit musical whose reputation has survived until Cagney's return to the form nearly a decade later in the Oscar-winning *Yankee Doodle Dandy* (1942), a picture that returned some of that famous old Warner grit and patriotism to the musical format. Cagney, the star who had caused the most labour troubles for them (aside from possibly Bette Davis), the star who reflected more than any other the hard-bitten aesthetic that defined the studio during the 1930s, succeeded for them again. Why did it take Warners nearly a decade to cast him in another musical after his dynamic and profitable turn in *Footlight Parade*? This omission was a source of 'bitter frustration' for Cagney,[24] and for his fans too, then and now. Applying Cagney's abundant musical talents to new films seemed like a natural move in the wake of the strengthening of the PCA censors, when irredeemably violent plots were curtailed, and Cagney was forced to abandon playing ruthless gangsters for FBI 'G-men' during the mid-1930s. The tighter production code hit the Warner studio harder than any other because of the kinds of unsentimental adult themes and films that brought them their initial notoriety; the exit of envelope-pushing executive Darryl F. Zanuck almost certainly exacerbated this situation as well. Perhaps this corporate omission of Cagney as a musical foil represented another sign that something was amiss, some bit of company soul lost, at the Warner studio in the years following the NRA code fights and the PCA revamp. Few great or memorable films emerged from the Warner lot during the 1934–5 period.

The events of 1933, as seen in the Great Depression Musicals and real life, combined to form the beginnings of Hollywood's own 'new deal' between its artists and the moguls who ran the studios. Starting that year and continuing through the 1950s, the big eight studios would increasingly have to share more money and control with their artists and creative staff, and allow programming latitude for the theatres that played their films. In the opening years of the consolidation of the studios during the 1920s and in the first half of the 1930s, studios could dictate the terms of how their product was packaged and sold, but in the long run their business practices would be forcibly directed away from the dominating institutions they had constructed for themselves.

By 1950, block booking would be declared illegal by the Supreme Court, the studio's thousands of film theatres (not to mention the valuable real estate beneath them) stripped away.[25] They would have to deal with powerful unions representing their creative personnel, and their prohibitive seven-year contracts would be declared unconstitutional. Stars were beginning to insist upon lucrative box-office percentage deals in exchange for their appearances, which awarded them more of the profits. Television was permanently altering America's viewing habits. And the foundation for these earth-shaking changes was laid in the divisive events of 1933, and reflected in *Footlight Parade*.

But not all portents surfacing during 1933 were positive. The various Hollywood labour conflicts of that year eventually inspired a conservative counter-reaction by publicity-hungry politicians and studio executives against those on the left –especially writers – who had fought for union recognition and better wages. In the late 1930s, the House on Un-American Activities Committee (HUAC) embarked upon a two-decade witch hunt for communists, real and imagined, serving in influential posts, whether in government, the aerospace industry or the motion-picture industry. The roughly 325 communists in Hollywood during the 1930s, particularly screenwriters, were persecuted for presumed transgressions, when most of them mainly supported communism as a remedy for the suffering they witnessed during the Depression, and none of them ever came close to advocating the overthrow of the US government. They were a threat to no one except the studio heads, who resented their role in the revolution against the domineering way they set up their business. Hundreds of the best Hollywood writers and other workers, including many active in the new guilds, were banned and blacklisted from the studios, their personal livelihoods and artistic careers ruined, with no ability to refute the almost always specious charges made against them. For the victories won by creatives during the NRA code experience and with the establishment of the guilds, terrible payback arrived for many in the post-war era. As David Thomson has argued and demonstrated, such anti-communist efforts by the studios were not only illegal and unconstitutional but served the political purposes of sometimes anti-semitic US congressmen and severely damaged their own industry at a time when their economic vulnerability was greatest – 'they declined to stand up for their own people and the law of the land'.[26] Anyone with knowledge of how the major studios used the NRA code negotiations to run roughshod over their employees would probably not be surprised with the outcome of the post-World War II Red Scare in Hollywood. The chill of the McCarthy era hit Hollywood particularly hard, but the major studios and their executives brought the damage down upon themselves.

By the late 1940s, as the studio system's hegemony over the market disintegrated, the agents for actors, screenwriters and directors, led by MCA's Lew Wasserman, would start gaining the power to assemble the packages of talents for films over which the studio moguls used to wield exclusive control. Perhaps the movies themselves suffered in quality as a result; they certainly suffered when multinational corporations took over the major studios beginning in the 1960s, often relegating the film business to just a small portion of a corporate portfolio. Perhaps the pendulum had swung too much the other way a half-century after Cagney's salary battles when stars such as Tom Cruise and Arnold Schwarzenegger were regularly pulling down $20 million-plus paydays for their film appearances, with some royalties continuing into perpetuity – but there was no turning back. The pioneers from 1933, such as Cagney, Cantor and Davis, demonstrated how unbalanced the system was and how leverage could be turned around on the bosses. Along with their compatriots, they unleashed a torrent that by 1950 could not be turned back; Hollywood's New Deal was there to stay, major studio hegemony crumbled and would never return. And no films of their era more embodied that tension surrounding the changes greeting the Hollywood system and the Great Depression than the Warner Bros. Great Depression Musicals.

NOTES

1. Edward G. Robinson with Leonard Spigelgass, *All My Yesterdays: An Autobiography* (New York: Hawthorne Press, 1973): 178–9; Cass Warner Sperling and Cork Millner with Jack Warner Jr, *Hollywood Be Thy Name: The Warner Bros. Story* (Rocklin, CA: Prima, 1994): 209–10.

   Though Harry Warner seems to blame FDR for the Sherman Anti-Trust Act, it became law in 1890. As was detailed in Chapter 1, Harry Warner's 1930 brush with federal law concerned 'insider trading'.

2. This account of the 1934 California gubernatorial election is based on the following sources: Ronald Brownstein, *The Power and the Glitter: The Hollywood–Washington Connection* (New York: Pantheon, 1990): 40–7; Greg Mitchell, *The Campaign of the Century: Upton Sinclair's Race for Governor of California and the Birth of Media Politics* (New York: Random House, 1992): Preface, 20–3, 31–2, 62–9, 207, 421–4, 530–6; Leo Rosten, *Hollywood: The Movie Colony, The Movie Makers* (New York: Harcourt, Brace & Co., 1941): 133–9; Mark Wheeler, 'The Political History of Classical Hollywood: Moguls, Liberals and Radicals in the 1930s', from Iwan Morgan and Philip John Davies, eds, *Hollywood and the Great Depression: American Film, Politics and Society in the 1930s* (Edinburgh: Edinburgh University Press, 2016): 32.

3. Wheeler, 37.

4. [Uncited authors], 'U.S. Sharpening Pic Axe; Sirovich Bill Being Revived', and

'Gov't's Film Salary Questionnaire Permits for No Evasions; Probably Also Utilized for Tax Check-up', *Variety* (16 January 1934); 'Government Launches Pay Quiz; 6,000 Signed Code Blanks Filled', *Motion Picture Herald* (20 January 1934).
5. Michael Hannon, 'Clarence Darrow and the National Recovery Review Board', from the University of Minnesota Law Library's Clarence Darrow archive website, available at http://darrow.law.umn.edu/trialpdfs/National_Recovery_Review_Board.pdf. (last accessed 15 August 2012); David Kennedy, *Freedom From Fear: The American People in Depression and War, 1929–1945* (Oxford: Oxford University Press, 1999): 185–7; William E. Leuchtenburg, *Franklin Roosevelt and the New Deal, 1932–1940* (New York: Harper & Row, 1963): 67–8.
6. Sources for this section on Darrow's NRA board findings: Bernard Bellush, *The Failure of the NRA* (New York: Norton, 1975),142–50; [uncited authors], 'MPTO Blast Allied as Film Code Obstructor; Flay Group in Letter Broadcast to Exhibs', *Daily Variety* (12 March 1934); 'Clarence Darrow's NRA Review Bd.'s Power Has Film Codism Nettled' and 'Darrow Assails Pic Code: Rosy in Battle with Review Bd.', *Variety* (27 March 1934); 'Calls Coders in Quiz to Answer Charges or Face Roosevelt', *Daily Variety* (27 March 1934); 'Indie Exhibs Charge Rosenblatt Ignored Them, Code Gives "Big 8" Stronger-than-ever Dominance', *Variety* (3 April 1934).
7. [Uncited author], 'Code Splits Review Bd.; Darrow's Comm. in Two Factions', *Variety* (10 April 1934). Michael Hannon's research indicates six people served on the Recovery Board, but *Variety*'s report says that only five made the decision described in the article above.
8. Hannon; Cap Hill, 'NRA Tops Scoff at Socialistic Ideas, Charge Soreheads Lied', *Daily Variety* (21 May 1934); [uncited authors], 'Despite Producers' Opposition, Judge Lindsey Hears Code Wails', *Variety* (10 April 1934); 'Major Producers Attack Integrity of Indie Squawks in Lengthy Brief Supporting Code Authority', *Variety* (17 April 1934); 'Rosie Accuses Darrow of Bias, Malice, Slander, Negligence', *Variety* (21 May 1934); 'Darrow's Attack; NRA Rebuttals', *Variety* (22 May 1934); 'Senator Accuses Rosy of "Extravagant Lies"', *Daily Variety* (24 May 1934).
   To confirm the ridiculousness of the major studios' claim that '89.5% of the [motion-picture code] clauses' were drawn up for the benefit of independent film interests, peruse the previous chapter and consult: *Code of Fair Competition for the Motion Picture Industry* (Washington, DC: US Printing Office, 1933).
9. Hannon; Kennedy, 185–7; Leuchtenberg, 67–8; [uncited author], 'Gov't Depending on 63 Observers to Check on the Picture Code; Gets Real Lowdown That Way', *Variety* (24 April 1934).
10. [Uncited author], 'Salary Control and Anti-raiding Provisos in Pic Code Discarded by NRA; Industry Will Regulate 'Em', *Variety* (11 September 1934).
11. Sol Rosenblatt, 'Report Regarding Investigation to be Made by the President in His Executive Order of November 27, 1933, Approving the Code of Fair Competition for the Motion Picture Industry' (Washington, DC: National Recovery Administration, US Government) 7 July 1934: 5–12, 21–2. Of course, the top fifty movie stars in Hollywood made much more money than the majority of other actors working in Hollywood. Overall, they averaged between $3,298 and $4,197 in salary per year during 1931–3, while executive salaries at 'Producing-Distributing Companies' averaged between $53,000 and $92,000 each during the same period, rounded off.
12. [Uncited author], 'Code a Lovely Dish of Alphabet Soup, Only Labor and Extras Win Spelling Bee', *Daily Variety* (1 October 1934); The Analyst, 'Film Shares $106,614,125 Higher in Market Value than Year Ago', *Motion Picture Herald* (5 January 1935).

13. This section on the post-July 1934 Production Code Administration is based on the following sources: Thomas Doherty, *Pre-Code Hollywood: Sex, Immorality, and Insurrection in American Cinema 1930–1934* (New York: Columbia University Press, 1999), Chapter 12; Joseph Breen to Will Hays, 3 August 1934, Production Code Administration Collection, Margaret Herrick Library, Academy of Motion Picture Arts and Sciences. For additional documents pertaining to the Production Code Administration's approval of *Dames* (1934), as well as the concerns of local censorship boards, see: *Dames*, file 1851, Warner Bros. Archives, University of Southern California [henceforth WBA/USC].

Not everyone in the studio system was thrilled about the stricter censorship regime. RKO producer Pandro Berman remarked near the end of 1934: 'Things like the Legion [of Decency, a major national film censorship advocate] always come to an end, and it will be doubly so in the case of motion pictures when audiences are faced with a steady flow of saccharine material.' An editorial in *Motion Picture Herald*, probably written by Terry Ramsaye, upbraided the 'very young producer' for his remarks, but one could imagine Darryl F. Zanuck harbouring the same kinds of thoughts: [uncited author], 'Pandora Berman's Box', *Motion Picture Herald* (5 January 1935).

Though it was not known at the time, numerous documents from 1932–4 unearthed by scholars in recent years have demonstrated that Breen, who administered the Production Code on behalf of film studios run by Jews, was a 'rabid anti-semite', using words such as 'rotten', 'vile' and 'perverts', among others, to describe Jews as a group in letters to Catholic prelates: Gregory D. Black, *Hollywood Censored: Morality Codes, Catholics and the Movies* (Cambridge: Cambridge University Press, 1994): 70–1, 170–2.

14. While working on *Dames*, Warner Bros. head of production Hal Wallis forced Berkeley to excise a number entitled 'Come Up and See My Pussy Sometime' even though it was made clear that a cat was the subject of the song. But still, a female character apparently sang the song and the lyrics did indicate that the 'pussy cat ... wants to eat her little white mouse' – perhaps Wallis had a valid point after all. Berkeley's sex obsession could theoretically be taken too far: Inter-Office Communication, Hal Wallis to Busby Berkeley, 19 March 1934, from *Dames*, file 1851, WBA/USC.

15. [Uncited authors], 'New Dealers' Film Threat: Congressional Pic Biz Probe', *Variety* (13 November 1934); 'US After Films' Scalp: Pix As Possible Political "Goat"', *Variety* (15 January 1935); 'Code A Lovely'.

16. Giuliana Muscio, *Hollywood's New Deal* (Philadelphia: Temple University Press, 1997): 101–2, 115–17, 131.

17. Brownstein, 78–9; Paul Buhle and Dave Wagner, *Radical Hollywood: The Untold Story Behind America's Favorite Movies* (New York: The New Press, 2002): Muscio, ibid.

18. Ellis W. Hawley, *The New Deal and the Problem of Monopoly: A Study in Economic Ambivalence* (New York: Fordham University Press, 1995): 97; Arthur M. Schlesinger, Jr, *The Age of Roosevelt: The Coming of the New Deal* (Boston: Houghton-Mifflin, 1960): 160–7 [quotation from p. 167]; Jean Edward Smith, *FDR* (New York: Random House, 2008): 343–5; [uncited authors], 'Biz-Gov't in Double Harness from Now On, Is Washington Dope', *Variety* (21 August 1934); 'Pic Code Another 2 Yrs: NRA's Extension Leaves It As It Is', *Variety* (3 April 1935).

19. [Uncited authors], 'Show Biz's NRA Rebound: Labor Relations, H'Wood Chisel', 'Don't Chisel' [editorial] and 'Continuing Bull Movement Halts for a Day on NRA Blow-up Decision', *Variety* (29 May 1935); 'NRA Lid Off, Films Fears: Exhibs

Run Wild on Premiums?', *Variety* (5 June 1935); 'Handling a Headache', [editorial], *Variety* (12 June 1935); 'Films' Voluntary Code: Substitute for NRA via F.T. B'ds', *Variety* (19 June 1935); 'Board Studying Records of NRA Film Code for Probable Future Use', *Variety* (18 Sept. 1935).

20. Tino Balio, *Grand Design: Hollywood as a Modern Business Enterprise 1930–1939* (New York: Scribner, 1993): 153–5; Danae Clark, *Negotiating Hollywood: The Cultural Politics of Actors' Labor* (Minneapolis: University of Minnesota Press, 1995): 59–60; Marc Norman, *What Happens Next: A History of American Screenwriting* (London: Aurum, 2008), Chapter 9: 204; Rosten, 158–60; Nancy Lynn Schwartz, *The Hollywood Writers' Wars* (New York: Knopf, 1982): 171–9.

21. Inter-Office Communication, Hal Wallis to Busby Berkeley, 31 March 1934, *Dames* file 1851, WBA/USC.

22. The seven 1934 Warner Bros. musicals in chronological order: *Harold Teen, Fashions of 1934, Wonderbar, 20 Million Sweethearts, Dames, Happiness Ahead* and *Flirtation Walk*. The latter film was nominated for the Best Picture Oscar of 1934.

    Steve Farrar, from the 'What the Picture Did for Me' column, *Motion Picture Herald* (1 April 1933).

23. Jack Warner with Dean Jennings, *My First Hundred Years in Hollywood: An Autobiography* (New York: Random House, 1965). It should be noted, however, that the Warners were in sync with Roosevelt later in the 1930s in their opposing of the Nazi regime, and did their part in supporting Roosevelt's approach to World War II.

24. Patrick McGilligan, *Cagney: The Actor as Auteur* (San Diego, CA: A. S. Barnes, 1982): 76.

25. As Iwan Morgan argues, stripping away the major studios' exhibition businesses largely did not spark new independent competition as hoped. Instead, it empowered large theatre chains controlled by national distribution companies: Iwan Morgan, 'Introduction', from Morgan and Davies, eds, *Hollywood*, 21.

26. David Thomson, *The Whole Equation: A History of Hollywood* (New York: Vintage, 2004): 274–83.

GENERAL INDEX

FILM INDEX